Crossroads of Family Businesses in China

Succession and Transformation

Crossroads of
Family Businesses
in China
Succession and Transformation

Jean Lee
China Europe International Business School, China

Yan Anthea Zhang
Rice University, USA

NEW JERSEY · LONDON · SINGAPORE · BEIJING · SHANGHAI · HONG KONG · TAIPEI · CHENNAI · TOKYO

Published by

World Scientific Publishing Co. Pte. Ltd.

5 Toh Tuck Link, Singapore 596224

USA office: 27 Warren Street, Suite 401-402, Hackensack, NJ 07601

UK office: 57 Shelton Street, Covent Garden, London WC2H 9HE

Library of Congress Cataloging-in-Publication Data
Names: Lee, Jean (Jean S. K.) author. | Zhang, Yan Anthea, author.
Title: Crossroads of family businesses in China : succession and transformation / Jean Lee,
    China Europe International Business School, China, Yan Anthea Zhang, Rice University, USA.
Description: 27 Warren Street, Suite 401-402 : World Scientific Publishing Co Pte Ltd, 2021. |
    Includes index.
Identifiers: LCCN 2020051972 | ISBN 9789811229404 (hardcover) |
    ISBN 9789811229411 (ebook) | ISBN 9789811229428 (ebook other)
Subjects: LCSH: Family-owned business enterprises--China. |
    Family-owned business enterprises--Succession--China. | Organizational change--China.
Classification: LCC HD62.25 .L4334 2021 | DDC 338.70951--dc23
LC record available at https://lccn.loc.gov/2020051972

British Library Cataloguing-in-Publication Data
A catalogue record for this book is available from the British Library.

当传承遇到转型—中国家族企业发展路径图
Originally published in Chinese by Peking University Press
Copyright © Peking University Press, 2017

Copyright © 2021 by World Scientific Publishing Co. Pte. Ltd.

For any available supplementary material, please visit
https://www.worldscientific.com/worldscibooks/10.1142/12073#t=suppl

Translator: Jun HE
Desk Editor: Lixi Dong

Typeset by Stallion Press
Email: enquiries@stallionpress.com

Printed in Singapore

Preface

Over the past 30 years, China's private businesses have developed rapidly and at their very core are the family businesses in various sectors. Similar to many family-owned workshops in Europe, family businesses in China have withstood the test of the times under the leadership of the first generation of entrepreneurs — after the reform and while opening up. After having flourished through economic openness and having survived the ups and downs of the financial crisis, they have become increasingly powerful and have gradually formed family-based business groups.

The process of breaking through the growth bottleneck and addressing the issue of succession have always been the focus of family businesses for generations. How is the younger generation going to take over the family businesses from their parents successfully? Family businesses in Europe and the United States may have found the solution through professional governance and the widespread use of professional managers. Yet, for a large number of family businesses in China, this is still a problem that needs to be solved urgently.

There are three obstacles that family businesses in China face. Firstly, the industry is backward. Most of the family businesses are concentrated in low-end manufacturing. In recent years, the turmoil brought about by industrial upgrading is very obvious. Secondly, the governance structure is chaotic. Family businesses have long relied on the decision of the "big boss", leading to unnecessarily excessive reverence for the most powerful individuals. In the process, opportunities to formulate rules that give play to talented personnel and sound decision-making mechanisms are lost. Finally, the impact of the Internet era and the upgrading of the profit-making model in the market have overwhelmed many traditional entrepreneurs in recent years. In the face of new competition, the experience that traditional businesses value so much has turned out to be their weakness in terms of further development.

In Europe, there are many great family businesses that have grown out of small workshops. In China, I have met many hardworking family business owners in the industrial sector. They have many things in common: Wholehearted devotion to their career and a strong sense of responsibility for their family and business. On one hand, family is the most important aspect in their life and they have developed their own careers around the family. On the other hand, in order to expand their business, they have to sacrifice some of their family interests. This conflict between family and business bears on the relationships between family members and the allocation of interests and power. The interplay between the two keeps the owner of the family business thinking constantly about making appropriate changes. Similarly, they have to think how to foster and select the right successor to the family business before it is too late.

Most of the family businesses in Europe are now in the hands of the fourth or fifth generations. Because of their early beginnings, the first two successions between the generations occurred at a time when no big changes took place in the businesses and when the overall economic environment remained relatively stable. Thus, the succession from one generation to the next did not greatly overlap the development bottleneck of the business. On the contrary, family businesses in China are immature, and the continuation of the family is excessively intertwined with the development of the business. In addition, due to the special development background of the economic environment, the intergenerational transition of the family almost occurs at the same time as the transformation and upgrading of the businesses. Faced with a succession problem within the family and the business, the first generation entrepreneurs are lost. Like all parents, they pin their hopes on the next generation. The change of the economic situation and the transformation and upgrading of businesses are inevitable in the development of enterprises. However, the first generation of entrepreneurs are beginning to seem less capable of handling problems in management, and it would affect whether succession to the second generation will be smooth — a question that must be answered regarding intergenerational succession. Thus, the inheritance of China's family businesses is now standing at this special crossroads.

We need to pay more attention to this issue because most of the first generation owners of family businesses in China are now aged between 55 and 75, and finding the right successors to their businesses is imminent. It is very difficult and stressful when the two major international problems of succession and transformation fall on family businesses at the same time. Whether the next generation can successfully take over the businesses and lead the transformation and upgrading of the family businesses is a new topic. How should they transfer power from one generation to the next and where are the family businesses heading while standing at the crossroads? This is an era when traditional businesses are facing transformation and upgrading and when family businesses complete the succession and inheritance. Are China's first generation entrepreneurs and wealthy second generation well prepared?

Pedro Nueno
Honorary President (Europe)
China Europe International Business School
January 2017

Foreword

Over the past three decades and amidst reform and opening up, plenty of influential family businesses have emerged in China. They are found in all sectors and industries, demonstrating extraordinary vitality in a time of unprecedented change. Many of these family businesses are industry leaders, and as a whole, they play an important role in the private economy and even in the entire national economy.

Nevertheless, as China's first generation of entrepreneurs reach the age of 60, passing on and sustaining the businesses they manage has become an urgent task. According to the "China Family Business Development Report" released by the All-China Federation of Industry and Commerce in 2012, 85.4% of China's private enterprises are family businesses and about 3/4 of the family businesses will face the succession problem in the next 5–10 years. Whether the family businesses can be passed on to the next generation and developed further has a vital bearing on not only the fate of individual family and business, but also on the overall operation and prosperity of China's private economy.

"Passing on the family business from father to son" seems to be the most traditional and natural way of succession. Yet, finding the right successor is no easy task. It requires attention on the part of the first-generation businessmen, the desire to succeed on the part of the second generation, and the long-term joint efforts of the two generations. Many entrepreneurs do not own or have yet to work out a systematic succession plan, while other entrepreneurs have made great efforts to train their successors, but the result is far from satisfactory. The biggest obstacle to succession is that the wealthy second generation is not willing to take over the family businesses. Even if they are, they lack the ability to do so.

As a scholar who has been paying much attention to the management and succession of China's family businesses, I am very pleased to witness the ongoing succession process of family businesses at its peak and share the pros and cons in this process. Over the years, my research team and I, alongside my collaborator Professor Zhang Yan, have had in-depth exchanges with the founders, leaders, managers, and heirs of China's family businesses. This includes getting to know their views, concerns and prospects from different perspectives and summarizing some valuable practices and experiences in the succession of family businesses.

In 2012, with the support of many parties, we launched a survey on family businesses that were undergoing succession and those that had completed the succession, studying the factors affecting the succession of Chinese family businesses in the current context. The project surveyed 114 enterprises and 504 related personnel in China, hoping to crack the code of successful succession of family businesses. We also recorded many cases in terms of succession and made a series of discussions on the intergenerational succession of family businesses.

How can Chinese family businesses successfully carry out intergenerational succession? This is a proposition of our time. As the saying goes, "The way ahead is long, I shall search high and low." The handover of Chinese family businesses from the first generation to the second generation has only just begun and there are still many things that we need to study and conclude. As China's economy has entered a period of industrial restructuring, family business owners in China need to deal with the major issue of business transformation in addition to finding successors. It is of great significance for many family businesses to realize the strategic transformation within their business and simultaneously complete the succession between the two generations. At such a crossroads, where should the second generation go? How much maneuvering do professional managers have? Is there only a thin line between the transformation and upgrading, and diversification? How should family businesses utilize the Internet and international markets to continue their expansion? It is already difficult to start a business, and it is even harder to keep an existing business going. It is certainly challenging to promote the sustainable development of family businesses while passing on entrepreneurship in the family, while respecting and maintaining the family traditions. These considerations are new topics for today's Chinese family businesses. For the two generations, they have encountered many unprecedented challenges in their initial attempt for succession. We hope that the publication of this book will bring some enlightenment to the succession of family businesses in China.

Anthea Zhang Yan is a professor of strategy at the Jones Graduate School of Business at Rice University in the US and she has done many original researches on corporate governance of listed companies. When she was working at China Europe International Business School (CEIBS) from 2013 to 2014, she began to turn her attention to the succession of family businesses in China, and wrote, among others, the case of "Midea changing leaders", and opened a course on the succession of business executives in the school. When I invited her to write this book together, she readily accepted. Since I lived in China, I made the interviews and collected materials for many cases. Anthea is better known for her clear logic, solid theoretical foundation, and a deep understanding of China's phenomena and problems. There have been endless discussions between us about the framework of the book, the refinement of cases, and the induction of theories. I delve into the stories, while she thinks from a theoretical height. Therefore, when revising the manuscript, her ability to provide a clear theoretical conclusion of many of the details impressed me strongly. Hence, in this book, "I" am the storyteller and she is the person expounding on the rationale.

The overall structure of the book is as follows: First, we focus on several challenges in the "succession" and "transformation" of family businesses in China (Chapter 1). We then discuss why the second generation is not willing to take over the family businesses, and explain the challenges and conflicts between the two generations in the process of succession (Chapter 2). The process of reinforcing the willingness of the second generation to take over the family businesses is closely related to family relations and family values, thus the power of "family culture" should not be ignored (Chapter 3). A good method for smoother succession is to engage the future successors in the startup of family businesses and the succession of Fotile is a good exemplary (Chapter 4). But in reality, there are also many cases like Huamao — the succession had to be carried out when the second generation was not prepared. This process is very painful and poses a great challenge to the successor; it is also the most memorable learning experience through which the second generation can grow from (Chapter 5). The succession of businesses is different from inheriting wealth. Fotile followed the "pocket theory" to give its successor clear equity and decision-making power, while Huamao chose to "divide the family but not the property" and stipulated that the family property should be trusted. There are pros and cons in dividing or gathering. The key is the value orientation of the family, especially the values of the founders (Chapter 6). Some founders of family businesses believe that "family is business and business is family", while other founders want to separate their businesses from the family and hire professional managers for specialized management. However, the reality is often unsatisfactory. The limitations of professional managers in terms of concept and personal quality often convinced the first generation of entrepreneurs to turn to their children when it comes to the succession of their businesses. Neoglory Group appointed three professional managers, but ultimately it was the founder's son who ended up taking over the business. Instead of "separating family from business", "the family ties were reinforced through business" (Chapter 7). Which is better? A CEO selected from within the family or a professional CEO from outside the family? The research literature has never given a conclusive answer, but each option has its own cultivation and selection path (Chapter 8). Midea has certainly done well so far in the shift to professional managers regarding the succession of family businesses, but it is undeniable that this is also a tortuous road (Chapter 9). The model of "mother to daughter inheritance" has begun to challenge the traditional concept of "transferring the leadership from father to son" in China. Moreover, in the case of Wensli, "the daughter took over the business from her mother", showing the different charms of two generations of Chinese women. The son-in-law played a positive role in leading Wensli to brand internationalization amid conflicts and compromises (Chapter 10). Red Collar is another case of a daughter's succession. The father and daughter of a family business jointly promoted a revolution in the traditional clothing industry and established a new industrial model in the Internet era (Chapter 11). The last part (Chapter 12) summarizes the four models of succession of family business in China and the four types of strategic transformation models that go along with it.

Throughout the book, the cases, stories, theories, and practices intertwine. We hope that readers can obtain some information and ideas about this topic through an enjoyable reading experience, and find food for thought on the succession and transformation of family business in China.

Jean Lee
January 2017

Contents

About the Authors

Dr Jean Lee is the Michelin Chair Professor in Leadership and Human Resources Management, Professor of Management and Co-Director of Center for Family Heritage in China Europe International Business School (Shanghai).

Her research interests include leadership, corporate culture, women in leadership, family business and cross-culture management. She has published extensively in local and international journals, such as *Human Relations, Family Business Review, International Journal of HRM, Asia Pacific Journal of Management, Financial Times, Forbes, Harvard Business Review (China)* etc. She serves on the editorial board of *Asia Business Review* and *Journal of Chinese Human Resource Management* and has served as the Associate Editor of *Asia-Pacific Journal of Management*. She is the author of *Wealth Doesn't Last 3 Generations* (2009) and *Chinese Women Business Leaders — Seven Principles of Leadership* (2018).

Prof Lee has consulted and conducted training programmes for many multinational, local and international organizations in Southeast Asia and mainland China. She also serves as Independent Director of several companies. She has received several Teaching Awards and Service Awards based on her excellent teaching and outstanding leadership and contribution in the profession. She was listed as top 25 influential scholars in the field of family business in 2015.

Dr Yan "Anthea" Zhang is a professor and the Fayez Sarofim Vanguard Chair of Strategic Management at the Jones Graduate School of Business, Rice University, USA. Her research focuses on CEO succession and corporate governance of public-listed companies and family-owned firms, and foreign direct investment and technological entrepreneurship in emerging markets (notably China). She is a prolific scholar ad has published many research articles in top academic journals in the business field, such as the *Academy of Management Journal* and *Strategic Management Journal*. Her research has been widely cited in top business media outlets such as *Harvard Business Review*, *Economist*, *Business Week*, *New York Times*, *Wall Street Journal*, *Washington Post*, *USA Today*, and *Financial Times*. She has served on the boards of directors of Strategic Management Society and International Corporate Governance Society. She received her PhD in business administration from Marshall School of Business, the University of Southern California, Master of Philosophy in international business from City University of Hong Kong, and BA and MA in economics from Nanjing University. She was on the faculty of China Europe International Business School and held visiting professorships in Tsinghua University, Fudan University, Shanghai Jiaotong University, and Sun Yat-Sen University.

1

Challenges to Family Business

Origin

I began to show serious interest in my family's business at the age of 28. I was studying for a doctoral degree at university and I chose overseas Chinese family business as the topic of my thesis. At that time, I had left Singapore for the US to pursue my PhD and I didn't expect that this topic would accompany my research for so many years.

I grew up in a typical Chinese merchant family in Southeast Asia. My grandfather and his fellow villagers left China for Southeast Asia in the 1940s in search for a better job and they engaged in business in various fields in Indonesia, Malaysia, and Singapore. When my father was 11 years old, he was taken to Singapore by my grandfather from his hometown, Hainan. People of that generation suffered much hardship and the devastation of war; thus they were very tough. My father was a very self-disciplined businessman. Upon the death of my grandfather, he began to take charge of the family business — a catering services chain. He worked with my grandfather's business associate, a widower and whom I called "Grandpa". My father went to work in the morning rain or shine, came home to rest at noon, went to the enterprise to handle business in the afternoon, and returned home in the evening. In fact, my father did not need to go to work daily. Yet, he always set an example by working hard day in and day out — dressed neatly and talked softly — to keep and develop the family assets passed down from his father. He never talked about business at home, but he liked to discuss the current situation with us and comment on political figures. He respected Lee Kuan Yew and regarded him highly. People of that generation did not talk about idols, but I think that Lee Kuan Yew was my father's idol. He even had Lee's demeanor in dressing style, speech, and behavior. My father was always strict but not harsh, so we never dared to mess with him. We respected him but we were not afraid of him. He neither smoked nor drank, instead he liked to take a stroll in the park every day. After he was diagnosed with pancreatic cancer, he died in peace, leaving behind the unchangeable diligent figure in our heart.

My father never wanted us to do business. He hoped we would receive good education and find jobs in government agencies or foreign enterprises. In the post-British colonial era of Singapore, being fluent in English and wearing a suit and tie to work was a matter of pride for the family. My eldest younger brother majored in architectural design and worked in a government agency for ten years before he decided to start his own business and establish a design company. That, however, did not last long. At the end of the day, he opened a pastry bakery chain. It was a process full of twists and turns, as my brother's intention was not to follow in my father's footsteps. In the end, the family business was passed down to the third generation anyway. I grew up in such a family, so I have a relatively good understanding of the handover of family business, and the challenges within. However, daughters are rarely considered successors in the Chinese families in Southeast Asia, which is different from the situation in contemporary China. We have some cases in which daughters are taking over the family business and will be discussed later in this book.

My first interest in family business came from my father and his family background, while my deep understanding of this topic derived from my first consulting project — working as a consultant and director in a family business ranking among the top five in Indonesia. After graduating from university in the US with a Ph.D., I returned to teach at the National University of Singapore. Since my doctoral thesis was published in the *Straits Times*, Mr. Hadi Wang came all the way to Singapore from Indonesia to meet me, hoping that I could help his family business.

Seven brothers were responsible for the different sections of the family business, covering forestry, timber, furniture, mining, agriculture, aquaculture, shipping, shipbuilding, finance, etc. I became involved not only in the management of his family business, but also in the communication with his wife and the education of his children, thus becoming a veritable "family consultant". I served as consultant for the Wang family for nearly a decade, during which I experienced all the difficulties encountered by this family business, the problems in business management, and compromises between the brothers.

During my teaching at the National University of Singapore, I was exposed to more Chinese family businesses in Southeast Asia. In the process of communicating with the family business leaders, I saw many cases of family business succession through three or even five generations, and I was also told about the troubles, struggles, and joys of many entrepreneurs. The most well-known example was Yeo's Group,[1] a family business with nearly a hundred years of history that was being passed from the third generation to the fourth generation. The name of the group represents the joint efforts of the family to pursue success. However, due to the divergence of ideas and the rupture of relations, the internal problems and disputes in the Yeo family were brought to the court and the Yeo family holding company was disintegrated as the judge announced his ruling. This classic case was written in one of my earlier books — *Chinese Family Business — Wealth Goes Beyond Three Generations*[2]. Later, many Chinese scholars often use this case to remind Chinese family businesses of the trap that "wealth never survives three generations".

Coming to China

In 2004, I decided to go to China and settle in Shanghai because of my work. At that time, I was full of curiosity about this birthplace of Chinese culture. Especially when I witnessed the rapid rise of China's economy

---

[1] Lee, Siew Kim Jean. (2005). Understanding Family Business from the Rise and Fall of Yeo's Group. *Oriental Enterprise Culture*, 10, 9–14.

[2] Lee, Siew Kim Jean. (2007). Chinese Family Business — Wealth Goes Beyond Three Generations. Shanghai People's Publishing House.

after its reform and opening up, the fast expansion of the Chinese market and China's transformation from the "world's factory" to the "world's market", I was very curious about the important force behind these changes, namely, the private entrepreneurs and their management skills that constituted the main body of China's private sector. The first time I got in touch with Chinese entrepreneurs, I suddenly realized that the concept of "family business" was taboo at that time and they did not have the same sense of honor as that of Southeast Asian or European family businesses. Instead, they thought that "private business" was synonymous with a level of unprofessionalism and non-standard management, nepotism, giving priority to family interests, or such short-sighted behaviors as cronyism and the distrust of outsiders. Lots of private entrepreneurs were reluctant to admit that their enterprises were family businesses, so at that time, the subject of family business was rarely mentioned, and data and cases in this field were hard to get. This was not until the financial crisis in 2009 when people around the world began to realize the resilience of family businesses. When many businesses fell apart in the financial storm, some family businesses showed their indomitable will. A well-known example abroad is the US Ford Motor Company in the financial crisis. Two other US auto businesses, General Motors and Chrysler, filed for bankruptcy protection, so the US federal government had to invest huge amounts of money from taxpayers to support the two companies. General Motors even became a state-owned company controlled by the US federal government. Ford Motor Company, as the only family business among the three leading US auto businesses, insisted on not filing for bankruptcy protection and sold all of its luxury car business to save its most important brand, Ford. It sold Volvo to China's Geely Automobile Company and Land Rover and Jaguar to India's Tata Group. A large number of scholars have begun to pay attention to the cultural foundations of family businesses, and attempted to find an answer to this question: Why some family businesses that do not normally find themselves in the spotlight and are relatively conservative in strategy turn out to be more resistant to risks in times of crisis?

Family business is one of the most common forms of business in the world. Even by the most conservative estimate, family-owned or operated businesses account for between 65% and 80% of the world's businesses, and 40% of the world's top 500 businesses are owned or operated by families. In China's economic composition, the private economy and the state-owned economy have maintained a long-term ratio of six to four, while the proportion of family-owned businesses in the private economy is as high as 80%. In terms of economic contribution and employment opportunities offered, family business is a force that should not be ignored. For more than ten years, I focused my research efforts on the operation of Chinese family businesses in Southeast Asia, the comparison of Eastern and Western business cultures, and the leadership of Chinese business owners. I also conducted long-term studies on such Chinese businesses as Yeo's, Acer, Giti and so forth. In 2007, I published *Chinese Family Business — Wealth Goes Beyond Three Generations*, in which I expounded on the origin, evolvement, and characteristics of Chinese family businesses, compared the similarities and differences between family businesses on the Chinese mainland, Taiwan, and Southeast Asia through many case studies, and discussed the succession of some typical family businesses in Europe. The book reaped a lot of repercussions in the market. I was later delighted to find that family business became a hot topic, and more and more people began to pay attention to this business model.

China is a country with a long history of "family culture", so family is the foundation of ethics, customs, social organizations, governance of country, and business development. The model of family business is consistent with China's "family culture", and management based on the family has a strong vitality in the beginning stage of a business; it can reduce costs, enhance trust, and solve conflicts to the greatest extent. Therefore, many businesses established by the Chinese people adopt the form of family business. The Chinese economy has entered a period of unprecedented rapid development in history, and Chinese family businesses are booming in this context. As my contact with Chinese family businesses increased, I began to study the problems and challenges they faced. In the past few years, my research team and I interviewed over a hundred domestic family businesses and collected data for analysis. I then recorded the research results in several white paper reports[3] and academic articles. In the process of research and in my interviews and conversations with

---

[3] Lee, Siew Kim Jean, Rui Meng, Lu Yunting, Cui Zhiyu. (2014). Will and Commitment of Successors: White Paper on the Inheritance of Chinese Family Businesses. Family Inheritance Research Center of China Europe International Business School.

entrepreneurs, I found that Chinese family businesses seized the opportunity of reform and opening up after a long period of disruption due to historical reasons and experienced more than 30 years of vigorous development. Although we have not seen the re-emergence of the big family, the concept of family business has gradually taken root in people's hearts. However, after more than 30 years of development, the first generation of entrepreneurs are already in their twilight years, and many family businesses are hovering at the crossroads of intergenerational succession.

Succession: The Challenge Facing Chinese Family Businesses

Family businesses on the Chinese mainland lag far behind the developed countries in Europe and the United States, and they are also far behind their counterparts in Southeast Asia, Hong Kong, and Taiwan. While family businesses in those countries and regions have reached the stage of professional management after four or five generations, most family businesses on the Chinese mainland still face two challenges. The first is succession, especially that from the first generation to the second generation. This poses a challenge because Chinese family businesses are facing the first shift in power, leadership, and management, and perhaps the inheritance and dispersion of wealth. The second is transformation. Due to the economic characteristics of the reform and opening up, the advantages of the traditional industries that had been growing rapidly for decades no longer exist. When family businesses are facing the challenge of succession, business transformation only makes things more complex and difficult.

I believe that the challenge to Chinese family businesses is largely the same as that of many foreign family businesses. The most fundamental issue is whether or not to pass the businesses to their children. The complex process of succession requires orderly planning and control, including the succession plan, the distribution of ownership, and the employment of professional managers, each of which affects the success of intergenerational succession. Psychologist Ivan Lansberg maintains that it is human nature for parents to pass on the business they have established and engaged in throughout their lives to their offspring, which is also the best way to keep their hopes and dreams alive. Hence, I believe well-planned training and education of the prospective successor is an important factor for effective succession. For the second generation born with a silver spoon in their mouth, life holds numerous possibilities in light of what their parents have already achieved, and succession is just one of the options. However, the traditional culture of Chinese society has always attached importance to clan, family, and family ethics. From feudal dynasties to family businesses today, there is a traditional ethic of "regarding the family as the world", so "transferring the leadership from father to son" is a sustainable development model favored by most family business founders. That process is not only done out of emotional need, but also as a practical matter. However, for the second generation, two possibilities exist when it comes to succession. One, they have the ability but lack interest. Two, they have the willingness to take over but lack the ability. Therefore, the leaders of family businesses are always struggling with these problems: Should they pass on the family business to their children? Are the children qualified and ready to take over?

In addition, whether to hire a family member or a professional manager is also a problem that has troubled many family businesses. In the course of interviews, I have heard too many stories about the failure of professional managers, perhaps more than the stories of unsuccessful succession by their own children. After all, the succession of family businesses is actually the transfer of business ownership and control rights. In China, it is difficult to clearly distinguish between the two. As we know, the first problem that professional managers face when entering a family business is integration. Their identification with the emotional orientation of the family or the management mode of the family business will directly or indirectly affect their devotion and performance, and decide whether they will be accepted by the family. In a complicated family business, the identity of professional managers as "outsiders" can be a double-edged sword. First of all, there is an innate conflict of interest between professional managers and family members, and family businesses are bound to face the problem of decentralization of power with the introduction of professional managers. Sometimes, it is difficult for the older generation to delegate power to their own children, so delegating power to an "outsider" requires even more trust and faces greater psychological resistance.

Similarly, if a professional manager does not feel he has won the trust of or has been integrated into the family group, his commitment and loyalty will be greatly reduced, thus forming a vicious cycle. Secondly, most of the assessment indicators of professional managers only reflect quantifiable performance, which may lead professional managers — in the process of management — to ignore the long-term interests of the family business or result in their lacking the drive to maintain the intangible wealth of the families. Instead, they will try to pursue immediate, short-term gains to prove their capabilities and get good remuneration through rapid growth or market expansion. However, everyone is familiar with the story of "pulling up seedlings to help them grow". In many cases, the short-term rapid development will cause the business to lose the opportunity to take a steady stance and dig deeper into the market. It will also harm the development of businesses in the long run. For instance, a professional manager employed by Neoglory Group[4] set up self-operated stores in large scale across the country during his tenure. This action virtually replaced the local dealers who used to be partners of Neoglory and turned them into its competitors in the local market. In the short term, Neoglory's sales soared due to the expansion of stores and its gross profit increased greatly as local dealership was bypassed. However, competition with local dealers in regions where the market and consumers were unfamiliar to Neoglory proved hard and ineffective, and the huge inventory surplus brought by the expansion of stores greatly increased Neoglory's operating cost and restricted its cash flow and turnover rate. Therefore, the professional manager's seemingly gorgeous performance left behind a heavy burden to Neoglory.

Nonetheless, we should not ignore the positive significance of professional managers for family businesses. Professional managers need a relatively complete and standardized platform to enter family businesses, which can, to a certain extent, promote the sound management of family businesses. Because of the absence of nepotism, professional managers can adopt an objective and rational style of work in handling some business management issues. Currently, the market of China's professional

---

[4] Lee, Siew Kim Jean, Zhong Wanwen, Lu Yunting, An Jing. (2015). Neoglory Group: Inheritance Selection. Global Platform of China Cases.

managers is not standardized, and the relevant laws and regulations need to be improved. Other issues such as the quality and integrity of professional managers are factors that must be considered. Therefore, there are many topics worth discussing regarding the challenge to family business succession.

It is a very complicated and lengthy process for family members to put their trust in an "outsider" and hand over the power of business management to him with confidence. This not only requires careful planning and consideration of the business founders, but also tests the ability, ethics, and wisdom of professional managers. The employment of professional managers is still a tricky dilemma for family businesses in China. The superior management skills of professional managers may protect businesses from family infighting, but simultaneously, whether professional managers will regard the family businesses as their own is a matter of concern. In the face of huge wealth or power, executives from outside are not bound by family missions, so some of them will inevitably seek personal gains at the expense of the development of family businesses. Even if equity incentives are used to tie the interests of professional managers with those of the family businesses, professional managers may still pursue rapid growth and short-term profits that turn out to harm the long-term development capability of businesses. Therefore, Chinese family businesses are currently facing a dilemma: The "wealthy second generation" lacks strong will or ability to take over, and professional managers cannot meet the requirement of the "first generation entrepreneurs" for dedication due to their lack of integrity and motivation. The dearth of both internal and external successors is likely to continue for some time.

Strategic Transformation: Another Challenge

Another challenge to family business is strategic transformation. Although all businesses find this transformation difficult, there are some particularities for family businesses. First of all, the founders themselves need to deal with the transformation. To the founders of the business, the strategic transformation and the power transfer seem like some sort of self-denial, in which they find hard to accept and therefore result in the refusal to let go of the business. This only makes succession more difficult. Of course, many first generation entrepreneurs are willing to try and change, and their inherent entrepreneurial spirit and keen sense of business opportunity will not weaken with age. But they may also have limitations as to what they should do and where they should head for. Hence, it is crucial that the "first generation entrepreneurs" face their own limitations and give their successors the freedom to explore the new direction of business development, while they serve as consultants to help the successors make sound decisions.

The birth of most family businesses in China benefited from the opening-up policy and the market economy. In the early days of reform, market opportunities abounded, and the first generation of entrepreneurs showed their business acumen in all types of undertakings. However, due to the limitations and influence of the overall economic structure, most started their businesses in low-end manufacturing industries, which were generally labor-intensive industries that employed no advanced technologies. After more than three decades of development, most of the businesses that survived competition have been expanded several times in scale, and have amassed large amounts of corporate assets and family wealth along the way. However, with the development of the market and the rising labor costs, many of the labor-intensive industries must make necessary adjustments and use more effective and economical methods to generate greater benefits in order to survive and develop in a fast-growing market. Meanwhile, in a fully open market with international competition, businesses have reached the point of transformation and upgrading. Faced with the impact of the Internet era, the leaders of businesses should change strategies from the low end to the high end. Many second generation of family businesses have received their education in the West, so they have easy access to better resources and platforms that provide the latest market information and they tend to prefer high-tech or investment industries. The process to help the family businesses realize the favorable cycle of "making money with money" through capital operation and better promote the transformation and development of businesses is a common topic for both generations. In the process of transformation, family businesses need to find better growth opportunities and drivers for development. The difficulties and challenges involved are one of the fundamental obstacles hindering the development and succession of family businesses.

Chinese family businesses are groping their way forward in spite of the two challenges. While succession is as important as starting a business, the transfer of power from the first generation to the second generation is the most vulnerable moment of family businesses. Unsuccessful succession will often be the turning point from boom to bust for a business, or even worse, result in the family losing the power of control of the business. I have heard so many such stories that it is necessary to explore the lifeline choices in the continuation of family businesses: How the businesses will be successfully passed from one generation to the next generation at different stages of development. Foreign family businesses, even those in Hong Kong, Taiwan, and Southeast Asia, have many successful experiences that we can draw on. What are the key elements in these two challenges? I believe that if we can find the relevant paths and rules and sum them up, they can be used as the guideline for the future development and succession of Chinese family businesses.

In China: When Succession Meets Transformation

The expression *fuerdai* or "wealthy second generation" emerged in 2007, when the public and the media began to notice the children of the first batch of private entrepreneurs in China. Most of them were born in the 1980s and can expect to inherit over 100 million yuan of family wealth each. As the heirs to family fortune and successors to family business, they are expected to carry the family tradition forward. After more than 30 years of reform and opening up, the emergence of the "wealthy second generation" has become an inevitable and extremely important topic. Owing to the impact of China's unique economic development and environment, they are destined to be a generation with special features. Wealth and stress go hand in hand through their life.

Due to the special economic environment in China over the past three-plus decades, the development of the private economy, especially the family businesses, has formed a huge difference between the two generations. The sparks of succession and transformation are also different in form. Many prospective successors from the "first generation entrepreneurs" who started their own business on the already-built foundation of their parents' business are known as the "1.5 generation". Fotile Group[5] as a typical representative is co-founded by Mao Zhongqun and his father Mao Lixiang.

I have known Mao Lixiang for many years and he is a "first generation entrepreneur" whom I admire very much. He started new business three times in his life and became the "King of the World's Gas Igniters" on account of his first venture. The succession and transformation of his family business began earlier than many other entrepreneurs. In 1994, when many entrepreneurs first started their businesses, his business had already gone through several ups and downs. When business was down once again, he thought of his son Mao Zhongqun, who had just graduated from Shanghai Jiao Tong University with a master's degree. Thus, Fotile began its succession and a bold transformation as well. The young Mao Zhongqun made an agreement with his father to directly take over the family business in the way of transforming the business and reinventing a new brand Fotile. In the process, Mao Lixiang accepted his son's advice and gave him full support despite numerous arguments on several occasions. He properly dealt with problems left over from the old business, including matters concerning former employees. He utilized all the resources he had gathered over the years to help his son develop his new business. I am also impressed that Mao Lixiang's daughter, Mao Xuefei, gave her father a helping hand when his business was in trouble for the first time, by establishing a factory with her husband to produce parts and components for her father's business. When her brother Mao Zhongqun decided to undergo industrial upgrading and create new industrial modules and brands, she took over the old family business from her father, which helped in a smooth succession within the family. Many of Mao Lixiang's experiences in family business succession were obtained in the process of creating Fotile with his son Mao Zhongqun and handling the division of family fortune among his children. Other Chinese family businesses can draw lessons from Mao's experiences when it comes to succession and transformation. In the later chapters, I will go into details about

---

[5]Lee, Siew Kim Jean, Zhong Wanwen, An Jing. (2015). Fotile Group: Father-Son Entrepreneurial Succession of Mao Family. IVEY.

the specific practices of Mao Lixiang, and discuss the efforts and ideas contributed by Mao Zhongqun as the second generation.

The second generation like Mao Zhongqun was prepared to take over the family business when he co-started the new business with his father. On the other hand, Xu Lixun of Huamao Group[6] was not given the choice of whether or not he should take over the family business, nor was he given the opportunity to work for the family business before he was placed in the position of successor. In 1999, Xu Lixun graduated from Rice University in Houston, USA with a degree in business administration and returned to China. He did not have time to decide whether he would work at the headquarters of Huamao, let alone consider his real interest. A sudden family crisis pushed him to the forefront. On April 30, 2000, Huamao suffered the biggest crisis in its development — the Huamao American crisis. Xu Wanmao, founder of Huamao, was involved in a lawsuit in the US and someone in China must step up to lead the corporation. Thus, 26-year-old Xu Lixun received the authorization from his father to work on his behalf. Junior Xu, who took over the family business unprepared, experienced trials and tribulations in the first 6 years in control, including industry downturn, suffering from deficit for the first time, internal conflicts, clashes between father and son, and so on. Succession like this is not uncommon in China. I have seen many family businesses by which succession had to be carried out hastily because of some unexpected incidents when neither the first nor the second generation were prepared for it. Some of them suffered greatly as a result, and even led to the closure of businesses and the decline of family fortunes. We should not shift the entire blame onto the second generation for their incompetence. Reasons for the failure can be attributed to the poor planning and preparation on the part of the first generation in many cases. However, such circumstances provide a real test regarding the soundness of the system of the family businesses and the ability and resilience of the successors. In the following chapters, I will elaborate on how Xu Lixun gradually gained a firm foothold, overcame the challenges, and helped Huamao transform and develop. After a lengthy discussion with his father over a period of

---

[6]Lee, Siew Kim Jean, Zhong Wanwen, An Jing. (2015). Huamao Group: Common Agreement of the Xu Family. IVEY

two years and at the suggestion of Xu Wanmao, they invited Huang Dongli, a member of the WTO Law Committee, lawyer of international law and professional lawyer of the Chinese Academy of Social Sciences, to draft the "Common Agreement of the Xu Family" which made clear agreements on the three core issues of "the family intervening in businesses", asset dispersion, and the ability of heirs. This case is the first of its kind in the development of Chinese family businesses and provides a valuable reference for succession and transformation of family businesses.

Compared with Chinese family businesses in Southeast Asia, the status of women in China's family businesses is relatively higher. Of course, there is no shortage of shrewd female entrepreneurs in China's family businesses. Wensli Group[7] in Hangzhou, for example, has two generations of outstanding women leaders. In 1975, the enterprising Shen Aiqin, together with 22 farmers, saved a small factory from bankruptcy. Their products were made using 10 machines discarded by a state-owned factory and the leftover bits and pieces that were sold at the local fair or through door-to-door marketing. The factory gradually developed and emerged as the Wensli Group. Shen Aiqin is a tough iron lady and her love for silk and dedication have enabled her business to grow incrementally. Shen Aiqin has two daughters. When the youngest daughter Tu Hongyan started work in the family business, Wensli was already a business group engaged in multiple sectors. Tu Hongyan's succession lasted for more than ten years, starting from the lowest position to the CEO and later, to chairwoman. Her mother's influence on the business remained after she succeeded. Her succession was a process of constant wrestling with her mother; she was duty bound to maintain the family fortune, and more importantly, to adapt to new social and economic changes. Fortunately, her husband Li Jianhua was very supportive and very passionate about the silk industry. Together they worked hard to promote the transformation of Wensli. Unlike Mao Zhongqun's radical change to Fotile, Tu Hongyan gradually reduced the diversified elements of Wensli and worked with her

---

[7]Lee, Siew Kim Jean, Zhong Wanwen, An Jing. (2015). Wensli Silk. Inheritance of Mother-Daughter Entrepreneurs, Brand Internationalization. Global Platform of China Cases.

husband to build a brand culture around the main silk industry. After the completion of the reduction, Tu Hongyan acquired a leading French brand and employed the former CEO of Hermes to help improve the overall industrial structure of Wensli, realize the dream of going global, spread the silk culture overseas, and make Wensli a synonym for good silk. The story behind the succession and transformation of Wensli is rather unique, and it is one case that can be copied by other family businesses. We will elaborate on it in later chapters.

Over the past two years, I have also visited many family businesses that have been inherited by the second generation, some of which are leading companies like Fotile and Wensli. Red Collar Group[8] in Qingdao, Shandong Province left a deep impression on me. This is a traditional family in northern China — a dignified father, a son, a daughter, and a business that grows with the children. Red Collar is a typical model of family business in China, in which parents start their own businesses when their children are young. With the development of the business and the growth of their children, they gradually pass the day-to-day management responsibilities to others and retire behind the scenes. They are not only faced with the question of who will be taking over the businesses, but also the transformation challenge posed by the impact of the Internet era. The founder Zhang Daili was a private entrepreneur in the garment industry, and at the beginning Red Collar took the traditional path of mass production, original equipment manufacturing (OEM), and shopping mall sales. In those days, China's garment industry had great growth potential. It was very easy for garment companies to make money as the demand was higher than supply. However, Zhang Daili saw a different future with the business acumen of a pioneer entrepreneur. He foresaw the challenge that Red Collar would face in the future. As a manufacturing industry, the cost advantage of the traditional garment industry was gradually fading, so Zhang Daili always believed that the best clothes are those that fit one best. In 2003, he decided to change the Red Collar Group from large-scale manufacturing to personalized customization. His courage to change from a low-end OEM industry to a mass customization model is

---

[8] Lee, Siew Kim Jean, Zhao Liman. (2015). Red Collar Group: Father-Daughter Relay, The Ongoing Strategic Transformation (A) (B). Global Platform of China Cases.

worth studying. Does technology lead business transformation or does a leader's insight determine the transformation of the businesses? What are the essential elements that decide the transformation and succession of traditional businesses like Red Collar? Zhang Daili, who used to be a carpenter, was modest to say that he did not receive much education and his initial motivation for starting the business was nothing more than a desire to improve his family's standard of living. However, the vision of an entrepreneur determines the height that his business can reach. In the following chapters, I will take the readers to Red Collar to take a closer look at how Zhang Daili advanced in the forefront of the times, and how his chosen successor, his daughter Zhang Yunlan, inherited the business under the guidance of her father and continued to complete the transformation of the family business.

Generation Gap Standing in the Way

For the first generation of entrepreneurs, their first foray into business ventures and subsequent decisions to look for change when the size of their companies has expanded are driven by entrepreneurship, which in itself is motivated by their responsibility for the family. The vast majority of first generation entrepreneurs started business in an attempt to improve their families' standard of living. Zhang Daili once said that when he was young, the construction of a small house could not be completed because his family had no money to buy another three purlins. This incident had a great impact on him, so he resolutely decided to seek an opportunity for change. Zhou Xiaoguang from Zhejiang Neoglory Group is also the same. Zhou was the eldest child in a family of seven. When she realized that no matter how hard her parents worked all year round and they still could not make ends meet, the 16-year-old girl decided to leave her home in the Zhuji mountains to make a fortune in the outer world to support her family. It should be said that in addition to their love for their families and a sense of responsibility, the first generation of entrepreneurs also have to own the courage to change. In the face of family burdens, they did not choose to escape, but actively sought ways to alter the status quo and take up the heavy responsibility for caring for their families and improving their quality of life.

Almost all the first generation of entrepreneurs have strong leadership qualities. With the development and expansion of businesses, they find themselves closely attached to their businesses, employees, industries, and even local water and soil. The element of emotion is important to family businesses, so relationships are the driving force for the initial development of business and at the same time, they also play a unique cohesive role. Under the leadership of the first generation founders, everyone is united around the core of family leaders. Apart from seeking personal interest, personal relationship and kinship are key factors supporting the development of family businesses, the latter being more important than the former. To every member of the family business, especially the old employees who have been engaged from the very start of the business, the family has a special emotional bonding. The business and employees are bound by common responsibilities and obligations. Moreover, Chinese entrepreneurs with a nostalgic complex from the ancient times are willing to develop locally and repay their hometowns, which may be related to the influence of the traditional culture. Family businesses actively participate in programs for public good, assume social responsibility, and benefit the local people, which when becoming a virtuous circle, can enhance the reputation of the business and family, increase the intangible assets, and improve the stability and continuity of family businesses.

The one-child policy poses a very particular challenge to the succession of Chinese family businesses. The first generation of entrepreneurs worry about how years of entrepreneurial effort will be wasted if the only child is unable to take over due to the lack of interest or ability. As prospective successors to family businesses are limited, the first generation of entrepreneurs must consider the interest, willingness, and ability of their children in succession and weigh the corresponding issues of business development and family inheritance.

Many first generation entrepreneurs are still troubled by whether they should pass the business to their son, defining the role of the son-in-law if their daughter takes over, cultivating their interest if their children don't want to inherit, or even helping them achieve success elsewhere. Moreover, most of the first generation entrepreneurs in China started from scratch, and the management and decision-making model of "one person alone having the final say" has made businesses overly-dependent on individual leaders. Most of them spend much more time and energy on business than on their families and are accustomed to the round-the-clock pace of working. The enterprises will hence not be able to develop in the founders' absence, and in turn it seems almost impossible emotionally for the founders to let go their business. As a result, many of the first generation entrepreneurs have not considered seriously about succession, much less about selecting successors or making long-term plans for their families and businesses until one day the issue is forced on them. Whether it is the temptation of the rapidly developing industries or the pressure of the ever-changing market, Chinese family businesses are rising due to the opportunities and exponential growth under pressure. Faced with a host of emerging market opportunities in China and the global platform that is being fully opened, the first generation of entrepreneurs are really overwhelmed. However, as the old saying goes, "If a worker wants to do something good, he must first sharpen his tools." A sound succession plan will lay a solid foundation for the sustainable development of the businesses. No matter what path is chosen to complete the handover of the businesses and the inheritance of family wealth, the "first generation entrepreneurs" must prepare for succession in advance. Family business succession planning and arrangements cannot be deferred until the last moment; rather, the plan for succession must be worked out at least 10–15 years in advance.

A gap that cannot be ignored on the way to the succession is the inevitable conflicts between the two generations. I once met an entrepreneur and his son in Shandong. The son described the difference between himself and his father as "we are not only different in our business concepts, but almost in everything". This is the most common and dominant issue among many family entrepreneurs I have interviewed; the agreement and harmony within the family and business retains importance on the road to succession. Whether at home or in the business, if fatherly authority is used to demand the children's absolute obedience, it will have an adverse impact on the relationship between the two generations, compromising the decision-making and development of businesses. The constrasting background in which the two generations were brought up will definitely result in the generation gap, and the differences in environment, educational level, and philosophy mean that their values will differ greatly.

Ultimately when the second generation enters the business to prepare for succession, the views of the two generations on the management and development of the industry will inevitably clash. Thus, it is extremely tricky whether the two generations can cooperate to find the right pace and balance between the degree of authorization on the part of the first generation and the ability to bear responsibilities on the part of the second generation.

Regarding the succession of family businesses, the major problem between the two generations is reflected in the following two aspects. The first is management philosophy. Since the "first generation entrepreneurs" typically invest a lot of energy and time in businesses, they pay relatively little attention to the family and spend less time with their children. Many of the first generation entrepreneurs created their business out of nothing, and over time, a paternalistic management mode is formed, which places emphasis on personal relationship. On the contrary, many of the second generation have received Western education on corporate governance and prefer a law-based and rational management philosophy, especially in employment of people, to personal relationship. Sooner or later, all family businesses will undergo the transition from the management mode based on personal relationship to one based on law and reason, and this is one of the bottlenecks that the first generation needs to break through. It is very challenging to strike a balance between "family" and "business" and this effort normally entails all types of problems and conflicts. However, "family business" naturally ties both "family" and "business" together. Once the second generation begins to take over, family relations will be involved in work, and disagreements at work may turn into disputes or even quarrels at home.

The second is the way of communication. Parental authority exists universally in Chinese families. As stated in *Luxuriant Dew of the Spring and Autumn Annals*, "Ruler guides subject, father guides son, and husband guides wife." Such a concept has deeply influenced Chinese families and also shows the authority of the parents in Chinese families. When the younger generation expresses their own views that are different from those of their parents, it creates conflicts in the family when an appropriate form of communication is not used, especially if the parents are conservative. If family members are not well-equipped with communication, the first generation will find it difficult to pass their values on to the next generation, and the positive changes by the next generation will not exert the expected influence on the first generation. In the long run, the family cannot form effective family values and pass them on from generation to generation. The failure of succession of many family businesses is mostly due to improper handling of internal conflicts.

The vicissitude of the Chinese society and the replacement of regimes also reflect the ups and downs of Chinese family businesses. In terms of intergenerational succession, Chinese family businesses have historically been reborn from scratch. From the embryonic form of pan-family businesses in the Ming and Qing dynasties, to the family businesses in the capitalist economy during the Republic of China, and then to the current family businesses in China after the reform and opening up, they have actually just undergone one generation of growth and development, so more than 80% of China's family businesses are just coming to the point when the first generation is going to pass on the family business to the second generation. As far as intergenerational transition of family businesses is concerned, we are still far behind the developed countries in Europe and America, as well as Southeast Asian countries. Can the experience in the succession of family businesses in those countries and regions serve as reference to China? The successful successions that occurred in many large family businesses outside China have not only made great contributions to the economic development of the country or region, but also symbolized the enterprising spirit and the sense of responsibility of their younger generations. For example, Wal-Mart in the US, Porsche and BMW in Germany, and LG Group in South Korea are internationally renowned family businesses that have been passed down for generations. Lee Kum Kee, the most famous food brand in Asia with a history of 120 years, has now been passed down to the fifth generation. The key to their success lies in the right succession and distribution mechanism.

Business owners in the US and Europe exercise management of their own businesses through a well-defined, law-based managers system. They generally do not care whether the daily management is exercised by a family member or anybody else. If there are no suitable candidates in the family, whether it is because of lack of interest or ability, they will hire a professional manager to manage the business, or form a team of professionals including lawyers, bankers, and professional managers to assist the heirs in managing the businesses through a reasonable and standardized governance mechanism. Of course, this is because there are sound legal and credit systems in Europe and the US, which is not available in present-day China.

In the present, the development of family businesses in the world, especially in Western developed market economies, shows the following trends: First, the ownership and management rights are separated. With the expansion of the scale of businesses, the intensification of business competition, the transformation of concepts of family and clan, and the rise of professional managers, family-based operations cannot keep up with the development of post-industrial society. Well-established family businesses in the West have taken the initiative to adapt to this trend and given the management rights to the management experts to ensure their continued development. Secondly, pan-familism management is prevalent. The West advocates a family spirit in teams but opposes paternalistic management. Third, there is further socialization of family businesses. By issuing stocks and bonds into the general public, transferring shares to their employees, and investing in social welfare programs, family businesses have furthered the socialization of ownership. The socialization of businesses is not only reflected in the dispersion of equity, but also in the emphasis on corporate social responsibility in terms of management purpose.[9]

At present, there is a low number of Chinese family businesses following this model, with perhaps the exception of Midea.[10] As the only son of He Xiangjian, the founder of Midea Group, He Jianfeng has been detached from his family business since he started his own business in 1994. He did not want to undertake his father's business and had his own career pursuit — he established the Infore Group. His entrepreneurial spirit certainly came from his father. Although he did not inherit the resources of

---

[9] Wang, Ting. (2010). The Status Quo of Group Relay and Approach Research on the "Wealthy Second Generation" of Family Businesses: Taking the United States as a Reference. *Internet Fortune*, 19.

[10] Lee, Siew Kim Jean, Zhao Ziqian. (2015). Midea: Succession of Professional Managers. Global Platform of China Cases.

the home appliance industry from his father, he achieved success in capital operation and the acquisition of the equity of Shangfeng Hi-Tech and E Fund in 2007.

Perhaps because He Jianfeng had expressed his reluctance to take over the family business early, He Xiangjian had enough time to look for professional managers in the process of business development and expansion. By adjusting the internal organization of the business alongside establishing and improving the company's mechanisms and systems, he made plans and arrangements for the future succession well in advance. In 2012, when He Xiangjian officially retired from Midea, his successor was not his son He Jianfeng but Fang Hongbo, a professional manager who rose from the ranks in Midea.

After his father handed over the business to the professional manager, He Jianfeng officially entered the Midea board of directors as a director. The son inherited the equity, the family shared the wealth and at the same time, the management right of the business was delegated to the professional manager. This practice is still a precedent in the succession of Chinese family businesses, and we are looking forward to seeing if the Midea model can be applied to more Chinese family businesses in the future.

Turning our attention to other parts of Asia, we find that Japan, a neighboring country of China, also has many family businesses, and their most distinctive feature is longevity. "The World's Oldest Family Business List" released by Hurun (Rupert Hoogewerf) Report[11] in 2011 showed that the top-ranked Kongo Gumi, a temple construction company from Osaka, Japan, has a history of more than 1,400 years and has now been passed on to the 40th generation. Japanese businesses like Mitsui, Mitsubishi, Sumitomo, and Yasuda are family businesses with centuries of history and they basically implement the "single inheritance system", in which the family businesses will only be passed on to one member of the next generation and other members will "be prohibited from entering the businesses". The purpose of it is very simple: to prevent "infighting". In general, the successor of a Japanese family business will be the eldest son of the next generation, or other competent descendants. However, if the

---

[11] Hurun World's Oldest Family Business List. (2011). Hurun Report — The Richest People in China,

founder believes that his son does not have the capability to take over the business, or that his son is unwilling to do so, he will then find the most capable man among the young people in the business and marry a daughter to him. Finally, a ceremony about "adopting a child" will be held, and then the "adopted son-in-law" will become the head of the family and officially take charge of the business. For instance, although Yasuda Zenjiro, the founder of Yasuda Zaibatsu, has a son, he chose his "son-in-law" as his heir. Matsushita Konosuke, the founder of Panasonic Company, also handed over the company to "adopted son (his son-in-law)" Matsushita Masaharu (his original surname is Hirata).

China's one-child policy has left the first generation of entrepreneurs with the choice of having only one daughter, so in recent years, more and more women are engaged in business. One example is Liu Chang, who is the daughter of the chairman of New Hope Group Liu Yonghao; another is Zong Fuli, who is the daughter of the chairman of Wahaha Group Zong Qinghou, and so on. Whether it is through the way of co-CEO to assist the daughters to take over, or to open new markets to let them take the lead alone, or to turn them into professional managers, the second generation of women like Zhang Yunlan who inherit the traditional businesses are numerous and the daughters inheriting businesses has become a feature of Chinese family businesses. Tu Hongyan of the Wensli Group and his husband Li Jianhua jointly inherited the business. As an expert in the silk industry, Li Jianhua has contributed greatly to the handover and internationalization of Wensli. In addition, although Lu Guanqiu of Wanxiang Group handed over his business to the youngest son Lu Weiding, his three daughters' contribution to Wanxiang should not be ignored, especially the youngest daughter and her husband Ni Pin who have taken on the responsibilities of expanding the international market for many years. Furthermore, Ni Pin is the spokesperson for Wanxiang in the US. Due to the great difference between China and Japan in the view about family consanguinity, it may be difficult to truly employ the practice of "treating the son-in-law as the adopted son" in China, but it is an indisputable fact that the role of a son-in-law is becoming increasingly important in Chinese family businesses. Compared with the incompetent or reluctant sons, selecting sons-in-law may be a turning point in the development of family businesses.

To Succeed or Not: The Dilemma of the Second Generation

I feel particularly sad when I notice how the inheritance of family businesses cannot be carried out smoothly due to various constraints. Likewise if the two generations are so conflicted in the process of succession that they do not know what to do and relations between family members become strained. A novel *Buddenbrooks*[12] written by the famous German writer Thomas Mann tells about the rise and fall of a bourgeois family in Lubeck, Germany in the mid-19th century. Elder Buddenbrook was born in poverty, but he founded a large grain company and became a local tycoon through hard work. Until his later years, he always regarded this company as his whole world and left it to his son Thomas Buddenbrook after his death. However, Thomas, who had been born into a wealthy family, was no longer interested in pursuing money, and saw the grain business as a duty to his family. Then, he focused on pursuing social status and later became a senator. The son of Thomas, the grandson of the elder Buddenbrook, was born in a family with both money and social status, so he was interested in spiritual life and music rather than money and social status. After the death of Thomas, the food company founded by the elder Buddenbrook closed down, the property was sold, the servants were dismissed, and the Buddenbrook family went into decline.

This is a typical story of "shirtsleeves to shirtsleeves in three generations", but there is also a Buddenbrook-like impetus in the Buddenbrook-like decline. The everchanging process of a family over several generations can also reflect the change of a society. The driving force of social development is also derived from this intergenerational change. Each generation has their own goals, so what we have to do is figure out how to calibrate this goal and promote each generation to build their own businesses based on the principle of maintaining the prosperity of family businesses. It is understandable that the older generation of entrepreneurs want their children to follow in their footsteps, and desire for the business empire they have built over the course of their lifetimes to continue to grow in the struggles of future generations. For a long time, family

---

[12] Mann, Thomas. (1901). Buddenbrooks. S. Fischer Verlag, Berlin, Germany.

businesses have continually embodied the law of "both prosperity and decline can appear rapidly". In particular, whether a person can become an entrepreneur depends on talent, interest, and even opportunities. The second generation will not always find the road ahead full of roses merely because their family businesses are thriving. The opportunity of transformation is like the current, which can simply either carry the boat or overturn the boat. When the successor Zhang Yunlan of Red Collar went abroad to study or even when she found a job in Shanghai after returning from abroad, she felt that her life would be as peaceful as ever, and the idea of succession never occurred to her. However, when her father asked whether she could inherit the family business, she felt it was her duty to take over the family business. Even though she did not understand the garment industry or the IT-based transformation her father planned, Zhang Yunlan felt that she should shoulder the responsibility no matter how difficult it was and withstand the pressure together with her father, younger brother, and family. In my perspective, the second generation born into affluent families requires more courage to shoulder this responsibility, and this courage mostly comes from a sense of responsibility to their families. Compared with the first generation of entrepreneurs who have no other choices, the second generation shouldering the family responsibility is not only the specific result of the one-child policy in China, but also the attachment and identity of the second generation to their family and blood relationship. Both generations recognize the huge influence of family edification in the process of inheritance. Although the second generation leads an affluent life in their childhood, the hard work of their parents and the edification of business thinking have left an indelible impression on their childhood, and that identity with the family will greatly embolden the second generation.

As a second generation successor, Zhang Yunlan was brave enough to take on the responsibilities and did not shrink from the pressure imposed on her by this big corporation with thousands of employees. The family responsibilities and her father's love helped her grow. In addition, it is rare in the inheritance of family businesses in China in recent years for a daughter to inherit the business from her father all by her own. As a young university graduate who had just returned, she had no experience in the industry. With her father's full support, Zhang Yunlan persevered despite all the difficulties and setbacks. She once said that she was duty-bound to help him when her father needed her, so I think that the valiant fighting spirit in the second generation is very valuable. In fact, she is not an impulsive person who takes reckless actions. As the saying goes, "Newborn calves are not afraid of tigers." What force is behind this unhesitating decision? Perhaps it is filial piety deep-rooted in the Chinese people's heart, the family concept, and national values that combined to promote the inheritance of family businesses. The one-child policy has an impact on many private entrepreneurs and the traditional concept of transferring the leadership from fathers to sons limits successor choices. The hesitation of the second generation, with so many possibilities in their life, about whether they should inherit the family businesses or not is also an issue worthy of our attention and thinking.

It is obvious that the second generation has to give up an otherwise carefree life and many fields of interest when deciding to enter the family businesses. Nowadays, most of the second generation have received education overseas and this background has an impact on their decision to inherit family businesses in traditional fields. This is especially in the face of pressure in business transformation and upgrading due to the temptation of making quick money in the market, thus many of the second generation choose to venture into finance and investment. Compared with Chinese family businesses in other countries or regions, the "wealthy second generation" on the Chinese mainland has a strong sense of resistance to inheriting the family businesses. In addition to the conflicts in values, the second generation also struggles to inherit the family businesses due to the rapid economic changes in China and the decline of the career of the older generation. As the "only" successor from the second generation in the family in many cases, how does one handle the conflict between family mission and their own interests? Filial piety is a traditional virtue of the Chinese nation. No matter where it comes from — childhood education or the long-term impact of family atmosphere, among the Chinese entrepreneurs I have come into contact with, filial piety has always been the national value respected by everyone. The ethical concept that "filial piety is the foundation of all virtues" has always been advocated by the Chinese nation. In the face of the differences caused by the times, the family is the best bond, which is the basis for the particularity of family businesses compared with other types of business.

In fact, most of the second generation enjoy good material conditions while also having strong learning ability and social adaptability. This kind of learning ability is not simply reflected in test scores or school rankings, but more about having a keen sense of new things and business opportunities. Of course, given the impact of China's booming economy and advanced Western concepts, their thinking — including their creativity — is certainly very different from that of the previous generation. They are averse to the constraints of traditional industries or rules, but their family identity will never change. Scholars have pointed out that the power structure and emotional relationship of the family determine the complex family obligations among family members. I personally believe that the outstanding second generation often has a firm belief which is both innate and acquired, and they are the hope of social change and business innovation.

Due to the differences in growth environment, education, opportunities, and challenges, the two generations differ in thinking, values, and world outlook. The blood connections in the family is inseparable, yet when the businesses are intertwined with the family, the friction between the two generations will not only affect the development of the businesses, but it will also affect the unity of the family. Concluding this analysis, the reason why the second generation is willing to take such challenges under such circumstances is because they are driven by the sense of family responsibility and their own willingness and ability to inherit.

The second generation who has the responsibility and ability to take over the family businesses should have a positive driving force for their inheritance and development. According to the Matthew effect in economics, the more resources people have, the more resources they can use to create opportunities for themselves and for the development of businesses. A life of plenty, good education, commercial edification, and family capital give the second generation a unique competitive edge. Moreover, in addition to the transfer of management rights and equity, there is family-specific knowledge transfer (not costly) in the handover process. This advantage, in which the second generation can share the "special knowledge" of the family businesses, namely the intangible assets of the family, is unmatched by external professional managers.

On the issue of inheritance, the first generation of entrepreneurs should not only set out requirements for the second generation, but they should also conduct an introspection: Do I often neglect my family, and to some extent, it leads to a lack of family responsibility and unwillingness to take over? Am I too authoritarian to see or recognize the second generation's ability to take over? Have I not brought the business into the stage of standardized management, which has hindered the ability of the second generation? In many cases, the mentality and conduct of the second generation is a mirror of the values and style of work of the previous generation over a long period of time. When the inheritance is not going smoothly, the first generation can make a self-examination to identify the underlying causes of the succession problem.

Succession doesn't simply mean the pass over of the businesses to a person, but more importantly, the establishment of institutions and the succession of the business culture. Teaching by precept and example and the instillation of correct family values is the basic skill in family business succession. Especially in today's special era in contemporary China when succession meets the time for transformation, China's family businesses have become the focus of attention. The first generation of Chinese entrepreneurs started from scratch in an age of opportunity and built a business kingdom with their own diligence and courage. While seizing the opportunities, they also struggled to stay alive. However, when the economic situation changes, and the businesses face the challenge of transformation, most entrepreneurs of the first generation are in their twilight years and have to face the problem of whom to hand over the business to, which highlights the particularity of succession in Chinese family businesses. We often talk about European and American family businesses which have been passed down for hundreds of years, and the inheritance of dozens of generations has been very successful. Nonetheless, we must realize that most of them do not face the challenge of transformation at the juncture of inheritance. For Chinese family businesses, this is the first time when intergenerational succession occurs in decades and it happens to coincide with another difficult issue of business transformation. The destiny of Chinese family businesses hinges on whether they can tackle the two problems effectively. Failure in either one can lead to the decline of family businesses. In these circumstances and environment, Chinese family businesses seem to have no other overseas models to refer to and they must rely on their own strength to find a path of inheritance and transformation with Chinese characteristics, so as to break through the bottleneck and move on to the next platform.

2

Richness Stands for Willfulness?: Why Does the "Wealthy Second Generation" Love the Financial Investment Industry?

The vast majority of family businesses in China are still in the hands of the first generation entrepreneurs but they will soon face the problem of finding successors. The intergenerational succession of family businesses has gradually become the focus of attention in the past few years. The intergenerational succession aims to achieve a smooth handover of businesses and the transference of power. The importance of succession is sometimes even greater than the creation of a business. For family members, the power transfer between generations is the most vulnerable part. Failure in succession could become a turning point in the business' decline, and result in the family losing control of the business.

Are the second generation of successors ready to take over? Do they have the ability to take over the businesses from their parents and further continue their development? How do they transform their roles from the "wealthy second generation" to the "second generation entrepreneurs"? In the case of different industries and businesses, properly handling the factors affecting the succession and finding the right path of succession require the joint effort of both generations.

"Transferring the leadership from father to son" is the most traditional and natural succession model of family businesses in China. The development and selection of successors is however not an easy task. It requires particular attention of the first generation of founders, the willingness of the second generation of heirs, and the long-term joint efforts and integration of the two generations. I visited many entrepreneurs and found that they do not own or have not begun to formulate systematic succession plans. Some other entrepreneurs, although having made great efforts to develop their successors, produced final results that were not satisfactory.

After more than 30 years of hard work, China's first generation of private entrepreneurs have accumulated a certain degree of business assets or family wealth, and the development of family businesses has entered the inheritance stage. Compared with the developed countries in Europe and America and our neighbor Japan, all of which have inheritance experience over three to five generations, the inheritance between the first and second generations of China's family businesses is facing many difficulties.

The "Report on the Development of Chinese Family Business"[1] jointly published by the All-China Federation of Industry and Commerce Research Office, Research Centre for Chinese Family Firm of Sun Yat-sen University, Family Business Research Institute of Zhejiang University City College and Lee Kum Kee Family in 2011 showed that only 35% of the second generation have a willingness to take over family businesses. Much of this is owed to the legendary entrepreneurs who are not willing to fade out of the power center and who are not fully aware of what they should do in raising successors. Moreover, the stark difference in ideas between the first and second generation also makes the second generation resistant to succession.

Over many years of research into the management and succession of Chinese family businesses, I found that there are two main reasons for the unsuccessful succession between the two generations. First, in regards to transferring the leadership from father to son, there are obvious differences in values between the two generations. Values do not only decide an

---

[1] Research Group of Family Business of China Private Economy Research Association. (2011). Report on the Development of Chinese Family Business. CITIC Publishing House.

individual's behavior, but they also affect the relationship between family members and the decision-making of the whole business. This eventually affects the economic benefits of the business. Second, the two generations have different perceptions and preferences for business ideas and management methods. The management models and business ideas favored by most of the second generation are significantly different from the common practice of "one person alone having the say" preferred by their parents.

The root causes of these two main differences are highlighted in the following:

Firstly, the age and experience gap of 25–30 years between the two generations of Chinese family businesses correlate with the social and economic transformation of contemporary China. The huge transformation of this environment has resulted in a vast difference between the second generation and their parents in their growth, background, and values. The background which one grows up with determines one's values. The greater the difference in social experience between the two generations, the more rebellious the second generation is to the traditional conducts and concepts of the first generation.

Secondly, the level of education affects the entrepreneurs' cognitive ability and the capability to collect information and deal with problems. Most of the first generation entrepreneurs in China were from humble family backgrounds and benefited from the opportunities of the market in that particular period. Most of their experience and leadership ability comes from actual business transactions, while the second generation are often highly educated with in elite institutions, with a large number of them having had the experience of studying abroad. Such stellar educational background and experience have given them different experiences and broader perspectives. The big difference in the level of education between the two generations means that they also differ greatly in business management and decision-making. More importantly, the first generation belonging to the "empiricists" can't help but educate the second generation, while the second generation belonging to the "academics" often scorn the experience of the "empiricists". Subordinates who do not recognize the boss's ideas can resign and leave, but when one's father is the boss, the second generation child finds it hard to leave with easy grace, and the first generation also finds it difficult to be truly rigorous with their children.

Thirdly, it is precisely because the first generation of Chinese entrepreneurs, after having caught up with the first wave of economic development and reform and opening up while relying on their own efforts to start businesses, put their lives into a state of going all out and rushing around. There is a large number of entrepreneurs who sacrifice family life for the sake of business development, hence they have little communication with their children — the environments in which they live in and grow are separated. Simultaneously, in the period of rapid economic development, the influence of utilitarianism also results in the reduction of interpersonal communication and the inculcation of values and cultural concepts, thus neglecting the establishment and unification of the core values within the family.

Of course, the second generation who grow up in an era of rapid economic development have more choices and most of them prefer to develop their own careers according to their own wishes and interests. More than half of the students and interviewees I talked to are reluctant to work in their parents' company for two reasons. First, they have no interest in the businesses of their parents. Second, they think the family businesses are so wide-ranging and messy that it would be difficult for them to take over and face the old staff. After the reform and opening up, the impact of Western culture was strong throughout the years when they grew up, and their overseas education background led to differences in values and concepts between the two generations which further affected the inheritance of family businesses. Meanwhile, they are eager to be independent and to prove their self-worth and do not like being called the spoiled "wealthy second generation". Most of them prefer to do things that they are interested in, and many of the first generation entrepreneurs are, in turn, happy to provide the necessary financial support to their children as they pursue their interests.

The Second Generation's Preference for Financial Investment

The result of our research cases showed[2] that many of the second generation are far more interested in financial investment than in succeeding

---

[2]Lee, Siew Kim Jean. (2015). The Second Generation Prefers Financial Investment — Richness Stands for Willfulness? *Forbes* (Chinese version), 9, 64–66.

their parents' businesses. Many of the "second generation entrepreneurs" are also inclined to start their businesses in the fields related to financial investment. In more than 60 cases I interviewed, at least three-quarters of them are more or less involved in financial investment. Some of them work full-time in financial institutions, some started financial companies in partnership with friends, and some help family businesses manage financial investment projects. With the development of market liberalization, family businesses are indeed faced with many different challenges and temptations. While the real economy finds it difficult to make a profit and get loans from the bank, there exists the temptation of making quick money with high risks and high returns. Therefore, many family businesses follow the trend of the times, jumping into the fields of real estate and financial investment which are outside their former range of business. Our research finds that although the second generation loves the financial investment industry, they have different options in investing and handling the enterprises created by their parents. Their options not only affect themselves, but also the future of these businesses.

The Willful Second Generation

Let's take a look at a case of a rich and willful second generation. Haixin Steel, created by Li Haicang, was the second largest steel company in Shanxi Province, and Li Haicang was known as the "King of Shanxi Steel" for his good management. After Li Haicang died in an accident in 2003, the family business — the largest private company in Shanxi Province — was taken over by his son Li Zhaohui at the proposal of his grandfather. However, Li Zhaohui had no interest in the real economy but attached great importance to the capital market, making the Haixin Steel an "ATM" for his financial investment.

On November 12, 2004, the first year of his succession, Li Zhaohui became the tenth largest shareholder of Minsheng Bank by buying 160 million shares of the bank held by NFC (China Nonferrous Metal Industry's Foreign Engineering and Construction Co., Ltd) at a price of nearly 600 million yuan, paid for with Haixin Industry, a subsidiary of Haixin Steel. At the peak of the bull market in the first half of 2007, Haixin Industry sold nearly 100 million shares of Minsheng Bank and cashed out more than 1 billion yuan, so the investment in Minsheng Bank was the most successful investment of Li Zhaohui in the capital market. He also invested in China Everbright Bank, Industrial Securities, Shanxi Securities, and other companies, and cashed out after they went public. Furthermore, in the secondary market, he also invested in listed companies such as Chinalco, Yimin Commercial Group, Industrial Bank, and Luneng Taishan. Compared with his huge gains from the investment in Minsheng Bank, Li Zhaohui's subsequent transactions in the capital market did not achieve desired results.

Li Zhaohui continued to take money from Haixin Steel to invest in the capital market, but a large sum of money vanished and did not return to Haixin to support its development. From the end of 2013, the production at Haixin Steel was in trouble. After the Spring Festival in 2014, the six blast furnaces of the factory were discontinued. In late March 2014, Haixin Steel was completely shut down, totaling up to billions of debts. At the end of 2014, it began to enter a formal bankruptcy process. Recently, a bribery scandal was exposed in Haixin Steel.

Due to his excessive enthusiasm for capital operation, Li Zhaohui was actively involved in transactions in the capital market in the past ten years. After the succession, he completely ignored the development of the enterprise and the main business of steel. He did not withdraw money from the stock market in time to help the steel company overcome difficulties. All this led to the final decline of Haixin Steel. Ten years at the helm of the family business, Li Zhaohui was regarded as a real disappointment. In the early days of Li Zhaohui's succession, sales and profitability of the company were satisfactory thanks to the influence of his father and family, the good economic situation, and the big bull market in 2005–2007. The economic downturn followed, and the capital market fell rapidly. It was not shocking that Haixin Steel collapsed without the support of the real economy.

The Second Generation Who Take over Their Family Businesses and Open up New Prospects

Xu Lixun of Ningbo Huamao Group was in a similar position to Li Zhaohui when he took over the family business from his father. Unlike Li, he was very successful in the field of financial investment. He returned to China after graduating from Rice University in the US in 1999 and was not planning to work at the family business. On April 30, 2000, Huamao suffered the biggest crisis in its history — the Huamao American crisis. His father Xu Wanmao was involved in a lawsuit in the US and a replacement in China must come forward to lead the corporation. Thus, 26-year-old Xu Lixun became the designated authorizer and agent of his father, but he soon suffered an industry slump when he took office. At that time, students were the targeted users of one of Huamao's key products. It happened that the Ministry of Education introduced a policy aimed at reducing students' burden, hence production at Huamao had to stop. Profits fell consecutively year in and year out. By the end of 2005, Huamao faced a deficit for the first time in more than 30 years since its establishment. In order to prove his ability and have the final say in the business, Xu Lixun, who was sensitive to the financial market, began to set foot in the capital market in 2004. Taking advantage of the restructuring of Ningbo Bank Co., Ltd., Xu Lixun invested 161 million yuan to increase his stock, holding 162 million shares and a 2.5-billion-yuan credit line. In 2005, he obtained another 17 million shares. In July 2007, Ningbo Bank went public, which brought lucrative profits to Huamao. In 2007, the investment sector created 80% profit for the company. Later, with a series of successes in the investment field, Xu Lixun was recognized within the company. After that, he made frequent investments in the capital market and became a shareholder of Ningbo Construction Company and Ningbo United Communications.

Having gained a firm foothold in the company through excellent performance, Xu Lixun did not give up his father's business, which was the education industry. He made great efforts to hire and train new professionals within the company, reviewed and improved company rules, exercised delicacy management featuring the motto "rules are more important than the group's president", liquidated the company's assets, cleared up equity ownership, addressed the problem that some assets had not been accounted for, and so on. Xu Lixun constantly sought breakthroughs in industrial development by learning from successful foreign models. He also diversified Huamao's business, by not relying solely on the previous model of tendering in the field of education. Today, under the leadership of Xu Lixun, Huamao has not only formed an investment industry chain mainly based on equity investment and secondary market securities investment, but it is also a diversified group based on the education industry.

As a representative of the post-1985 successors, Yu Jiangbo was considered a success. As the eldest son of Jewelry Queen Zhou Xiaoguang, the head of the Neoglory Group and to take over the responsibility from his parents, Yu Jiangbo studied in the UK for seven years before returning to work in the family business in 2008. First, he served as the assistant to the vice-president of marketing. In 2011, he was appointed as the general manager of Neoglory Jewelry and began a series of radical reforms, such as outsourcing non-core production and establishing a high-end multi-brand strategy, which achieved good results. He not only upgraded the company's existing business, but also carried out a new e-commerce business expansion, thus establishing three vertical integration businesses: Taoqu Network focused on the establishment of online stores, Warehouse Technology's main business involved logistics warehousing and diversified services, and Taoci Technology was positioned as an e-commerce software provider. Starting from the industry was his own choice, because he believed that one should achieve a good understanding of industry before one could make a worthy and good investment. With the transformation and stabilization of the jewelry business, Yu Jiangbo began to get involved in the investment field. On the evening of June 9, 2015, Sichuan Jinlu Group, which was suspended for nearly five months, issued a restructuring plan. It planned to respectively purchase 100% stock in Wansha Real Estate and Neoglory Building Materials at a price of 11.214 billion yuan. However, this move was hindered by non-market factors at the threshold of listing. After several twists and turns, it was not until May 2016 when Neoglory once again carried out asset restructuring through the backdoor listing of FY Precision Machinery. Finally, through the newly-established company Neoglory Prosperity, some of the assets of Neoglory Group went public, and Yu Jiangbo and his parents led Neoglory to the broader capital market.

The Innovative Second Generation

Xu Lixun and Yu Jiangbo chose to take over the family business from their parents and at the same time got involved in financial investment to pursue their own interests. They worked hard and became more mature after being tested in difficult circumstances. However, not all second generation children are willing to take over the enterprises created by their parents. Perhaps many of them want to follow He Jianfeng, who did not take over the management of the family business, but instead set up his own investment company instead. Eventually, as a shareholder, he became a non-executive director on the board of directors of the family business.

As the only son of He Xiangjian, the founder of Midea Group, He Jianfeng started his business in 1994. Initially his business focused on OEM production of small household appliances, which constituted the upstream and downstream industry of Midea. After ten years of development, he made the business transformation by gradually withdrawing from the OEM appliance manufacturing and circulation industry to focus his energy on the capital market. He began to set foot in the securities investment industry through acquisitions and other means. The Infore Group created by He Jianfeng gradually shifted away from his father's influence. In the following years, he gained a lot in capital operation, such as the acquisition of the equity of Shangfeng Hi-Tech and E Fund in 2007. As the unquestionable successor to his family business, He Jianfeng had his own career pursuit; he did not want to inherit his father's business but desired to establish his own business kingdom.

Perhaps because his son had indicated that he was unwilling to take over the family business early, He Xiangjian had publicly stated on many occasions that Midea would not become a family business, and that he would not allow his children to work or participate in Midea Group. Through a series of well-thought-out measures, He Xiangjian made sure that Midea would be ready for succession when it was time for him to retire. The measures included cultivating professional managers in the process of business development, adjusting internal organizations, creating conditions for the development of professional managers, building and improving the mechanisms and systems, and more. In 2012, he officially stepped down as chairman of Midea Group, and only served as the controlling shareholder of Midea Group and the chairman of Midea Holding Company. His successor and new leader of Midea Group was not his only son He Jianfeng but a professional manager called Fang Hongbo, who served as the chairman and president of the listed company Midea Electric Appliances.

He Jianfeng, who kept a distance from the family business since he started his own business in 1994, officially joined Midea's board of directors after his father passed on the scepter to a professional manager. He inherited the equity and wealth from his father, leaving the management of the business to the professional manager. This practice is a special case of family business succession. In the foreseeable future, the He family will withdraw behind the scenes and Midea Group will surely turn into a public company. We would like to witness how the influence of the He family on Midea will change in the future, and how long He Xiangjian's influence will remain in the future development and culture of Midea.

Why Is Financial Investment So Popular with the Second Generation?

Firstly, they are unwilling to earn money the hard way as their parents. Currently, most of the family businesses entering the generation transition period in China were established around 1978 when China introduced reform and opening up. At that time, market opportunities were everywhere, so how the first generation of entrepreneurs made their fortune was obvious to all. Although they were subject to the limitations of the overall economy and the market, they managed to survive, develop, and grow in the market over the past 30 years and more. Now, when the market is fully open with competition from all over the world, these businesses have reached the stage of transformation and are constantly upgrading. This is a fact that cannot be ignored. In the face of the weak economy and the declining industrial development, what the second generation of entrepreneurs are taking over is in fact a huge business; they not only need to handle the complex relationship within the businesses, but also have to cope with the external pressure for change. In addition, within the development of private businesses, the "first generation entrepreneurs" often started from scratch and went through all the hardships to build up today's huge empire from a small business with small profits. The second generation has witnessed all the difficulties, the hard work, and sacrifices experienced by their parents, so it is reasonable that they are unwilling to take over the industry. By the same token, many of the first generation of entrepreneurs are reluctant to let their children take the same old path after their painful experiences, preferring to give them the freedom to develop their own interests.

Secondly, the second generation has already gained the "first pot of gold". For many of the "wealthy second generation", family business is a responsibility and obligation, but involvement in the field of financial investment is more about developing their own interest. Their parents' business success gives them the "first pot of gold" that can be used for investment, as well as the good resources that will help them find investment projects. They are provided with a platform for a smooth start and the ability of capital operation. The family also brings good connections to the second generation, making it easier for them to access good resources when making investments, which is undoubtedly one of the unique advantages vital to the second generation as they enter this field. Whether the second generation is starting their own business or engaging in financial investment, the starting funds, in most cases, come from their parents. With all the funds accumulated by their parents at their disposal, "making money with money" is a road to get rich quickly. With the expansion of family businesses and the accumulation of wealth over the years, it is necessary for the first generation to consider investment and financial management. The second generation's involvement in financial investment can satisfy their interest and explore new fields on behalf of the first generation. If the second generation can make good use of their resource platforms, "making money with money" will not only put their parents' wealth into good use, but will also meet the demand of asset preservation and appreciation. On the basis that the wealth is accumulated by the parents over the past 20 to 30 years, the second generation is likely to make substantial profits after a few years of operation.

Third, the second generation applies what they have learned and enjoys the lifestyle of investors. Most of the new generation of successors are influenced by the experience of studying abroad and a large number of them have studied banking, economy, finance, and other related disciplines, either by their own choice or at the suggestion of their parents. Their academic qualifications and the accumulation of resources are also one of the reasons for them to engage in the financial industry. The years they studied abroad are a time when they form and establish their values and the impact of the "Spirit of Wall Street" convinced them that they would not suffer the hardship as their parents in the early days of their business. They want to make money in a relaxed and leisurely manner. Therefore, the capital operation mode of "throwing a sprat to catch a herring" has gradually become their favorite and they prefer to stay in first-tier financial centers such as Beijing, Shanghai, and Guangzhou to realize their dreams of capital operation and financial investment. Obviously, the second generation wants to prove their ability through capital operation and apply what they have learned; they also want to maintain their comfortable lifestyle formed in the superior environment from childhood and interact with the rich and the powerful. Therefore, engaging in financial investment seems to be the best choice for them.

Fourth, the second generation goes with the flow in accordance with the development of the times. Since the reform and opening up, China's private economy has experienced four wave of opportunities under different stages of development: The tough start-up period, the passionate period of "venturing into business" in 1992, the peak period of the survival of the fittest of the Internet era and the emerging period of the last seven or eight years. The first batch of "wealthy second generation" started around 2000, and many of them are the "second generation entrepreneurs" who relied on venture capital and Internet economy to develop rapidly with the rise of the new economy. The vigorous development of China's financial capital market in the past 15 years has also provided a fast lane for the second generation to enter the investment field. Financial reform has promoted the mass listing of financial enterprises, and large quantities of private capital has entered the fields of banking, securities, insurance, venture investment, etc. After the economic development reaches a plateau, the real industry faces the pressure of transformation and upgrading, and the profit margin of businesses can no longer rival the high rate of return brought by financial investment. In contrast, banking remains an industry with rapid and high rates of returns. As the financial market matures, a multi-level capital market gradually comes into shape, and Internet-based finance has become a hot topic in the past two years. The temptation of the market environment and the development of emerging industries have strong attraction for the second generation who are "born with a silver spoon in their mouth". Moreover, the collision between traditional industries and emerging industries is also an important reason for the second generation to choose financial investment. Faced with the rapid development of the high-risk and high-yield financial industry, it is reasonable for the second generation to attempt to take advantage of the trend.

Financial Investment as an Alternative

Based on the above reasons, the second generation's preference for financial investment seems to be a natural response to the prevailing trend. At present, China's economic development has reached a plateau, and businesses are facing the challenging processes of transformation, upgrading, and globalization. The second generation is happy to leverage their overseas study experience and the advantage of being familiar with the overseas market. They are not fettered by any traditional models or thinking. It is valuable for them to seize the opportunities and reap the benefits just by following the tide. The financial market is skyrocketing; hence, risk also means opportunity. It is again justifiable for the second generation to stand on the shoulders of the first generation, make use of their knowledge and resources, and turn their strengths into actual wealth.

What does it mean for the inheritance of a family business when the second generation chooses to enter the financial investment industry for capital operation?

From the cases above, we can see that the second generation has two successful modes of capital operation. One is the combination of traditional business and new business. The succession of family business is an eternal theme for the owners who desire the everlasting development of businesses. In general, most entrepreneurs have only one or two children, hence, the options for successors are very limited. Then, if the second generation prefers to engage in financial investment, it creates a problem of finding someone who should take over the enterprise. Taking Xu Lixun of Huamao Group and Yu Jiangbo of Neoglory Group as examples, the second generation can use investment as one of the strategic expansion measures behind the group while taking over the main business. The accumulation, integration, and utilization of family resources, reputation, brand, and personal connections can help the second generation to improve the financial leverage of family businesses through financial investment, enhance profitability, advance the diversified development of businesses, and foster the ability to resist risks in times of economic fluctuations. The other is the total separation of the family business from the successor's investment practice as He Jianfeng did in Midea Group. This is perhaps the choice that many of the second generation prefer. However, this approach requires that the head of the family must make an early plan for the development of future successors and have a corporate culture well established. If the second generation is actively engaged in the investment industry but his practice is not clearly separated from the business entity and is not subject to effective checks, there is the danger of repeating the failure of Haixin Steel.

When the second generation steps into the financial investment field, it is not difficult to find that the risk of the capital market should not be underestimated even if they start on the shoulders of the first generation. "Losing money from investment in the financial market" is something that every pioneering entrepreneur or a person who wants to be a "second generation entrepreneur" tries to avoid by all means. Therefore, the second generation must take risk control when entering the investment field. The experience of China's rapid economic development in the past three-plus decades has raised people's expectation for return on investment unrealistically, which may compromise their judgment on investment risks. We must always be aware of the risks of the capital market and the unsustainability of long-term high returns.

At the same time, in order to establish a better risk prevention mechanism, family businesses need to set up a sound governance model to guide and manage investment and avoid making decisions subjectively. For example, the Mulliez family in Europe regulates family business funds by establishing a family committee to guide and manage the investment practice of family members. Since transactions in the capital market need to be professional and standardized, they should turn to professionals and investment institutions for advice before making the final decision. This will allow them to avoid irreversible losses brought to the family business due to an individual's unsound judgment.

Finally, it all comes down to the fundamental issue: If money is not given any value, then a family business that possesses a lot of money will ultimately have no value. A business must have a clear governance structure and professional management in order to protect family wealth and business assets. This is of vital importance in the development and inheritance of family businesses. The cornerstone for a family to last a century and beyond is not wealth itself, but family values and a sense of responsibility to the family business. The best gift for the new generation of trendsetters who grow up in abundance is to inculcate family values in them and a strong sense of responsibility to the family business. Being affluent does not mean one can act willfully, instead they should act sensibly. Family and social responsibilities are the best constraints when the wealthy second generation wants to act willfully. If family wealth is not endowed with family values and responsibilities, acting wilfully with money will result in families suffering the "Shirtsleeves-To-Shirtsleeves" curse.

Cultivation of Interest

Among many family businesses, one common and important reason why the second generation engages in the financial investment industry is that they are not interested in the main business of the family. The question is: Is interest so important in the succession of the second generation? Can interest be cultivated? As they get older, the interest of the second generation may also change. I understand that there were some people of the second generation who had showed zero interest in the family business early on but changed their mind and eventually turned out to be a great success after the succession.

Li Yunfeng Builds Ships

I know Li Yunfeng, the young president of Marco Polo Marine in Singapore. To my understanding, many young people have heard of him because his wife is Vivian Hsu, a pop star. His growth and succession experience should be instructive to many of the second generation. I once invited him to be a guest speaker in the successor course of CEIBS — "Creation and Inheritance". I also specially invited him to Shanghai to share his experience of growing up in a typical family business with the audience at the forum of Chinese family business inheritance in 2015. Li Yunfeng was born in Indonesia, the world's fourth most populated country and one of the world's fastest-growing economies. His grandfather was born in south China and started his business by trading commodities, such as sugar and salt. His father took over the trading of bulky commodities, and subsequently entered the real estate industry when the opportunity arised. In fact, their first pot of gold came from real estate. Li Yunfeng's father can be truly regarded as a first generation entrepreneur. After getting involved in the real estate industry, the Li family began to engage in infrastructure construction. In the 1960s, Indonesia was a land of opportunity. It is interesting to note that Indonesia is a country with a large Chinese population and the whole society is influenced by Chinese culture. Connections are very important in doing business. Through said special connections, Li Yunfeng's father obtained a large number of contracts for the business, so the second pot of gold of the Li family came from infrastructure construction and engineering projects. After that, his father entered the mining industry, which is currently the core business of Marco Polo Marine.

Although Li Yunfeng was born in Indonesia, he moved to Singapore with his family when he was 8 years old and later went to Australia to study. He spent most of his childhood, adolescence, and college years in Australia. As the second generation of the family business, he returned to Singapore after graduating from university, which was certainly not his own choice. Li Yunfeng said that his father raised him in a very traditional way because the father himself came from a very traditional family, which seemed to be a kind of family heritage. His father was very strict in doing everything. He remembered very clearly that at the age of 8, while other parents took the children to play in different places on weekends, his father took him to the construction site. He had been exposed to life on construction sites since he was a child, with only sand and architectural workpieces in his memory. His "boring" childhood made him lose interest in the family business. He did not find life interesting until he went to Australia, where his father was absent. When he was 16 years old, Li Yunfeng returned to Singapore for a holiday. His father still insisted on taking him to the mine and hoped that he would learn the entire mining process, which was a really bad experience for young Li Yunfeng. His father asked him, "Do you like it?" He did not hesitate to answer,

"I certainly don't like it because I like to chase girls and hang out with friends." After all, he was only 16 that year.

By the time he was 21, he passed the exams and completed his studies. As a wealthy second generation, he started to delineate his future of infinite possibilities and felt that the real interesting life which really belonged to him was unfolding. However, a phone call from his father completely changed his life trajectory, "You have completed your studies and should come back. Come back soon!" So, the day after the exams ended, he returned to Singapore, where the family business was located. Many people admired that Li Yunfeng was so obedient.

From then on, Li Yunfeng began working in a mining company, starting at the grassroots level. When he was in charge of a mine, he faced a lot of pressure, especially from the old staff who had followed his father for a long time. Handling any relationship with them posed as a huge challenge for Li Yunfeng. An old staff member would say, "I watched you grow up. You shouldn't do that." But Li Yunfeng stuck to his own opinions as long as he believed that they were doing things incorrectly. As a result, his relationship with the old staff was very tense and they would complain to his father about this. He could only make a pledge to his father, "If you want me to do this, you must trust me and I will prove to you that I can do it right." Fortunately, he proved himself and convinced the old staff. Relations between them improved, and the business reaped progress. This example tells us that the second generation must prove themselves through good performance. As their power increases, they can do more in managing their family business their own way.

Later, Li Yunfeng went to work at the shipping company that is part of Marco Polo Group. It was so small that many people did not know that they had a shipping business. At that time, the shipping section of the Marco Polo Group was mainly responsible for transporting bulk commodities, such as minerals, and because it was a supporting service, the family did not attach much importance to it. When he got there, he found that the company had only six ships. The general managers and CEOs of different business units had a meeting every three months. As Li Yunfeng remembered clearly, at a meeting he said, "We can afford to buy more ships." His father asked, "How much do you know about shipbuilding and shipyards?" It was obvious that his father was not very supportive of his ideas, so he did not refute at the time. After another three months, they had a meeting again and his father said to him, "Son, I have bought a piece of land. You want to build a shipyard, don't you?" Li Yunfeng was surprised that his father bought the land he wanted and gave it to him, because he merely mentioned it thoughtlessly three months before. This incident had a great impact on him. He felt extremely diffident: "This land means a lot more to me than what it actually is." His father then said to him, "Son, this is the cheapest piece of land I can find. You have no choice and should start from here." Subsequently, Marco Polo established a shipyard and began making ships. Li Yunfeng received funding of 15 million yuan and 20 million Singapore dollars from the parent company, but after the shipyard was built, it had no business and no income. This was a heavy blow to him.

At that time, many banks were not optimistic about this business and were unwilling to invest in it. Li Yunfeng did not give up. When he contacted the Bank of Indonesia, which had long-term cooperation with his family, it agreed to provide a loan with an 18% interest rate and requested that his father be his personal guarantee. At that time, Li Yunfeng could feel the important influence of family reputation on business development. He was very fortunate because the shipyards were built at a time when market was good, and things were turning for the better.

Looking back, Li Yunfeng realized that his father had made a good plan for his development in advance and trained and educated him since he was a child. Therefore, even though he found the construction sites boring, with his father's instruction and encouragement, Li Yunfeng became more and more interested in the family business through actual practice and eventually found his right place in a supporting industry of the family business. The number of ships in Marco Polo Marine has increased from 6 to 106 today and the company has been successfully listed. This is not only a successful story of Li Yunfeng; it is also a successful case of family business inheritance.

Liu Chang Raises Pigs

Liu Chang of New Hope Group was typical of the second generation who had no interest in their parents' businesses. The "post-80s" young girl who received education abroad since childhood had a beautiful and unrestrained youth. No one would expect her to be linked with her father Liu Yonghao's feed business. Someone asked Liu Yonghao, "What about the inheritance of your business?" Someone said, "Give your chairman's position to Liu Chang and the succession is completed." To Liu Yonghao, these views were one-sided. In his eyes, Liu Chang, who is a girl and is much younger than him, has received better education than him, speaks and writes English much better than him, has traveled to as many places as he has, and is quick at learning and absorbing new things. He is particularly impressed by his daughter's communication skills. After Liu Chang took over as Co-Chairman of New Hope Liuhe for more than a year, she won the recognition of everyone in the company. She is now very passionate about the family business and loves the industry of New Hope.

However, Liu Chang was not born like that. More than a decade ago, when Liu Chang came back from studying in the US, Liu Yonghao took her to their factory. She went there once and refused to go the second time. She said that pig farms were stinky, instead she liked fashion, internationalization, and modern and foreign things. She did not like raising pigs or New Hope's feed industry. What should he do at this time? Instead of forcing her, Liu Yonghao asked her what she liked. He lent her 1 million yuan to help her open a shop with some friends. When she didn't know where to stock up, her friend told her to go to Wenzhou. Then she actually went there, brought the goods back and sold them in her shop. At the time, there were few shops like hers in Chengdu, so she made some money and found out that the selling price of many items was three or four times as much as the cost. For a while, she loved her company and shop very much and Liu Yonghao felt that this was very important. In his view, a smooth inheritance required the second generation to like the family business, and he should not force the business on her. After a period of carefree time, Liu Yonghao told his daughter that their dairy company was doing well and asked her if she would like to work there. She thought for a moment and agreed. Then she started work at a low position in the dairy company. She used an alias, so people in the company didn't know that she was Liu Yonghao's daughter. Unfortunately, this trial did not last long, because at that time Liu Chang had just returned from abroad and was not really interested in traditional industries. She opened an advertising company in

Beijing with her friends. The advertising company did some planning, publicity, and promotion for some famous companies, and gradually she gained a better understanding of the market.

After his daughter was tempered in the market, Liu Yonghao patiently waited for her to return to the dairy company again and made her office director. Seven or eight years later, Liu Chang became a Peking University student under renowned professor Lin Yifu before she went on to study at Tsinghua University. After all those years of work and study, she was slowly progressing and maturing. A few years ago, Liu Yonghao asked her again, "I am old! Are you willing to do something for the family business?" This time Liu Chang said that she would like to start in agriculture. Liu Yonghao was surprised and pleased, "So, you are not bothered by the stinky pigs?" Liu Chang, who had been through adversities in the world, replied, "No! To me all industries are the same. I don't believe that some industries are more decent than others. On the contrary, I think agriculture has great development potential and our industry is very important. Moreover, we are already in a leading position in the country. Our company is now the world's largest feed company and the largest supplier of meat, egg, and milk in China." Liu Chang genuinely changed. A lot of friends said to Liu Yonghao, "You are amazing, and your daughter is outstanding, because she is willing to do it. Even though my son is a grown-up, he doesn't want to take over the business. Many of the second generation are like this. They despise the work and think that they should enjoy life and go their own way."

From the cases of Li Yunfeng and Liu Chang, we can see that the interests of the second generation can be developed incrementally. This requires the patience and gradual guidance of the first generation and not force the industry on them. Liu Yonghao was a successful example. At the same time, the experience and courage of the second generation are indispensable. In my research over the past three years, I also studied some of the personal attributes that affect the willingness of the second generation to take over.

The Need for Cultivation and Edification of Time

The succession process of Li Yunfeng and Liu Chang has been tortuous: Reluctance at first but resulting in their willingness to take over. This corresponds with my research findings. I have interviewed nearly one hundred families with the second generation already working at the family businesses. In my research I found that the education level and age of the second generation are two important factors that affect their willingness to take over and organizational commitment. With the rise of academic qualifications, the willingness of the second generation who received college education to take over their families' companies has increased. When the second generation continues to pursue advanced studies and receives postgraduate education, their willingness to take over increases significantly. In addition, with the rise in age, the second generation will have a higher sense of identity and commitment to family businesses. This means that young people may express no interest in family business and succession and prefer to do things as they wish. But with the passage of time, they tend to change their mind. Therefore, the first generation of entrepreneurs should have enough patience to train and guide their successors, just as Liu Yonghao did with his daughter. It takes time for the second generation to assimilate themselves in the world and rekindle their interest in the family business.

Society is the best teacher and truth comes from practice. In addition to academic qualifications, the second generation can prepare for the succession and increase the willingness to take over by participating in some training courses on business management, receiving the guidance of senior employees within the family business or other successful entrepreneurs and working in other businesses. People of the second generation who are well prepared demonstrate a stronger willingness to take over than those who are not. This shows that the second generation is very concerned about self-assessment when considering whether to take over or not.

To the second generation who already are working in the family businesses and are preparing themselves for the succession, the difficulties, challenges, trials, and tribulations in the succession process will help them learn and grow. In general, as succession time increases, the willingness and organizational commitment of the second generation to take over the family business increase significantly. In the process of succession, the second generation can learn and accumulate business management experience and transform the knowledge into their own experience and ability,

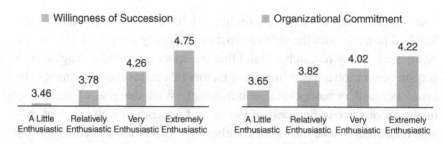

Figure 2.1 The Impact of Growth Experience of Succession on Willingness and Organizational Commitment

Note: The values in the figure are the mean comparison coefficients.

which will help them enhance their self-affirmation and give them a sense of involvement in family business, thereby increasing organizational commitment. In the *Willingness and Commitment of Successors — White Paper on the Inheritance of Chinese Family Business*[3] published in 2014, I shared some of my research results (see Figure 2.1) in this area and considered the factors affecting the willingness and commitment of the second generation to return to family businesses.

Self-efficacy Is Crucial

If a good educational background lays the foundation for the second generation, then working in businesses provides an environment for testing their capabilities. Business experience can be divided into two categories: One, the prospective successor works in other enterprises; two, the prospective successor works in the family business. Our research has found that the experience of working "outside" in other people's business does not enhance the willingness to inherit the family business, but working in the family business and growing up with it does strengthen their willingness to stay and take over the family business. The growth experience of

---

[3]Lee, Siew Kim Jean, Rui Meng, Lu Yunting, Cui Zhiyu. (2014). Willingness and Commitment of Successors — White Paper on the Inheritance of Chinese Family Business. Family Inheritance Research Center of China Europe International Business School.

potential successors within the family business is very important. Challenging work in the family business provides prospective successors the opportunities for trial-and-error. This will test and improve their abilities. If in this process they get positive feedback from others, it will bolster their confidence in carrying forward their family business and enhance their willingness to stay for the succession. The more confident the successors feel about the family business, the more efforts they will make. Meanwhile, the enhancement of their ability means their efforts will have good results, thus forming a virtuous circle, so that they will have greater organizational commitment after taking over.

It is hard to find an equivalent in Chinese for the English phrase "self-efficacy". In this context, I interpret this phrase as recognition of one's abilities and a demonstration of confidence in oneself, or a subjective judgment of the second generation about whether they can successfully inherit the family businesses. I found in this study (see Figure 2.2) that if the second generation has a higher sense of self-efficacy, their willingness to take over will be greatly strengthened and their organizational commitment will also increase accordingly. Even if their sense of self-efficacy has reached a high level, their organizational commitment will still rise.

It is worth mentioning that the second generation's sense of self-efficacy or self-confidence can not only directly increase their willingness to take over, but also reduce the negative effects that other factors may bring to them. For example, if the first generation has a relatively high level of education, less confident successors will be afraid to express their own opinions and demonstrate little enthusiasm for succession. If the number of siblings of the first generation is large, the second generation lacking

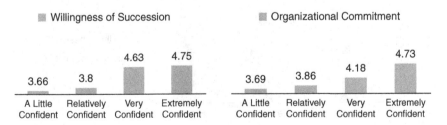

Figure 2.2 The Impact of Self-efficacy on Succession and Organizational Commitment

Note: The values in the figure are the mean comparison coefficients.

confidence may feel that there is always the possibility of being replaced and their willingness to succeed will not be strong. Moreover, the more senior executives there are in the business, the more challenges the unconfident second generation will face in all respects and the less willingness they will hold. Yet, for the confident second generation, these issues are not a challenge and will not have a negative impact on their willingness to succeed. This is because the second generation with high self-efficacy has a certain sense of confidence in their own abilities and believes that they are capable of taking over the business. At the same time, self-confidence can help them to rise up to the challenges in the face of difficulties and actively deal with them, thus creating a virtuous cycle in the process of succession.

So, where does the second generation's sense of self-efficacy come from? Our study (see Figure 2.3) found that, for the second generation, family factors have the greatest influence and enhancing the confidence of the second generation must be realized through the family. For family businesses, the degree of intimacy and the frequency of communication between family members have extremely important impacts on the growth and succession of the second generation. We generally use two indicators of family adaptability and cohesion to measure the degree of intimacy and effectiveness. In the next chapter, I will discuss in detail the importance of family culture for inheritance. In general, the stronger the family's adaptability and cohesion, the higher the self-efficacy of the second

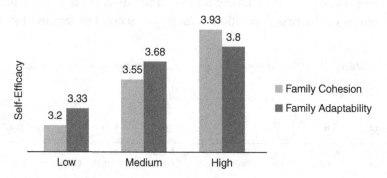

Figure 2.3   Family Relationship Affecting Self-Efficacy

Note: The values in the figure are the mean comparison coefficients.

generation. A moderate level of freedom and independence in the family is beneficial to the growth of the second generation and the harmony of the family.

Apart from family factors, other factors including level of education, overseas study background, and work experience in other people's businesses do not directly contribute to improving the confidence of successors. In other words, many parents think that sending their children abroad to study can increase their willingness and ability to take over. In fact, this is not the case. Family factors, in the final analysis, are most influential in shaping the second generation's self-efficacy and character. This shows how important family relationships are to family businesses. Family is the source of self-confidence and strength for the second generation.

In the next chapter, we will discuss the family factors and what constitutes traditional family culture in detail and how they affect family members, especially the growth and succession of the second generation. In such an ever-changing era, there are many traditional things that should not be forgotten or abandoned. On the contrary, how to use traditional strength to unite a family in the new era and how to carry forward the family spirit and fine traditions rooted in the blood of family is food for thought.

3

"Family Culture": The Evergreen Cornerstone of Family Business

According to *McKinsey Quarterly*, 37% of companies with annual sales of more than 1 billion US dollars in emerging markets will be family businesses by the year of 2025[1], which shows that the power of family business is constantly evolving. When it comes to family firms in the world, one-third of the largest companies publicly listed in the US in 2013 were controlled by families[2]: The total number of family businesses in Japan accounted for almost 95% of all companies nationwide. More than 6,000 family corporations in Europe, over 800 in the United States and 30,000-plus in Japan have a history of more than 100 years, but unfortunately there are none in China. However, in 2015, private enterprises accounted for 64.3% of all companies listed in China's A-share stock market, and approximately half of them were family firms, indicating that family business is a strong rising force in China.[3]

---

[1] Bjornberg, A., Elstrodt, H. P., & Pandit, V. (2014). The Family-Business Factor in Emerging Markets. *McKinsey Quarterly*, 4, 1–6.
[2] King, R., & Peng, W. Q. (2013). The Effect of Industry Characteristics on the Control Longevity of Founding-Family Firms. Journal of Family Business Strategy, 4(4), 281–295.
[3] Mao Jingjing (2015). Game Between Inheritance and Tradition: A Survey Report on Family Business. *Forbes* (Chinese version), 9, 52–59.

In the past, lots of family businesses, especially those in emerging markets, presented a negative image to the general public: Nepotism and cronyism prevailed; family interests were put above everything else; professional management was lacking; there were no well-defined rules and strategies; many of their activities were short-sighted; and so on. There were frequent reports in the media about disputes between father and son, husband and wife, and between brothers. As a matter of fact, these were not special phenomena on the Chinese mainland. They also occurred in other emerging markets, including Taiwan, Singapore, Indonesia, and Malaysia. Luckily, these problems are not unsolvable. In this section, we will utilize our own research and case studies to explain how family firms can work out solutions to these problems.

A large proportion of Chinese family businesses is based on marriage bonds, brotherhood, or parent-child relationships. When so many relationships co-exist in a single company, it becomes extraordinarily complex. In a typical business, everyone has a role. He may be the boss, employee, or shareholder, and even a professional manager may also hold shares to become a shareholder. However, in a family firm, due to the different organizational roles within the family and the company, family members often play multiple roles simultaneously, and need to constantly change from one role to another role, making it more complicated than it is in an ordinary business. That is to say, in addition to management right and equity, the family factor has been added. Sometimes people can misplay their role. For example, one may speak in the capacity of a father when he should do so as the boss, or the other way round. This complexity in personal identity makes members in family businesses often misplay their roles, which leads to conflicts.

Business management emphasizes rational decision-making, so the family business possesses rational and legal elements, but emotion plays an important part in the family. As a result, family business is often a combination of emotions, reason, and law. When emotions, reason, and law are intersected, things become very complex, especially when family members are also managers and shareholders, meaning that they have to execute three different roles simultaneously (see Figure 3.1).

Because family business will run into a variety of problems in the intersection between emotions, reason, and law, a large number of them

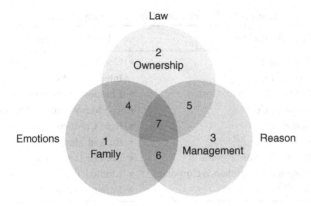

Figure 3.1 The Three-circle Theory of Family Business[4]

survive in the end mainly because they are able to straighten out the relationships in the process of enterprise development and inheritance. For example, many family firms end up being passed on to one heir, making him/her the only member to participate in the management of the family business on behalf of the entire family, which is conducive in resolving the conflicts within the company.

Family business is inherently a contradiction. On one hand, it has the advantages of strong cohesiveness, centralization of power, fast decision-making, low communication and management cost as well as high commitment. On the other hand, when corporate interests conflict with family ones, it is too emotionally oriented and has to meet many demands of the family. Additionally, it lacks innovation, limits talent development, faces complex relationships, and so on (see Table 3.1). Some believe that the two systems of family and business should be separated. Business should "de-family" and take the road of professionalized and specialized management, avoiding the involvement of family members as far as possible. If the two systems can be well balanced, the power it produces will be infinite.

Family business is known as a relationship- or *guanxi*-based enterprise, namely relationship is the core of a family corporation. Therefore, we

---

[4] Gersick, K. E. (1997). *Generation to Generation: Life Cycles of the Family Business.* Harvard Business Press.

Table 3.1   The Pros and Cons of Family Business

The Pros of Family Business	The Cons of Family Business
• Strong Cohesiveness • Centralization of Power • Low Psychological Contract Cost • Low Management Cost • Fast Decision-making • Dedication • Demonstration Effect of "Parents" • Family Reputation Can Enhance Corporate Reputation — Family Brand	• Conflicts Between Corporate Interests and Family Ones • Emotions, Relationship Orientation • Too Many Family Demands to Meet • Role Conflicts • Rule of Man • Lack of Innovation • Limited Talent Development • Intricate Nepotism

must pay special attention to family relationships in the inheritance. Without them, the problems of family businesses are no different from those faced by non-family businesses. Moreover, social relationships between family members often have the biggest impact on the operation of family firms. Only when you witness a great company being ruined by family members owing to their quarrels, slanders, or unresolved bitter conflicts will you understand the significance of family relationships to the success of family business.

Two Systems: Family and Business

When we study a family business, we are virtually studying the overlapping interactions between two social systems: One is the family system and the other is the business system. There are remarkable differences between the two systems: Their value orientation differs. The family system is more subjective and more emotional. It is relationship-oriented and tends to be rather protective and tolerant of its members. The business system, which emphasizes objectivity and goals, is utilitarian and features employer-employee relationships. As a result, the conditionality is relatively high (see Table 3.2). The overlap of these two systems will cause dislocations of their value orientation, which will result in conflict and confusion of roles. In the end, how do people make decisions? In accordance with family relationships or the company's goals?

Table 3.2 The Overlap and Differences of the Two Systems

Values Orientation of Family	Values Orientation of Business
• Subjectivity	• Objectivity
• Emphasis on Emotions	• Emphasis on Goals
• Relationship Orientation: Protection of Family Members	• Utilitarian Orientation: Employment Relationship
• High Inclusiveness	• High Utilitarian
• Unconditional	• Conditional

For this reason, family business, which involves multiple relationships, is much more complex than ordinary corporations. The complexity and intensity of family conflicts depend on the overlapping degree of responsibilities, ownership, and family relationship in the daily management of the enterprise. If multiple family branches and members get involved, the threat of family conflicts is simply a time bomb for the firm. In most cases, the bomb explodes when the second generation takes over after the death of the founding generation (usually when both parents die), or when the third generation of cousins takes over. This is because with the ties of consanguinity becoming more distant, people's interests are harder to reconcile. This also explains why many Chinese people believe in the proverb: "Shirtsleeves to shirtsleeves in three generations".

Because of the fundamental differences between family and business, "family" and "career" often collide, and there will be a variety of conflicts between the two. However, "family business" naturally binds "family" and "business" together. Once the second generation formally takes over the business, it is inevitable that family interests will be engaged in pursuit of business development. Disagreements in the workplace can turn into arguments at home, or even quarrels. In reality, when it comes to succession, most of us will consider factors such as the capability of the second generation, situations surrounding the firm and the industry, but tend to ignore the key element of family. In practice, family relationships add another element of concern to the second generation when they consider succession, so family support is extremely important to them. That is why we believe harmony of the family is a vital cornerstone in the expansion of family business.

The Power of Family: Resolving Conflicts and Enhancing the Willingness to Take Over

In the second chapter, we point out the high correlation between willingness of the second generation to take over the business and family relationships. Among the excellent family businesses I interviewed, many are good examples of smooth succession. The trust of the family in the second generation, the degree of harmony within the family, personal needs of the second generation, and financial returns brought by the succession have a great impact on the willingness of the second generation to take over the business. For example, in Fotile, Mao Lixiang and his son Mao Zhongqun did not have a plain sailing on the way to enterprise development and succession. On the contrary, there had been several major disputes between them. The unity of their differences and the solution to their problems did not merely rely on rules and regulations or authoritarian leadership, but their recognition of and identification with the family, as well as a harmonious and open way of communication. More specifically, we should note that Mao Zhongqun's mother served as a pivotal bond and bridge of communication between them. When a family enjoys harmonious and close relationships, it is easier for the two generations to connect and share ideas. Through continuous communication, they can find the best way to expand the family business. Besides, they are always committed to the common goals and values pursued by the family in this process, and they will stick together in spite of their diverging views.

Yu Jiangbo, young president of Neoglory, grew up in a big family. Even today, over 30 members of their family still live on the top floor of the group headquarters building with five or six large round tables in the living room. As long as they are at home, the family will dine together. It is this kind of growth experience in the extended family, as well as joyful and harmonious family relationships that instilled a sense of family responsibility in Yu Jiangbo. After completing postgraduate study at the London School of Economics and Political Science (LSE), he returned to Neoglory without hesitation to share the burden with his parents. Throughout his childhood, he had seen his parents take care of the family. Their model behavior taught him how to be a caring elder brother in the third generation of the family and help his cousins grow up. These cases truly reflect the impact of the family environment on the growth and succession of the second generation.

One of the major factors affecting the succession of family businesses is "family culture". In our growth process, family environment would leave an indelible imprint on us. The function of familialism is to promote harmony, unity, continuity, and prosperity within the family. Chinese familism and traditional values penetrate deeply into Chinese family businesses through pan-familism. Pan-familism in China is a process in which the structure of the family, its functional principles, ethics and role relationships, as well as concepts, attitude, and behaviors learned in family life are copied in a group or organization outside the family. Under the influence of familism, family relationships occupy a vital position in the process of succession of family business.

Among the family factors, there are two main aspects that have a significant impact on the inheritance: One is the spirit of family, i.e., family values; the other is family relationship (see Figure 3.2).[5]

Family Values

Chinese familism and traditional values have infiltrated deeply into Chinese family businesses through pan-familism and can be considered from the following four factors:

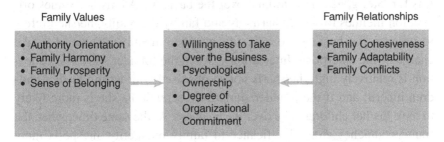

Figure 3.2 How Family Factors Affect the Willingness to Take Over the Business

---

[5]Lee, Siew Kim Jean, Rui Meng, Lu Yunting, Cui Zhiyu. (2014). Willingness and Commitment of Successors — White Paper on the Inheritance of Chinese Family Business. Family Inheritance Research Center of China Europe International Business School.

The first is authoritarianism. In the social context, it emphasizes sensitivity and dependency on the authority. People can clearly distinguish the authoritative representatives in the environment and generate worship and dependence.

The second is family harmony. In order to maintain unity and harmony, people demonstrate a proclivity towards forbearance and self-restraint and act submissively. Competition is not encouraged within the family, because as they say, "We are all family members and there is nothing to fight for."

The third is family prosperity. Family honor and wealth are valued, and family members are eager to work hard and fight for the good of the family. Priorities are given to family interests over individual interests.

The fourth is the sense of belonging. Family members are bonded by blood or marriage and they have a strong desire to unite as one. Individuals are always members of the family in which strong in-group favoritism exists.

The traditional values of the Chinese lay great emphasis on the authority of the parents, and Chinese familism includes family harmony, family prosperity, and sense of belonging. These three are pivotal elements of familism. The relevance of traditions, family harmony, and family prosperity to the way of succession of offspring is remarkable. Through research, we find that the more traditional the founder is, the more likely it is for later generations to take over the business. As his/her values orientation inclines to family harmony and family continuity, he/she prefers to pass on the business to a family member (members) who will take charge of the enterprise. Interestingly, when the founder's level of education is relatively high, he/she is not so obsessed with letting his/her children inherit; and if the founder starts from scratch, he/she is more likely to have his/her children take over the business. At the same time, when the founder attaches great significance to family prosperity, he/she is more likely to recruit good professional managers from outside the family to take charge of and expand the company.

Meanwhile, the more traditional the second generation is, the stronger their willingness to take over the business will be. The second generation who firmly believe in traditions will be more obedient to the will of the elder authority, and will be more ready to take charge of or (and) succeed the firm created by the older generation. In addition, the more the second generation cares about the family's happiness, the more they will enjoy the succession because this is consistent with the goal of family prosperity and proliferation.

The sense of family needs to be developed from an early age. Only in this way can philosophies established by the younger generation in the process of their growth be highly consistent with the development of the enterprise and family. Conflicts occurring in the succession will also be reduced. At the same time, our research indicates that the second generation with overseas education experience have a stronger willingness to return to the family to help with its business expansion, on the premise that they value traditions and maintain good relationships with their parents. Only in this way will they be ready to use what they have learned to promote the family business.

Family Relationship

Familism emphasizes family continuity, harmony, prosperity, and attachment. In the research[6], we discovered that family relationships play an important role in the handover of family business. Among the factors that affect family business inheritance, the key is the attitude of family members. If a prospective successor does not gain the support of family members, the likelihood of he/she eventually taking over the family business is very low. Many studies have confirmed that in order to succeed, the prospective successor must be trusted and supported by family members who are active in the family business.

As mentioned above, management costs of family business are relatively low and decision-making is fast. Family members have a strong dedication to the company and strong cohesiveness. The business is generally organized around an authoritative figure with low psychological contract cost. What's more, family reputation can enhance the credibility of the firm. The founders of the company are held as role models by the younger generation. Of course, we also see some of the drawbacks of

---

[6]Lee, Jean. (2006). Impact of Family Relationships on Attitudes of the Second Generation in Family Business. *Family Business Review*, XIX(3), 175–191.

family relationships, such as conflict between the company's overall interests and the family interests, emotions and relationships orientation, too many family demands, conflict between work and family roles, rule of man, and lack of innovation. Limited talent development means that the excessive participation of family members inevitably limits the development of professional managers. They will feel that there is not much room for professionals to develop their talents, and they need to deal with complicated relationships because of the intense involvement of numerous family members.

For family businesses, family relationships do not seem to be a key factor in business success in the short term. However, once quarrels, defamation, or direct conflicts between family members trigger a crisis, it may potentially lead to the downfall of the family business. Henceforth, for any family business, the biggest threats to survival and success are not the external factors — such as technologies, customers, and competitors — but the relationship between family members. The training and education of the heirs in accordance with a well-laid plan are generally considered to be the key to effective family business inheritance, and family relationships also affect the second generation's willingness to join the family business, the degree of their own happiness, and fulfillment from work.

The affinity and effectiveness of family relationships can be divided into two levels: The first is family cohesiveness and the second is family adaptability.[7] Family cohesiveness refers to the degree of closeness and emotional communication experienced by members of the family. At a degree of balanced cohesiveness, individuals can be independent of the family while being associated with it. Family cohesiveness reflects the amount of emotion the first generation feels towards their children. When family cohesiveness is high, it may mean that the first generation pamper their children as a way of showing their love but this does not necessarily mean that the children are more willing to devote themselves to the family business.

There are four types of family cohesiveness as shown in Figure 3.3. In the disengaged type, family members have little to no commitment to the family. There is often no communication between the father (mother) and

---

[7] Ibid.

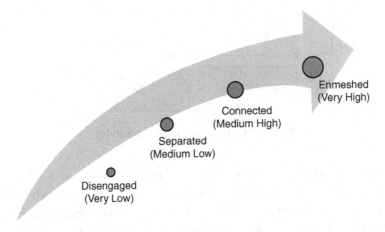

Figure 3.3   Types of Family Cohesiveness

the son (daughter). In other words, there is friction between them because they do not understand each other. Maybe the father does not know about his son's interests; neither does the son. Perhaps the father does not understand what his son's interests entail, nor does the son understand the significance of his father's career. In the separated type, there is some emotional separation between family members, but sometimes they still have discussions and support one another. For example, the father and the son is involved in each of his own business, which is relatively separated, but they will confer with each other over a meal or during a meeting about major issues and seek support from each other. In the connected type, the time spent together is seen as more important than the time spent alone, which implies emotional intimacy and loyalty. It also demonstrates that family members share common ground in both family relationships and career interests and are dependent on one another. In the enmeshed type, independence within the family is extremely limited, and the family relationship and the career relationship are intertwined. The disengaged and enmeshed types belong to the unbalanced state of family cohesiveness. Under these two states, corporate decision-making is likely to be influenced by the emotional aspect of family relationships, which is very unfavorable. In relationships of balanced family cohesiveness (separated and connected types), individuals can be independent of the family but associated with the family at the same time.

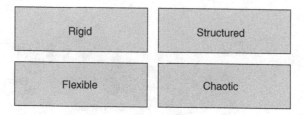

Figure 3.4 Types of Family Adaptability

Family adaptability refers to how a family operates as a whole, its flexibility in solving problems, the degree of preparedness when there are adjustments to change, and the way they makes decisions. Family adaptability is also divided into four types (see Figure 3.4). In a rigid family system, an individual takes control and restricts negotiations while roles and regulations are fixed and not allowed to be modified. In a family business, the founder of the business usually assumes this authoritarian role due to the background when he/she started the business. In those years, business leaders must be tough if they wanted to survive and develop. However, an authoritarian figure brings about negative impacts on the succession of family business. The structured family system is characterized by democratic leadership and partial sharing of roles, but everyone's identity and role are stable, and the rules are strictly enforced and rarely modified. For a flexible family system, the family head is equal in status to other members, decisions are made in a democratic way, identities and roles are shared, and rules can be changed. In a chaotic family system, the family head is unpredictable, a sound decision-making system is non-existent, and roles are not clearly defined with frequent shifts among family members. Structured and flexible family systems are regarded as balanced while rigid and chaotic systems are regarded as unbalanced. A study showed that it is family adaptability that affects a child's willingness to work in a family business. The second generation would choose to get involved in the family business because of the high degree of family adaptability rather than that of family cohesiveness.

We have seen the systematic model of family adaptability in which the founding generation takes control of everything in the corporation. In this case, the second generation is reluctant to get into their families' corporations. The standardization in this case means that the rules are formulated by one individual and are effectively executed without flexibility. Therefore, the second generation will think that there is not much room for them to display their abilities as it is already so well-developed, hence they are not willing to enter the company. The business flexibility we expect can be realized through equal and democratic decision-making, meaning that rules can be changed. At the same time, too much flexibility can lead to confusion, vague roles, and ambiguously defined rules, resulting in an unbalanced system. In a chaotic and unbalanced system, no one has a clear idea about his role and his role in the family may affect the decision-making in the company. For example, the person of the second generation who has taken over must take his uncles' suggestions, which sometimes not only adversely affects family relationships but also leads to chaotic management. It is thereafter crucial to find an adequate balance between family and business in this intersected relationship.

A family system with a rule-based structure and relative flexibility is balanced. Maintaining such a system is vital for a family business. A balanced family system enjoys a democratic leadership style, open communication, clearly defined role sharing, and active participation in decision-making by family members. In such a family system, the second generation normally has a fairly high degree of satisfaction and greater commitment to the family business. Conversely, if one individual has power of control, or if the role definition is ambiguous, the degree of satisfaction of the second generation will be severely reduced. A democratic leadership style and open coordination will help the younger generation maintain their commitment and heighten their willingness to enter the family business.

Family Factors Influencing the Willingness to Take Over the Business

In order to further assess the influence of "family culture" on the willingness of the succeeding generation to inherit, we spent two-plus years visiting more than 100 Chinese family businesses. The following results reflect the cognitive differences between the two generations on family culture and family relationships during the handover period. They also show how "family culture" affects the handover. In the research[8], we discovered that the following factors affect the willingness of the second generation to take over:

- The values of the two generations are beginning to converge. Among the family businesses where succession is taking place, the family values of the first and second generation are relatively high and very similar. Both generations think highly of family harmony, prosperity, bringing honor to their ancestors, and possessing a strong sense of belonging. Yet, in companies that have not considered succession and companies where succession has yet to take place, family values are fairly low on the agenda of first-generation entrepreneurs. The family values of the two generations have a great impact on the succession of the second generation. When the values of the two generations are beginning to converge, succession will be smooth, and they find it easy to reach consensus on business philosophies and management methods.

- The authoritative orientation of the first generation. For the second generation with a high level of education or a background in science and engineering, their willingness to succeed will be weakened notably if the first generation emphasizes their personal authority. Most of the second generation with good academic qualifications have studied abroad. In terms of values orientation, they are more susceptible to Western culture and management thinking, which leads to disagreements and discourse with the first generation, including aversion to their authoritarian approach. This is particularly true for male heirs with a science and engineering background, perhaps because of their highly logical and rational thinking, who will show a strong dislike for the purely emotion-based authoritarian approach of the first generation.

- The family values of the second generation. The family values of the future successors directly affect their willingness to take over the business. Those who think highly of family harmony, family prosperity,

---

[8] Lee, Jean. (2006). Impact of Family Relationships on Attitudes of the Second Generation in Family Business. *Family Business Review*, XIX(3), 175–191.

and who have a strong sense of belonging demonstrate a strong willingness to inherit. Of the three factors, family harmony plays the crucial role, indicating that the unity and amity of the family has a great impact on the psychological willingness of the second generation. Coming in second is the sense of belonging, which gives the second generation a sense of integration with the family and the responsibilities associated with it. As they consider themselves to be an indispensable part of the family, they show a stronger willingness to assume the responsibility of the family business.

- Family adaptability. The higher the family adaptability is, the stronger is the ability of family members to resolve problems together, and the more likely the heir is to take over the business. In addition, the level of family conflicts will also affect the willingness of the second generation to take over the business. Frequent conflicts in the family will reduce the second generation's willingness to take over the business, and this is particularly true for the male successors.

- Family cohesiveness. Male and female heirs differ in their attitude to family cohesiveness when it comes to succession. The level of family cohesiveness has little influence on female successors' willingness to take over the business, but it is a strong factor which male successors will take into consideration seriously. Family cohesiveness has a greater impact on male successors than on female successors. In other words, male successors particularly need to feel the amicable relations and deep affection between family members before deciding to take over the business, otherwise they would rather carve out a career outside their own family business.

The Psychological Ownership of the Succeeding Generation

The importance of family factors in the inheritance of enterprises is not only reflected in its impact on the willingness of the second generation to succeed, but also on their psychological ownership and organizational commitment.

The process of succession is similar to that of a hurdle race: The willingness to take over the business is the first hurdle. Entering the corporation, devoting themselves to the family business, and getting approval equates to crossing the second hurdle. Still, he does not necessarily have the psychological ownership, or a sense of ownership of the business. Only when the heir certainly believes he is the real owner and proprietor of the enterprise, and is responsible for all the business activities and results of the enterprise, will he be considered to have officially taken over the business. The main determinants of the successor's psychological ownership come from the family, including family cohesiveness, the sense of belonging of the first and second generations.

Family cohesiveness is mainly manifested in the emotional closeness of family members, including their emotional depth and communication frequency and intensity. The stronger the family cohesiveness, the more both generations will value the family business. The emotional cohesiveness of the two generations will enhance their commitment to and recognition of the organization.

Founders' sense of family belonging is related to the way the family is involved. This means that when the founders pay more attention to the continuity and prosperity of the family, they are more willing to have family members get engaged or take control of the business. Therefore, the first generation will instill this concept into the second generation from an early age, thus increasing the second generation's identity with the family.

Similarly, when the second generation has a strong sense of belonging to the family — the belief that they completely belong to the family, that they acquire a great sense of security from their family, and that they are responsible to the family — they will regard the business as their own. When the heir feels that he is a member of the family, he will be willing to take the family business over; he will regard the family business as his own rather than working as an employee for other people. A sense of belonging will give the succeeding generation a sense of responsibility that is associated with family members while considering themselves an integral part of the business.

Interestingly, the actual ownership (the percentage of shares they hold) of the second generation is not directly related to their psychological ownership. In other words, it is not true that the proportion of shares they hold corresponds to how much they would regard the company as their own. The psychological ownership of the second generation is more of a feeling of "family" — family cohesiveness and a sense of belonging. The succession is based on the spirit and responsibility of the inheritance of family business and the successor possesses a strong sense of ownership. Another interesting finding says that when family cohesiveness is missing, the greater proportion the equities of the first generation holds, the stronger the willingness of the second generation to take over the business will be. This means that what the second generation inherits is only material wealth. For the successor to complete this transformation of psychological role, the combination of multiple factors is needed, all of which revolve around one key phrase — "the power of the family".

Regaining "Family Culture": Creating the Evergreen Gene of Family Business

"Harmony at home brings prosperity." A successor who devotes himself to the family business usually has a harmonious family behind him. Family cohesiveness, family adaptability, and the harmonious atmosphere will help the second generation implement ambitious plans with nothing to worry about, naturally increasing their commitment to the company.

We found that in families where smooth succession takes place, the two generations recognize the importance of family values. It is not directly related to their level of education or academic background of overseas study. Instead, they all think highly of family harmony, family prosperity, and possess a strong sense of belonging. They want to do well to bring honor to their ancestors. Obviously, familialism valued by both generations has a huge impact on the succession of the second generation. Therefore, in terms of family business succession, family education is more important than school education; teaching by personal example, verbal instruction, and spreading the correct family values is key to the successful succession of family business.

Between the three factors of family harmony, family prosperity, and a sense of belonging, the first has the greatest impact on the second generation when it comes to taking over the family business. A sense of belonging comes second, for it brings a strong sense of responsibility to the second generation.

In addition to family values, the way family members interact with each other largely affects the willingness of the second generation to succeed. Our research discovered that family cohesiveness and family adaptability have an impact on the children's willingness to take over the business and their organizational commitment after succession. Of the two, family adaptability exerts a greater impact than family cohesiveness. For the second generation, having families who are able to face and solve problems in an active, open, and flexible manner is more likely to determine their succession and organizational commitment than the depth of emotions. Therefore, when it comes to succession, it is not a problem of love, but of methods.

Family relationships play a key role in the second generation's sense of self-efficacy. The stronger the family adaptability and family cohesiveness are, the higher the self-efficacy of the successor will be. Other factors, such as level of education and background of overseas study, have little to do with self-efficacy. This demonstrates the importance of family relationships to the second generation and they are the source of self-confidence and strength of the future successors.

The psychological ownership of the second generation towards the family enterprise derives from their identity with the family — family cohesiveness and a sense of belonging. The succession is based on the spirit and responsibility for the inheritance of family business and the heir boasts a strong sense of ownership.

"Family culture" is of extraordinary significance to the succession of family business, and the family business with rich "family culture" is more likely to achieve long-lasting prosperity. Family business should recognize the crucial role of family culture and philosophy construction and ensure the smooth transfer of family business through a sound mechanism. The adherence to traditional culture by the Lee family of Lee Kum Kee (LKK) has not hindered its progress; on the contrary, it has regained enormous vitality because of the integration with modern management and technologies. LKK, which has experienced twists and turns over the decades, is a witness to the strengthening process of "family culture".[9]

A Good Example of "Family Culture" Inheritance: Lee Kum Kee, Thriving for Over Five Generations

A saying goes like this, "shirtsleeves to shirtsleeves in three generations." Here we discuss a case of a Chinese family business inheritance that has been going through five-plus generations — Lee Kum Kee. Since Lee Kum Sheung founded an oyster flavored sauce shop in Nanshui, Canton (now Guangdong), LKK has come through over the past 120 years and is a leading producer of Chinese-style sauces. From 1922, the second generation of the Lee family began to take over the business. At the beginning, the three brothers, namely Lee Siu Yung, Lee Siu Dang, and Lee Siu Nam, had a clear division of labor and each gave full play to their area of expertise. In the 1930s, they opened branches in Hong Kong and Guangzhou.

With the increase of members and the growth of the enterprise, the Lee family had to face the problem of inconsistent philosophies and divergent operational management ideas. In 1971, there was a major disagreement among the Lee brothers. Lee Siu Nam and his son Lee Man Tat suggested opening up the medium- and low-end market; Lee Siu Yung and Lee Siu Dang, who were not willing to take the risk, strongly opposed it and tried to maintain the status quo. At first, Lee Siu Yung and Lee Siu Dang intended to buy the shares from Lee Siu Nam, triggering a fight for family stocks. Finally, with the help of his son Lee Man Tat, Lee Siu Nam spent 4.6 million Hong Kong dollars purchasing the shares of his brothers. At the point, LKK was transformed from a holding company run by the three brothers to one run by Lee Siu Nam, the only inheritor of the second generation of the family business. With full control over the company, Lee Siu Nam was committed to improving the production process and product

---

[9]Lee, Siew Kim Jean. (2015). Regain Family Culture. *Tsinghua Business Review*, 12, 32–41.

quality, making its oyster flavored sauce and shrimp sauce popular in major cities in North America.

The lesson of the second generation brothers falling out did not prevent the third generation from being embroiled in conflicts. Lee Siu Nam has six daughters and two sons. One of his sons, Lee Man Tat became the chairman of the company in 1972. In 1980, Lee Man Tat's younger brother suffered from nasopharynx cancer. His wife, worried that she might lose her share of the family fortune, requested Lee Man Tat turn LKK into a limited company and to count his brother's equity in order to preserve her family wealth. In 1988, Lee Man Tat acquired his brother's shares with 8 million Hong Kong dollars. Despite the high price, Lee Man Tat, as a representative of the third generation, had the controlling stocks and ownership of the family business. However, the company was in risk of capital chain rupture. Fortunately, Lee Man Tat's five children returned home from studying abroad to help him overcome all difficulties and reinvigorate the business. In the end, not only did the company survive the crisis, but realized the dream of expanding the company.

In 2000, the Lee family was confronted with another challenge. Lee Man Tat's youngest son, Lee Wai Sam, decided to separate himself from the family business and to start up a business all by himself. Learning about this, Lee Man Tat talked to him, and persuaded his son to remain in the family business. But considering that he had five children, Lee Man Tat did not want to see the quarrels between his father and uncles repeat among his children, so he began to contemplate about the best way to maintain the long-lasting growth of the family business, and finally promoted the birth of LKK's rich "family culture". This time, the Lee family finally reached a consensus: The company is only part of the family; no matter what happen, family always comes first.

Lee Man Tat was not satisfied with the current situation of family harmony. He wanted to achieve family happiness and better business development by changing the family philosophy and the ways of interaction between family members. Consequently, he worked out a family "charter", set up a family committee, and stipulated that a family meeting be held every three months. The Lee family showed through concrete actions how the Chinese traditional culture of "cultivating the self and regulating the family" is applied in a family business.

The family committee is one aspect of LKK's distinctive "family culture". In 2003, the Lee family established a family committee, making it a platform of communication and consultation between family members. The committee consists of seven members: LKK's third generation Lee Man Tat and his wife and five siblings of the fourth generation. They take turns serving as chairman of the committee. The family committee convenes a meeting every three months, and each meeting lasts four days. Every member must attend the meeting, otherwise they will be punished. Together they will review the family business in an open and transparent atmosphere. They also discuss issues relating to their families and children together. Intimacy and thoughtfulness provide the warmth of the family.

The Lee family does not limit family activities to the conference table. They arrange family trips every year, and all the 26 family members from the third to the fifth generation will participate in each trip. They play golf, tennis, and enjoy the amity of the whole family in a relaxed atmosphere. The trend of profit-seeking in modern society has caused many people to be indifferent to the congenial climate of family reunion. Luckily, the Lee family has found a way for the whole family to share happiness.

With the guidance of "family culture", LKK has become a good example of Chinese family business succession. It focuses on the family and strives to let every family member enjoy a balance between work and life. The tradition of good communication among family members is also applied in corporate governance. LKK is well prepared for the future; they are fully aware that they may have to hire an outsider to manage the family enterprise. From the fifth generation, the offspring's mission is not necessarily to succeed the family business, but to help the family with its sustainable development. If there is no qualified heir in the family, they will consider looking for a professional manager in the future, which, of course, is plan B. LKK's first choice is to retain the model of family-run business, and the inheritance of "family culture" will certainly benefit business development.

Over the years, LKK has remained a 100% family holding company and only allows people related by blood to hold shares. At the same time, it neither brings in strategic investors nor considers listing. The success of LKK has a lot to do with the tradition of continuous entrepreneurship and the full responsibility for the quality of products. The company's development proves the worth of "family culture". Under the influence of the family tradition, LKK continues to thrive, and the family's intangible assets have provided strong cohesiveness, powerful growth potential, and unique creativity to the company.

For successful family businesses, the idea of inheriting the same values system from generation to generation is at once fundamental and crucial. Many family businesses believe that one of the most primary things the family does is to pass on the values to the next generation. For them, one of the major roles of family business ownership is to help achieve the inheritance of values. They recognize that a family business is a solid and real stage where family values can be tested and practiced.

It is true that family and business are two mutually influenced systems. The favorable, transferable family values are the best lubricants of these two systems. The family works to establish credibility and positive image to promote the development of the enterprise. In turn, the enterprise brings better economic and social status to the family, thus making family members more dedicated to enterprise ownership. This is because family members regard the business as a vehicle or an example of family values practice, and they will show immense enthusiasm for carrying forward the family tradition from generation to generation.

In the case of LKK, we have discovered the vital elements for constructing a "family culture": Family creed, family "charter"/family governance, and family Chief Emotional Officer.

Family Creed

Professor John Ward, co-director of the Center for Family Businesses at Northwestern University's Kellogg School of Management, presented an example of "family creed" in his research.

It is beneficial to pass on the above ideas from generation to generation for the inheritance of the enterprise or its equitable interests. Family values and family harmony are the evergreen genes of family business. A healthy "family culture" is a cornerstone of the sustainable development of family business, and a fragile "family culture" is a latent threat. Therefore, the owners of family businesses need to carefully manage

---

Family Creed

As a family, we value excellence, trust, respect, love, and honor. We strive to:

- Act with integrity
- Promote self-esteem
- Cultivate "sense of family"
- Pursue the love of work
- Cherish individuality, independent thinking, and freedom of choice
- Encourage the participation and empowerment of every family member
- Commit to communication and the resolution of conflicts
- Serve as responsible "role models" of productive and creative people
- Create wealth responsibly and confront the challenges of wealth
- Acknowledge excellence as a personal expression, with freedom to learn from mistake
- Demonstrate pro-active compassion and generosity
- Focus energy on the enhancement of our community
- Create an environment for lifelong learning

Source: John, L.W. (2014). Perpetuating the Family Business: 50 Lessons Learned from Long Lasting, Successful Families in Business. The Oriental Press.

---

family relations and develop healthy family values. "Family culture" is not an abstract and unpredictable thing. It can be embodied in the family training rules, family "charter", family meetings, and in the words and deeds of the elders. It is the lubricant of family business succession. It is also an indispensable element in achieving long-lasting development of family business.

For the sustainability of good family relations, the way the two generations interact with each other is crucial. This is a process that requires mutual cooperation. First, the leadership style of the first generation entrepreneurs is important. Second, it is necessary to raise the second generation's awareness about the family tradition when they are young, so that they realize how hard their parents worked to build up the family business and be prepared to embrace the family philosophy through what they constantly observe and listen to. Finally, if the children go abroad to study, their willingness to take over the business will actually be enhanced.

The first generation entrepreneurs must show a strong willingness to accept the new ideas brought back by the second generation from abroad. The two generations should promote family stability through a balanced family relationship interaction under the guide of a sound family philosophy that has been developed and cherished over a long period so as to ensure the sustainable development of the company.

Family "Charter"/Family Governance

In addition to values and family relationships, the implementation and maintenance of "family culture" relies on sound systems and rules. The family "charter" and family governance constitute effective systems that need to be focused on and promoted by family businesses. Family businesses can invite their consultants to assist family members in understanding their roles and behavioral styles. Owners/founders of family businesses, in particular, need to understand their role as leaders and how their actions will affect the willingness and commitment of the next generation. Family consultants can also help family businesses to better draw up family "charters" and promote family members' understanding of "family culture" and their communication.

In fact, in this respect, besides Hong Kong's LKK whose story and practice can provide us with some references, we can also learn from family enterprises in other countries and regions. Japan, a neighboring country of China, is undoubtedly a role model of long-lasting family business. As a country well-known for their family businesses, Japan has a large number of family businesses that have lasted for many generations. According to the research of Professor Toshio Goto[10], who teaches in the Japan University of Economics, 25,321 family businesses in Japan have lasted for more than 100 years in the family. When calculated by Japan's standard of measuring the "longevity of a company" — 200 years, there are 3,937 family businesses. More extraordinary is that in Japan, 21 family businesses were set up more than 1,000 years ago.

---

[10]Toshio, Goto. (2014). Research on the Development of Japanese Family Business. Speech at Waseda University.

Japanese family businesses cherish the heritage of culture and philosophy and focus on the development of family philosophy. A strong and mutually recognized philosophy is the core of family cohesiveness. Two years ago, I went to Japan to visit a range of Japanese family businesses that have been passed down for generations. One hundred fifty years ago, the merchants from Ou-mi carried goods on their shoulders and peddled them on the street. The businesses have been passed on from one generation to another, owing to the first generations' hard work, firm family belief, and fine family tradition. They are beneficial references that Chinese family business entrepreneurs can learn from. I believe that many cases of inheritance depend on a kind of inheritance of family motto. Only when this kind of spirit, philosophy, and culture are carried forward can we guarantee the succession of family business.

Family Chief Emotional Officer

Family business is an enterprise of relationships in which emotional factors play an important role. In the Lee family, there is a family committee and family "charter", as well as the super mother committee composed of female members. Institutional communication and coordination from the female perspective deepen the emotional bond of the family.

Although the emotional connection of family members is based on blood and kinship, this connection needs to be maintained and strengthened. With the expansion of the enterprise and the proliferation of the family, the emotional ties within the family are both hampered by material interests and influenced by dilution of kinship. At this point, the Chief Emotional Officer needs to play the role of emotional bond, crisis communication, and even dispute arbitration. Female elders in the family are often the first choice for this type of officer. On one hand, female elders can pass on family values to descendants through words and deeds, thus stimulating the sense of responsibility and entrepreneurial spirit of the younger generation; on the other hand, they can utilize their prestige and affinity in the family to prevent or mediate conflicts between family members. For example, Kwong Ciu Hing, wife of the founder of Sun Hung Kai Properties, will step forward to help solve her three sons' problems when conflicts occurred among them. In this case, her influence is effected through informal emotional means rather than formal corporate power.

Is infighting inevitable in a successful family business? How do we maintain warm relationships in the family business, but also keep the family united alongside the enterprising and pioneering spirit? In this regard, the Chief Emotional Officer plays a pivotal part. Once a family business prospers, it tends to neglect love between its members. Conflicts and misunderstandings happen. There is a Chinese saying that expresses that family business suffers together but does not share wealth and joys together, which is rather pathetic. Therefore, family businesses need chief emotional officers so that wealth and love co-exist harmoniously.

In the next two chapters, we will discuss two Chinese family business cases in details. One is Fotile. We will have a look at how the founder, Mao Lixiang, persuaded his son Mao Zhongqun to come back from overseas to take over the family business, how they jointly overcame the obstacles on the way to succession and how, in the end, they realized a smooth shift of power and in the process summed up the "family culture" for Fotile. The other is Huamao Group. We will discuss how Junior Xu succeeded in a time of crisis, how he survived the conflicts and challenges, how Senior Xu realized his hindering of his son's inheritance, and why they started contemplating the significance of the family "charter" after the crisis. In these two cases, the families chose different paths in their succession, but through the joint efforts of both generations they eventually reached consensus and formed effective internal family governance. We will learn how these family businesses are passed on to the next generation.

4

"1.5 Generation" Entrepreneurial Succession

If a son succeeding his father's business is called the second generation, then Mao Zhongqun is a member of the "1.5 generation". His father, Mao Lixiang founded Feixiang Group the first time he ventured into business and became the "first generation entrepreneur". Mao Zhongqun created Fotile on the already-built foundation of his family's business. Being both a successor and an entrepreneur in his own right, he is a veritable "1.5 generation". The 1.5 generation phenomenon is a special feature in the inheritance and development of Chinese family businesses. As I have mentioned in the previous chapter, Chinese family businesses have re-emerged from a wasteland after historical disruptions. Most of the "first generation entrepreneurs" and enterprises experienced extensive growth in the past. However, after more than 30 years of economic growth and given the unique background of China's reform and opening up, the economic cycle has reached a point where major changes are taking place. Family businesses, at the juncture of succession, also face the challenge of transformation and upgrading if they want to survive. This gives rise to the "1.5 generation" with Chinese characteristics. Unlike the second generation who is waiting to take over the family business or the first generation who started from scratch, they stand on the shoulders of their parents and utilize their own strengths to innovate and transform the family businesses while the handover is going on. These excellent people of the 1.5 generation are both successors and pioneers.

For the second generation, succession not only reduces problems concerning the replacement of employees from the old business, but it provides them a chance to develop new businesses to their own liking. The business foundation built up by the old generation is put into good use while all family resources are utilized for the better and sustainable development of the family business.

The experience of co-founding Fotile with his son was Mao Lixiang's second venture, which made his son a true member of the 1.5 generation. To Senior Mao, this method had a clear direction of succession, and it was easier to relay his experience to his son through daily practices. At the same time, the father and son complemented each other in terms of resources and knowledge, and jointly created new ideas, new cultures, new experiences, and new modes. Mao Lixiang handed the old family business to his daughter Mao Xuefei, so that his son could spend all his time and energies on Fotile, so as to develop a strong sense of responsibility and awareness of risks. Of course, we must not ignore the problems associated with this mode. The growth backgrounds of the two generations are undoubtedly different. Many of their ideas in management differ and the methods adopted are also different. The two generations need to understand each other, communicate with each other, and find common ground. This is where the cohesive function of the harmonious "family culture" mentioned in the previous chapter comes into play. Otherwise, once there are two power figures, it will have an adverse effect on the daily management and long-term development of the enterprise.

The father and son of the Mao family have set a good example of this succession mode. The success of Fotile is not only a testament to the Mao family's entrepreneurial spirit, but also the result of the relay-like innovative transformation. Let's take a look at how Mao's family and Fotile prosper together in Zhejiang, a birthplace of private entrepreneurs.

The Family Business Started by Mao Lixiang and His Wife

After graduating from high school, Mao Lixiang made a living by being a middle school teacher and accountant in the village. He also worked as a salesman for 10 years. Mao gained a lot from these experiences. In 1985, he decided to start his first business in his 40s. He established Cixi Radio Nine Factory with 6 old punches and a small amount of money he raised to process TV parts. Unfortnately, in the second year, due to the state's macroeconomic control, sales of black-and-white TV sets decreased sharply, and so did the parts he produced. This was the first crisis of his business. Mao Lixiang's wife, Zhang Zhaodi, resolutely gave up her job at this difficult time of her husband's first venture to help him ride out the difficulties. She stepped down from the position of deputy director of a profitable knitting factory to serve as the deputy director of Cixi Radio Nine Factory. Mao Lixiang was responsible for the creation of new products and their sales, and Zhang Zhaodi was in charge of daily management. With the support of his wife, Mao Lixiang went all out without any worries. He then developed China's first electronic igniter which sold well on the domestic market. At the end of the 1980s, Mao Lixiang developed a new type of electronic gas igniter which was sold on an international scale. In 1989, Mao Lixiang attended the Chinese Export Commodities Fair in Guangzhou and completed deals worth 80,000 US dollars. From then on, the company officially turned into an export-oriented enterprise. It once occupied 50% of the global gas igniter market and was the world's largest manufacturer of gas igniters. Therefore, Mao Lixiang was also known as the "King of the World's Gas Igniters".

In 1992, Cixi Radio Nine Factory was renamed Feixiang Group. The word "Fei" (literally means flying) was taken from the name of his daughter Mao Xuefei, and "Xiang" (also means flying) was from Mao Lixiang's own name. Entrepreneurs must keep going on the road to success, because there are many uncertainties on the road to business development. When the gas igniter business was booming, the outsourcing factory suddenly tore up the agreement and Mao Lixiang suffered the second crisis of his entrepreneurship. At the 1991 Guangzhou Fair, another gas igniter booth was set up opposite Feixiang Group's booth, displaying the same products as those produced by the Feixiang Group at a lower price. Mao Lixiang had to lower the price of his own products, and yet still lost half of his customers. After observing his rival's products, he realized that the technical threshold of the gas igniter was too low. The factory that produced the plastic parts for him had mastered the technology of the entire production chain and decided to produce their own gas igniters. Therefore, his daughter Mao Xuefei and her husband resigned from their work in a bank and a hospital on the third day of marriage to create a plastic plant called "Lingke" to construct parts and components for the Feixiang Group. Due to the emergence of dozens of gas igniter manufacturers in China, the competition was so fierce that the price of a gas igniter dropped from 1.20 USD to 0.35 USD. At that time, the annual output value of Feixiang Group reached 150 million yuan, and the sales amount was approximately 50 million yuan. Mao Lixiang had to start looking for new products. He experimented with a new product that was similar to an audio-visual learning machine. He invited a dozen technicians, marketing personnel, and managers to start industrial and management transformation. The project was not a success, and eventually many employees left. Undaunted by the setback, Mao Lixiang called his son back. It was a risky move. Looking back, he thought that it was a critical period in the development of the family business. The success or failure of the project they were due to start would hence determine the success or failure of the company, the fate of the family, and the success or failure of his son's life as an adult at the initial stage. Therefore, the decision was very crucial at that time.

Mao Zhongqun: Should I Go Back to Continue My Father's Business?

In 1994, Mao Lixiang decided to call back his son who was going to graduate with a master's degree in electronics and power technology from Shanghai Jiao Tong University. Mao Zhongqun had three choices at that time: The first was to stay in the university to be a teacher, the second was to study abroad, and the third was to go back home to undertake a business. After six months of market research and consideration, Mao Zhongqun finally chose the third option. However, he clearly stated three requirements: "One, stop producing gas igniters; engage in the new project of the range hood; two, relocate the enterprise from the countryside to the city's development zone to start the new business; three, do not retain employees from the Feixiang Group; all employees will be recruited on the market."

As Mao Zhongqun recalled, he grew up in an environment like this: "My parents left home early in the morning for work and came back late in the evening. It seems to be a natural and normal way of life. My parents focused more on teaching by personal example than by verbal instruction. My father often went on business trips and did not spend much time with me. He regarded maths, physics, and chemistry as the most important subjects and believed that anyone with a good knowledge of the three would achieve success in the world. That's why I'm better at those subjects than humanities. He occasionally talked about establishing a corporate group of the Mao family in future. I often went to my father's factory to play. But as a child in the countryside, I did not know much about the company and was just growing up naturally."

For Mao Zhongqun, going back to work for the family business was a matter of course. Although he had made the decision, Mao Zhongqun had his own ideas. "I made it clear to my father at the start. I was not going to get involved in the gas igniter business. Fotile was a new business then, I would have the final say in decisions related to major issues. Reasons were as follows: First, I started the business from scratch and was personally in charge of it. Second, I would have confidence only if I was in control of major decisions and business operations. After all, huge differences existed between the two generations. My father's gas igniter did not employ any advanced technology and all products were exported. This was a rather simple way of doing business. Fotile is different. We would make Fotile a famous brand, a high-end brand at a time when the high-end market was dominated by foreigners. We had to make a lot of effort to do research and marketing. My father probably did not understand. These issues of great importance must be determined by me, otherwise the odds of success would be low."

After repeated discussions, Mao Zhongqun finally persuaded his father to establish Fotile, with Mao Lixiang being the chairman and Mao Zhongqun the general manager.

Mao Xuefei: Taking over the Feixiang Group

From 1995, Mao Lixiang engaged himself in co-founding Fotile with his son Mao Zhongqun. He gradually handed over the gas igniter business to his daughter. At the same time, Feixiang Group was no longer a township enterprise, which meant institutional hurdles adversely affecting the enterprise's employment and operation were removed. In 1997, the property rights issues of Feixiang Group were resolved. Mao Lixiang realized the transformation through buyouts and managed to solve the problems of the relationship between the company and its employees. Mao Lixiang said, "In fact, Feixiang Group is very special. It is the company that I contracted independently when I first started a business. It carried the label of a township enterprise. I brought it through restructuring, and after that what was left of the old company was but an empty building. Some of the former employees received compensation on the basis of their length of service."

In 1996, Feixiang Group underwent a restructuring. It adopted four different methods in relation to the employment of its staff: Those who were capable were welcomed to stay; those who were of very good character but not very competent were told to move to the group's subsidiaries; those with good abilities who wanted to start a business of their own either received a compensation for their service, or became a business partner of the group; and those who were of good character and ability were given the right to share the dividends if they expressed the intention to stay and contribute their bit to the new enterprise. Mao Lixiang set up six collaborative factories and put them under the charge of the founding members of the old enterprise. These factories only had business relations with Fotile and possessed no property rights. Mao Lixiang said, "Feixiang Group suffered losses for some time, but I am not willing to cut this business, because it is the fruit of my first venture. Then my daughter and her team take charge of the group. While they continue to produce this product, they develop new projects of their own. Although this product does not generate good profits, at least we do not lose money."

On the road of starting up her own business, Mao Xuefei inherited the entrepreneurial spirit of her parents. At the beginning, Mao Xuefei borrowed 50,000 yuan from her parents. She returned the money to her parents after her initial success. Mao Xuefei and her husband later took over the gas igniter business and developed new products such as outdoor ovens, fans, liners, etc., and established Ningbo Agsun Products. Inc. to engage mainly in ODM export, which maintained a steady growth.

The biggest crisis facing a family business is the conflicts surrounding property rights and the ensuing family division. There are two types of divisions: Active division and passive division. The effect of active division will be favorable. For example, the division of the four brothers of the former Hope Group headed by Liu Yonghao was an active type. After their division, they became independent and each brother got his own shares. On the contrary, a passive division would often endanger the entire enterprise and lead to its decline. Therefore, for a family business, the disposal and distribution of property rights at the point of intergenerational succession is a question worth scrutinizing. Aware of the critical importance of this issue to his family business early on, Mao Lixiang carefully weighed the possibility of family splitting that might arise from the conflicts surrounding property rights and figured out how to prevent it from happening after his daughter took over Feixiang and his son founded Fotile. During the eventual succession, Mao Lixiang worked out a set of theories to deal with the issue of property rights distribution of family businesses. He chose the method of dividing the wealth and splitting power among family members to achieve the goal of maintaining family property rights. Of course, Fotile's success does not mean this is the only method of succession suitable for Chinese family businesses. But first, let's take a closer look at Fotile's specific approaches.

Father and Son Partnership: "Three-thirds Systems" Succession

When Fotile was founded in 1996, Mao Lixiang served as its chairman and Mao Zhongqun as its general manager. Mao Lixiang said, "I decided to let my son deal with daily business matters. He was the general manager and I was the chairman from the start. This was unlike other bosses, who moved up the ladder from workshop director, team leader, assistant manager, and deputy general manager; we were starting from scratch."

At the beginning, many people (including relatives, friends, and old employees of Feixiang) had grave doubts about Mao Zhongqun's ideas. Mao Lixiang had to spend a lot of time gaining government and employees' trust in the new company. So, Mao Lixiang took charge of relations with associations, the government, and the media and communication with employees, while Mao Zhongqun was in charge of business and management. Mao Zhongqun recalled, "In the first few years, I rarely attended various events outside the company or worried about joining any association. But in recent years, I have joined more than 20 associations because my father has withdrawn from them one after another due to his age. Fortunately, everything in the company is on track now. At least for the first 10 years, I could concentrate on internal management and business; he gave me great support and enough time to do what I needed to."

Nowadays, Fotile is the leading brand of the Chinese kitchen appliances, and it has proved to be a strong rival in the competition with international brands. The two generations of the Mao family are good role models in the establishment, development, and succession of Chinese family businesses. Their joint efforts attribute to all their achievements. Some people may have doubts about this mode of business succession: Can everything really go smoothly? As the old saying goes, "If two men ride on a horse, one must ride behind." Is this saying applicable to a family business? Whose leadership should be followed? In fact, there had been disputes between father and son as they jointly established Fotile. Stark differences in the thinking of the two generations were also reflected in the decision-making concerning the enterprise's management and development.

Although Mao Zhongqun had a verbal agreement with his father that ensured he had the final say, problems and conflicts still arose when it came to management and decision-making. At the beginning, Mao Lixiang and Mao Zhongqun each led a team in conducting research on what new products to develop. Among cars, motorcycles, air conditioners, and kitchen products, both agreed to develop kitchen products. Mao Lixiang wanted to manufacture microwave ovens. His idea won the support of the Zhejiang provincial government, because they considered the microwave oven to be a high-end consumer product and there was no local producer in this field. Mao Zhongqun, however, had a different mindset;

he chose range hoods. Although there were more than 250 companies producing range hoods on the market at that time, including some popular brands such as ROBAM and Sacon, none of them catered to high-end consumers. According to market research reports, high-end range hoods were almost all produced by foreign companies. High-end range hoods suited to Chinese cooking habits were non-existent in the market. The son finally convinced his father that a range hood was what they should produce after showing him two market research reports completed by Zhejiang University and Shanghai Jiao Tong University. However, the local Zhejiang government did not approve the project at the beginning, so Mao Lixiang promised them that his company would also manufacture microwave ovens sometime in the future.

After that, a debate ensued between father and son which lasted several months surrounding the name of the range hood. Mao Lixiang wanted to use the name of Feixiang for the new product, and change the Feixiang Group to Feixiang Kitchen Appliance Co., Ltd. However, Mao Zhongqun argued that Feixiang was not a good name. He preferred Fotile, which was easy to write and remember, he said. Moreover, the femininity carried by the name made it a good name for kitchen appliances. The two men engaged in a fierce dispute. Mao Lixiang recalled, "The argument was so fierce that on one occasion he rose and left the house without finishing his meal. We were both intellectuals, so we did not make loud noises when arguing. Later, my wife asked me whether what our son had said was correct. I said 'yes', and we agreed to use the name Fotile."

Two or three years later, another major dispute erupted when Fotile was confronted with a price war in the industry. Father and son held different views as to whether they should stick to the high-end product strategy. At that time, sales staff on the frontline of the market phoned Mao Zhongqun and Mao Lixiang almost every day to request a price cut. Mao Lixiang went to discuss this with Mao Zhongqun, who was adamant that they should not lower the price. Mao Zhongqun prioritized the development of new products and the company finally survived the price war. After this test, Mao Zhongqun proved his own ideas right and consolidated his position in the company. Gradually, Mao Lixiang began to reduce his intervention in the company's management. In order to reduce the influence of family members on high-level management decisions, his mother Zhang

Zhaodi also withdrew from the daily management of the company. Mao Zhongqun recalled how he and his father got along in those years, "The most important thing is that the older generation should be open-minded. My father is indeed open-minded. Whatever he promised, he kept his word. He knows that I am stubborn, but he still trusts me, because there was nothing he needed to worry about me throughout my childhood. I am headstrong and no one can prevent me from doing things my way. Moreover, since we live together and could talk about business over meals, our communication is good. In the end, he would normally accept my point of view."

Mao Lixiang later summed up the experience as the "three-thirds system" in the succession: In the first three years he guided his son, in the second three years he supported him, and in the third three years he watched him. Since the founding of the company in 1996, it took nine years for Fotile to complete the inheritance of the family business over the course of the establishment, expansion, and transformation of the company. Mao Lixiang spent six years training his son. In these six years, Fotile witnessed rapid expansion, and wrestle and compromise between father and son. Superficially, it looked like Mao Lixiang made concessions to his son step by step, and he lost almost all the disputes with him. But all the arguments between them contributed to Fotile's succession and development, and the company and the entire Mao family proved to be the ultimate winner. In the final three years of mentoring, Mao Lixiang handed over almost all the management and decision-making powers to his son. Mao Zhongqun believed that for some big family businesses nowadays, three years of guidance after the child's graduation from university is certainly not enough. It may take five to ten years to further develop the ability of the next generation's successor.

Mao Zhongqun: Management Philosophy after Succession

Mao Zhongqun's vision for Fotile is to "become a respected world-class company". Mao Zhongqun said, "Fotile is a mission-driven enterprise. It is not simply a profit-oriented business. I have two missions. One is to make customers' homes better. By using our high-quality products, customers can feel better at home. Recently, we have added this statement: We strive to enhance the physical and spiritual wellbeing of all our employees. I think this is the value of the East, which is quite different from pursuing maximized profits in the West. Businessmen should not think of making money only. Because we have more than enough money, there is no need to focus on profit only. Bringing both types of happiness to our employees is of great significance."

Fotile's vision is composed of four elements: A model of high-end brands, excellence in management, standard of management aimed at winning national quality award, and a model of excellent employers. Mao Zhongqun emphasizes social responsibility and promotes it in all respects, instead of simple engagement in charity work.

Mao Zhongqun said, "The second generation of entrepreneurs have an advantage in that their family already has a lot of money, so they do not need to worry about money. They can pursue something more meaningful. On the contrary, most of the first generation enterpreneurs were born into poor families and their purpose of starting up business was to make money. I wanted to do something meaningful. That's why from the very beginning, I wanted to make my business a high-end brand. Foreign brands dominated the market of home appliances. We Chinese must have our own high-end brands as well."

Recruiting Talented People

Since 1999, Mao Zhongqun has gradually brought in people of talent to form a team of professional managers for departments of manufacturing, human resources, sales, procurement, logistics, etc. Many of them have worked in multinational coorporations such as Coca-Cola and Procter & Gamble. Mao Zhongqun took advantage of the experience and practices of these managers from different companies, merged them with features of Fotile, and summed up 25 management principles which were reduced to 20 a few years later.

Today, directly under Mao Zhongqun are seven vice presidents and two general managers. However, in terms of overall management, he insists on his hands-on approach, "If the founder does not spend all his energy on the enterprise, it will not do very well. I found that successful entrepreneurs in Japan, Hong Kong, and Taiwan all keep working until they reach the age of 60 or 70, some even into the 80s. I always think that with a good professional manager in charge, the company can get a score of 80, but if the founder devotes himself entirely to the business, the score can be as high as 95, a considerable difference. If the founder can make the enterprise grow quickly, it means he has strengths few other people have. It would be a shame if he does not put his particular strengths to good use and play golf or socialize instead."

Jiang Yi is the general manager of Fotile's Overseas Business Division. He joined Fotile in July 2000. He served consecutively as Director of the Quality Control Department, Director of the Comprehensive Quality Management Office, Chief of R & D Management of the Overseas Business Division and in 2010 Head of Overseas Business Division. He rested for two years during this tenure for health reasons. He also served as a private consultant for another company for some time before returning to Fotile. Jiang Yi said with a bright smile, "We often talk jokingly about how we are so accustomed to President Mao's leadership that it is difficult for us to work under other bosses. There are three reasons for this. First, our boss trusts us. He is not an authoritarian person and will not impose his ideas on us. He will listen to our ideas carefully. If he thinks appropriate, he will point to us the directions. Second, I really like the environment and atmosphere of Fotile. One person's ability is limited, so they require good resources and a good environment to complete one's tasks. Third, Fotile is not a company interested in office politics. I worked in state-owned companies before where people were divided into cliques and promotions were made in accordance with seniority. But things are much simpler here in Fotile. Everyone is honest and we all mainly focus on the company's business without worrying about other things."

Employee Incentives: Personal Share Policy

Since 2002, Fotile's sales revenue has maintained a yearly growth rate of 20%–30% for 12 consecutive years. Over the years, Mao Zhongqun has stuck to the three-point policy he formulated for Fotile — "Not engaging in price wars, not going public, and not resorting to deception". Mao Zhongqun has insisted on not going public, refusing share holdings or purchase by venture capital institutions, and keeping Fotile a 100% family holding company.

Mao Zhongqun said, "By not making Fotile a listed company, I can develop this business in line with my own ideas. Going public, getting a lot of money and making investment does not conform to my strategy. My strategy is to focus on one thing and do it well. I think it is enough, because in the home appliance industry desperate expansion does not make much sense."

In May 2010, Mao Zhongqun implemented the "personal share policy" within Fotile. Dividends were given to all employees who had been employed for two years. Twice a year, on events such as Dragon Boat Festival (5th day of the 5th lunar month) and Confucius' birthday (September 28th), dividends were paid out from about 5% of the company's net profit in the previous year. Employees did not need to invest in the company to get shares. Dividends were paid in accordance with what was known as an employee's personal shares which were determined by the performance of every individual and the department they worked for. Personal shares would become invalid once the employee leaves the company. The first group of employees who received the "personal share" certificates consisted of more than 1,300 people. Each held least one share to a number that was kept confidential. In 2010, Fotile's annual sales revenue exceeded 2 billion yuan, with a net profit of more than 100 million yuan. During the Dragon Boat Festival in 2011, employees including cleaners and production-line workers received dividends for the first time, ranging from 1,400 to 2,000 yuan per share.

The idea of the personal share policy came from the Shanxi Merchant Exchange Shop, commonly known as "labor-sharing system", which was to incorporate an important incentive mechanism for managers and employees. Since then, Fotile's personal share policy has continuously improved and the scope of issuance has continued to expand. Since 2011, this policy is extended from the headquarters to all business departments, including the 49 offices across the country, and more than 6,000 employees has received dividends. Assessment is made by the group in accordance with the group's total profit, and by each business department and subsidiary company in accordance with the remainder of the profit. Since 2012, all personal shares of the group's vice presidents are calculated independently, and the number of shares of department heads and directors has increased. The payment of dividends in branch and subsidiary companies across the country is decoupled from the group headquarters. The employees of these companies no longer receive personal share dividends from the group headquarters. After paying about 50% of their profits to the group, the branch and subsidiary companies then distribute the remaining 50% of the profits among the employees in accordance with the number of shares they hold, but giving preferential treatment to managers of the branches and subsidiary companies.

Li Zuguo, the vice president of Human Resources Department of Fotile, said that Fotile's stock document includes three parts, the stock of the headquarters, the stock of the retail business, and the stock of the frontline factory business. The distribution method of the headquarters is that the company promises to give 5% of the profits of the current year to everyone. Each employee holds 1 to more than 10 shares depending on their position (rank), work performance, and qualifications. The 5% of the headquarters' profits are distributed among staff members working at the headquarters and the three major business divisions. Employees working in the three major business divisions receive some dividends from the headquarters and some from their own division. The three major business divisions transfer some of the profits to the regional companies and the proportions of the profits are decided by the maturity of the business division concerned. For example, the most profitable business division is the kitchen appliance division. According to the ratio of 3:7, 30% of the shares receive dividends from the headquarters and 70% of the shares receive dividends from the kitchen appliance division. Although the Overseas Business Division is losing money, it is a long-term strategic investment department and it will probably take 5–10 years to achieve profitability. 20% of the shares receive dividends from this business division while 80% of the shares receive dividends from the headquarters. The Cabinet Business Division is a division which needs time to develop the ability to make a profit in the future. Therefore, 60% of the shares receive dividends in this business division, and 40% of the shares receive dividends from the group, and it will gradually increase the proportion contributed by the division itself. The specific ratio is discussed every two years. In addition, there is also a bonus system, under which one performance evaluation is conducted mid-year and another one is conducted at the end of the year. Yearly bonus is paid out in light of the two evaluations. People who get a C in the evaluations receive no bonus; those who get a B receive an additional two months' salary, and those who get an A receive an additional 4–5 months' salary.

At present, Fotile's employees enjoy a full-coverage benefits scheme consisting of social insurance, housing provident fund, "personal share" dividends, paid annual leave, and work subsidies.

After three years of implementation, the effect of the personal share policy is obvious. Li Zuguo said, "In 2013, Fotile's sales increased by 46%. The personal share policy has the most incentive effect on the middle- and high-level employees, as dividends from this policy account for about 30% of an already large annual income of the division (department) heads. Secondly, the dividends from personal shares have risen rapidly over the past two years along with the increase in our profit. In 2012, one share is worth 2,100 yuan as compared with only 1,000 yuan a couple of years earlier. If the profit reaches 1 billion yuan, it is 10,000 yuan per share. That is a lot of money, for the company's promise will remain unchanged and that is 5%. As you stay longer in the company, you will feel this more strongly. In this way, we are encouraging our employees to pay more attention to the company's overall profit."

Mao Zhongqun said, "The Confucianist idea that 'the benevolent love the people' requires us to take into consideration the interests of the employees. In China, the disparity between the rich and the poor is large. Those who genuinely need money are the employees working at the grassroots level. They also create value for the company — why not give them personal shares?"

Confucian President

When you meet Mao Zhongqun, you will think that he is more like a scholar than a businessman. He always wears a modest smile on his face. When taking questions, he always thinks for a few seconds before answering them. In 2005, Mao Zhongqun began to take traditional Chinese culture courses in Peking University and Tsinghua University, and introduced the ideas of traditional Chinese culture into Fotile's daily management, hoping to open up a new path of Chinese management. In 2008, he built a 200-square-meter Confucius Hall on the first floor of Fotile's new main building, and erected a statue of Confucius there. In this hall, ordinary employees and middle-level managers can study Confucianism and absorb the essence of ancient Chinese culture, and discuss how to transform the enterprise and make self-improvement. Every day from 8:15 to 8:30 a.m., employees and management executives begin reciting passages from the popular readers of traditional classics like the *Three Character Classic* and the *Standards for Being a Good Student and Child*. The induction training for new employees also takes place in the Confucius Hall where they recite Confucian classics. Mao Zhongqun believes that a classic book like *The Analects* will change one's temperament after reading it for a hundred times. If family members read it together, harmony runs in the family. Nowadays, standards of morality in our society are deteriorating. Reading *The Analects* can improve employees' moral standards. Mao Zhongqun believes that Fotile's idea is to achieve corporate excellence and social responsibility through the Confucian management model.

The educational model of ideology and morality is completely different from the educational model of technical skills. It cannot be instilled or enforced. Therefore, Fotile has established the Confucius Hall and adopted a method that does not require employees to undertake an assessment and write their thoughts after the study sessions. What Fotile teaches in the Confucius Hall is not how to work, but how to be a person, how to educate a child, and how to run a harmonious family. This is because it is best for a culture to influence people's way of thinking and behavior unconsciously. Moreover, the premise of Confucian "benevolence" is that it does not put pressure on employees but let them accept the ideas from the bottom of their hearts. It will actually give employees a sense of identity with the company.

In the company's newsletter "Fotile People", Mao Zhongqun has opened a column called "Confucian President" and writes articles on "Benevolence, Righteousness, Courtesy, Wisdom and Faith" — essential tenets of traditional Chinese culture. He feels that China is now at a stage where businesses like to resort to unfair competitions in order to increase sales. On the surface, this causes conflicts, but in fact, if a business can achieve the highest level and truly take into account the demands of customers in the whole process from products manufacturing to sales services, then it will certainly come out the final winner. Looking at this result, we may say that there should have been no conflicts. The mother of an employee said, "We have nothing to worry about when my child works in such a company. It is a trustworthy enterprise." A dealer from Singapore was received by Jiang Yi this year. Before he left for China, he was told that Fotile is a special company with a sound corporate culture. This piqued his curiosity. On the last day of the visit, the Singaporean said, "I was touched from the moment I got off the plane until the end of my visit. In terms of details, the people here are particularly polite, professional, and dedicated, from the start of the pick-up, to the arrangement of each itinerary, to the presentation of the company's products and image through to the new product launch, and so on. How come all of you say the same thing as Mr. Mao said?"

Of course, Confucianism is not the only effective method in enterprise management. Sound rules and regulations remain an important framework for enterprise development. How does Fotile balance the use of Confucianism and rules? That is to say, based on the strengths of Confucian thinking (emphasis on moral education, benevolence, and righteousness-based system), the essence of legalism is appropriately absorbed.

First, management effects must come from sense of shame and fear, because shame alone may prove to be unreliable in dealing with matters involving great personal interests. Therefore, Fotile divides errors into three categories: A, B, and C. Type A is a serious error, Type B is a moderate error, and Type C is a minor error. In general, Type-C mistakes can be managed with sense of shame, and Type-A mistakes must be managed with fear and sense of shame.

Second, punishment is meted out depending on the seriousness of the mistakes, that is, a Type-C error is mainly dealt with through education, and a Type-A error is mainly dealt with by heavy punishment (such as expulsion or punishment by law), which also serves as a deterrent. A Type-B error can be dealt with by light penalties (such as fines plus administrative sanctions).

Third, a supervision method combining self-monitoring, mass supervision, and special supervision is adopted.

Fourth, penalties should be imposed in strict accordance with the rules. Revisions will be made to existing rules that are found to be unreasonable. Otherwise, compliance with the rules is a must.

In short, in Fotile's view, giving Confucianism the primacy and supplemented by law is the best way to managing an enterprise. Western thought on the rule of law is similar to Chinese legalism (they are not identical, of course). Mao Zhongqun has always said that Confucianism is the foundation and law is for practical application; Chinese ethical knowledge is the foundation and Western knowledge and technology is for practical application. In this sense, if Chinese companies blindly copy Western management methods, they will certainly not go very far[1].

In Mao Zhongqun's view, the Confucius Hall is a manifestation of "benevolence" and is a small part of Fotile's education in Confucian culture. In addition to the tangible practices such as the establishment of Confucius Hall, Fotile also set up a related promotion group, planning to make Confucianism a procedure-based model and management system that can be put into practice. While carrying out Confucianism education, Mao Zhongqun has formulated rules and standards, hoping to establish a Confucianism-based Chinese-style management model. He believes that Confucianism will lack strength if it is only applied at the level of corporate culture. Only when it is truly integrated into management and forms a system that can be implemented on a regular basis will it become a management model.

Road to Innovation

Innovation is the primary driving force in Fotile's birth. Therefore, in the course of the company's succession and development, Mao Zhongqun has never forgotten that innovation is the key to Fotile's survival. Only through continuous innovation can enterprises survive and continue to develop. Fotile's road to innovation can be divided into three stages: First, the five years from 1996 to 2001 was a period for laying the foundation. The focus in this period was product innovation because only quality

---

[1] Mao, Zhongqun. (2010). Run Business with Confucianism. *PKU Business Review,* 8, 44–57.

products could help a new company gain a firm foothold in the market. The second stage featured management innovation that started in 2001. After several years of expansion, Fotile needed a better management model for the company to grow steadily further. Then after 2006, Mao Zhongqun led Fotile in making many attempts in cultural innovation. These three kinds of innovation are three different aspects of Fotile's overall innovation; they are not separated but interrelated. Management innovation will promote product innovation, and cultural innovation will promote management innovation. However, all kinds of innovation must contribute to product innovation and increasing customers' satisfaction.

Fotile is a leading company in high-end kitchen appliances, thanks to its technological and product innovation. In terms of technology, Fotile has more than 400 patents in kitchen appliances, including 48 invention patents, giving it a commanding lead in the industry. Its products, from the first type-A range hoods to the latest cloud magic cube/wind magic cube range hoods are all models of technological innovation, concept innovation, and quality and functional innovation, leading the industry of kitchen electronic appliances.

In Mao Zhongqun's view, product innovation is not difficult, the real challenge is technological innovation and conceptual innovation. Minor modification of other people's products may also be regarded as innovation and many companies are doing this, but this will not last long, because the needs of customers are always changing. After careful deliberation, Mao Zhongqun realized that Fotile's dilemma in product innovation was essentially a management problem rather than a technical problem. The company's strategy, system, management, and personnel were not conducive to product innovation, and as a result, the company lost its direction and motivation of innovation. Continuous product innovation should be based on management innovation, and innovation in management systems could inject new energy into product innovation. After making clear the strategic direction of the company through innovation, Mao Zhongqun and his team removed the products that did not conform to Fotile's strategy, established integrated product development process, shortened product development cycle, reduced development costs, and eventually achieved product innovation. Later, Mao Zhongqun came to a realization that only well-qualified and well-educated employees could produce high-quality products and create brands with cultural content. Ancient China had a splendid culture and it gave birth to the four great inventions, proving that Chinese people are as good as the Westerners in terms of creativity and innovation. Hence, as a company, the key is to create an environment conducive to innovation; as an entrepreneur, the key is to give a unique character to the enterprise, meaning the creation of a corporate culture. That is why Mao Zhongqun put forward the management thought emphasizing the combination of Chinese learning (which helps an enterprise's development on the strategic level) and Western learning (which is helpful on the tactical level). He makes great efforts to promote a Confucianism-based management concept to make the Confucian culture to become deeply rooted in the minds of the people and the soul of the company[2].

Giving up Diversification

For many companies that were established in the 1990s, diversification was the choice by most entrepreneurs, but Fotile had been known for many years in the kitchenware business. In fact, Fotile had once made a small attempt in developing other businesses, but Mao Zhongqun decided to stop it two years later. He said that he was a dedicated person. "In fact, I can't do multiple tasks at the same time. When I was a student, I was like that. I was interested in and good at maths and physics and I told myself that I must be the top of the class in these two subjects. But I hated Chinese language class, so I just gave it up. My personality determines that I can't choose diversification in my work."

In 2008, Fotile developed a "multi-brand specialization" strategy, launching the BORCCI, defining it as a "professionally-operated high-end integrated kitchen business". In 2009, it launched the Mibbo water heater, defining it as "providing solutions of hot water system at home to high-end consumers". In 2011, the Mibbo water heater business was discontinued. It was the second time that Mao Zhongqun cut down on his production

---

[2] Mao, Zhongqun. (2013). Modes of Fotile — From Product Innovation and Management Innovation to Culture Innovation. *Tsinghua Business Review*, 3, 22–30.

line after discontinuing the water dispenser and electromagnetic oven project in 2006.

He said, "This (multi-brand specialization strategy) lasted for a year or two. Finally, we decided to discontinue it after careful consideration. At first, a consulting company suggested that we should give it up to focus on kitchen appliances. The strategy had just been introduced for a little more than one year and we were quite enthusiastic about it. Giving it up was hard for us. Then we calmed down and weighed it over for about six months before making the final decision. This experience told me that there are few opportunities for new brands on the domestic market today. All industries are fairly mature with sufficient competition. Several leading brands are deeply engrained in the minds of consumers, so it is nearly impossible for new brands to enter the field; another reason is that the cost is so high that it is not worth the effort required. Secondly, our motive was not right at the time. We were eager to increase the size of the company. We did not fully comprehend why we should do it, or what was the significance of it. Third, the water heater industry was heading toward using technologies of air energy and solar energy, but there were very good companies in both areas then. In air energy, there was advanced air-conditioning technology, and basically there was no opportunity open to us as long as technologies were concerned. Moreover, we did not establish an independent organization for the water heater at that time. They were included in the sales team of Fotile. They couldn't do it well and was distracted in the meantime."

From then on, Mao Zhongqun decided not to pursue rapid expansion through merger and acquisition but to concentrate on Fotile's high-end kitchenware.

Road to Internationalization

Jiang Yi, general manager of the Overseas Business Division, went to the Division's R&D Department in 2007 and began to get involved in the discussion of overseas strategy. At the beginning, Mao Zhongqun did not pay much attention to overseas business. He often said, "I won't poke my nose into things I don't know much about. I don't know much about overseas business, so I just listened and observed. I didn't participate in the discussions." Overseas business strategy was discussed at Fotile's yearly meetings on strategy for three consecutive years. In 2009, Mao Zhongqun reviewed the company's corporate culture, values, mission, and vision. By that time, he was determined to implement the overseas strategy. He said, "Why do I want to do overseas business? This is because it will make Fotile a respected world-class enterprise. If our company only aimed at domestic market, it is quite limited. So, we don't need OEM. We should be firm in creating our brand independently, and we want to be a high-end brand, which is consistent with the domestic market positioning."

After the meeting on strategy in 2009, Fotile resolutely discontinued its OEM business, including some profitable ones, and began its overseas business in accordance with its strategic management model and promotion methods. Jiang Yi said, "We expand our business to overseas in a way that is rare in China. Leading brands like Midea, Haier, etc., in the home appliance industry expanded to the overseas market by way of scale, big sales, or OEM. The prices of their products are not high; even the pricing of their independent brands is very low. These inexpensive products, when being sold in a shopping mall, do not present a good image for their reputation. Fotile is not good in this manner and we are not going to use it. We are not able to compete with them for scale and speed, so we choose a road of our own that is intensive cultivation. We do not pursue large-scale at first, we focus on quality."

Fotile first overseas market is Southeast Asia, because there are many ethnic Chinese people who have similar dining habits and kitchen culture to China, which would highlight the strengths of Fotile's products. Malaysia, in particular, has become Fotile's benchmark overseas market, occupying the first place among the country's high-end brands. Fotile is now working to penetrate into the Indonesian and Vietnamese markets and has set up an overseas R&D center to establish a brand based on the mentality and needs of local consumers. In 2013, Fotile achieved 100% growth in Pakistan.

Jiang Yi said, "Fotile needs to gain a firm foothold in these countries before expanding to other countries. Although it is a slow process, every step is solid and we hope to gain respect internationally. The first three years has proved to be arduous. What we did was to cultivate the market and to gain customers' trust. We have to compete with European brands in these countries, which is really difficult. These countries were former colonies of European powers. Vietnam was a French colony and Malaysia a British colony. Yet, Mr. Mao insisted on this strategy. Our strategy is aimed at establishing our brand through quality products. We want to impress consumers with the products themselves. First our products and then our brand will be recognized by the customers. Fotile range hoods are unique in the world. This is our unique strength."

In 2008, Fotile's foreign trade amounted to around 100 million yuan. In 2009, the OEM business was discontinued, and Fotile focused on the promotion of its own brand, so overseas sales declined. To date, Fotile's foreign trade sales never exceeded those in 2008. In 2015, Fotile's total sales reached 6.6 billion yuan, and overseas business accounted for only 2%.

Mao's Family Governance

Fotile's shareholding structure at the time of its founding was: Mao Lixiang 35%, daughter Mao Xuefei 14%, wife Zhang Zhaodi 16%, and son Mao Zhongqun 35%. In 2010, Mao Lixiang transferred all 35% of his stocks to Mao Zhongqun, including the original 2% that belonged to high-level executives. Mao Xuefei held shares in Fotile and served on the board of directors but did not participate in running the business. Zhang Zhaodi was the vice chairperson and deputy general manager at the beginning of Fotile's founding. She was in charge of production, finance, and management. However, after the proposal of "emphasizing less the family factor" was put forward, Zhang Zhaodi withdrew from the management and is currently serving as the supervisor. Apart from these, no other members of the Mao family are holding senior management positions.

Mao Lixiang has a "pocket theory" about the equity structure of family businesses. This theory has three meanings: First, the majority, if not all, of the company's shares, are held within the family. Second, the successor to the family business should hold the majority of shares. Third, equity within the family should be clearly defined. If the brother and sister are both strong-willed people, they can hold shares in each other's company. However, they should not manage the same company together. It is best to put money in one pocket, otherwise it will be a "time bomb" in the business, eventually leading to the split of the family and business.

Mao Lixiang's "pocket theory" does not require to put all the resources in only one pocket, but to put the core resources in the most essential pocket to ensure the inheritance of the enterprise; at the same time, the enterprise needs to create other pockets to protect the interests of other stakeholders. For example, Mao Zhongqun agreed to serve as the general manager of Fotile on the condition that he would form his own management team that would operate independently. This meant that many senior members of the old enterprise were fired. Mao Lixiang created other "pockets": Six collaborative factories making parts and components for Fotile were founded, and were put under the charge of his "old courtiers". These manufacturers directly participated in market competition and only had business relations with Fotile, but possessed no property rights.

When explained via a modern corporate system, Mao Lixiang's "pocket theory" clearly defines the property rights. On the one hand, it avoids the conflicts of traditional family businesses and the disadvantages of rejecting talented people. On the other hand, it guarantees the interests of family members as well as founding members and senior employees of the old enterprise.

Mao Lixiang said, "There is a principle in the equity arrangement, that is, the successor must have holding interests. Why people say wealth never survives three generations? Because from the first generation, the second generation to the third generation, shares they hold may be reduced from 100% to 1/3, and then to 1/10. In that case, the authority of the successor will not be reflected in the equity. Hence, I must make proper equity arrangement."

Mao Lixiang once discussed his thoughts with her daughter. Both himself and his son co-founded Fotile, but he still gave 14% of the shares to his daughter, who had her own company. Senior Mao believed that the successor should have holding interests. This way his son would be highly motivated.

"If I gave half of my shares to my son and half to my daughter, it would be unfair to my son, so I gave all my shares to my son. As for his mother, she will work things out by herself. I have essentially completely delegated power to my children. We need to make preparations early so both children know our plans."

In accordance with a regulation laid down by Mao Lixiang, a conference of family members is held one every year. In addition, there is a family dinner once every month and a family gathering once every quarter.

Mao Lixiang said, "We often convene family meetings which are attended by my son, his wife, my daughter, and her husband. Perhaps this helps unify family members' mindset. At the meeting, everyone is informed of major events in the company and talks to each other about personal matters, including health preservation, nurturing of the third generation offspring, etc."

The management and investment issues of Feixiang and Fotile are also discussed at the family meeting. Mao Lixiang said, "We had previously considered investing in the name of Feixiang instead of Fotile when investing in the Hangzhou Bay Bridge, because Fotile did not want to invest in other areas at the time. However, during the family meeting, we decided to invest in the name of Fotile. This was because my daughter had Fotile's shares but did not have Feixiang's shares. If we invested in the name of Feixiang, my daughter would have no shares in the bridge, therefore we reached consensus and decided to invest in the name of Fotile."

Mao Lixiang attaches great importance to the family meetings. He said, "The purpose of family meetings is first to reach a mutual level of understanding among family members and not to complain in the company about the differing views, as it will do harm to the prestige of the family. Sometimes we have contrasting thoughts and we need to solve them at the family meetings. That's why I proposed the three-tier governance: Corporate governance, management governance, and family governance."

The purpose of promoting family governance is to prevent family conflicts from entering the enterprise, a common issue found in many family enterprises. Family conflicts are brought to the enterprise when a father quarrels with his son, or when a husband quarrels with his wife. The managers will feel that there is no hope and prospect in the company. Therefore, family governance is very important.

Mao Lixiang's Third Venture: Evergreen Family Business College

From 1999, Mao Lixiang was invited to be a guest lecturer by many universities in China, and he had taught more than 700 lessons to students in nearly 30 universities, including Peking University, Tsinghua University, and Renmin University of China. During this stint, Mao Lixiang came to realize the severity of the problem in family succession. After 2002, he gradually withdrawn from the daily management of Fotile and began to deliver lectures in universities. At the same time, he wrote a book and proposed a "modern family business management mode with Chinese characteristics", the main theme regarding how China's traditional family business should be transformed into a modern family business.

In the course of research and communication, he realizes that the challenge of succession faced by Chinese family businesses is serious. There are 5 million family businesses of a fairly large scale in China, and 3 million of them are facing the problem of succession. Many first generation entrepreneurs are between 55 and 75 years old, but the handovers are not going smoothly. The first generation complains while the second generation is not satisfied, resulting in a lot of problems.

In 2006, Mao Lixiang started his pioneering work for the third time. He founded the College for Successor of Family Business, the first one of its kind in China. In 2007, Mao Lixiang founded the Forum on International Family Business, which would present annual awards to theses and books that specially study the topic of family business.

The Future: Can Wealth Survive Three Generations?

In 2015, the Forum on International Family Business founded by Mao Lixiang entered its ninth year, and the "Mao Lixiang Family Business Research Excellent Paper Award" and "Mao Lixiang Family Business Research Monograph Award" were presented for the seventh time. I sincerely admire his devotion and enthusiasm to the cause. As an exemplary, Mao Lixiang, over the age of 70, is still giving impassioned speeches. The unscripted speeches are a stellar demonstration of his love and devotion for the family business. I also believe that Mao Zhongqun has surpassed his father. As a mature second-generation successor, after 20 years of experiencing ups and downs in the enterprise's development and immersion in the study of traditional Chinese culture, he has turned into a mature business leader who knows "what can be done and what cannot be done" while in pursuit of success. The clear and sound strategic planning and the continuous development of corporate culture are all centered around his management philosophy which emphasizes the combination of Chinese learning (which decides the direction for an enterprise's development) and Western learning (which excels in expertise). Mao Lixiang calls himself a "firm defender of the family business". He once said, "For family business inheritance, the first generation must be bold and determined; they must hand over the business to the next generation completely. If the first generation does not want or is afraid of making the transition, it will have an adverse impact on the second generation assuming the corporation responsibility."

Mao Lixiang often takes his 20-year-old grandson Yu Xinyuan to the factory and the showroom. At the age of 17, Yu Xinyuan made a speech in English at the 3rd Forum on International Family Business. Three years ago, he initiated a "wealthy third generation" organization in Shanghai, hoping to promote a sense of social responsibility in the third generation. He also established the Future Entrepreneurs' Social Responsibility Alliance. Even though there were not many members, Mao Lixiang encouraged him to do something useful rather than worrying about expanding the size of the alliance. Hence, they went to a poverty-stricken area in Yunnan Province to fund a primary school, bought books and stationery with their own pocket money, provided lucky money, etc. for students, and also launched events related to the low-carbon economy. These were all planned by the younger generation themselves. Yu Xinyuan does not like to mention his wealthy family background, because he feels that he has nothing to do with Fotile's success and discussion about the topic of "wealth never survives three generations" only puts him under pressure.

Mao Lixiang notices the big difference between his generation and the younger generation. The latter is well-versed with regards to the digital economy and investment tools, but are probably not interested in traditional industries since they have more opportunities to embrace new things. Compared with the second generation, the third generation will find it more difficult to understand the hardships experienced by the first generation. The second generation has witnessed how hard their parents had worked, but most of the third generation are concerned about only their studies. Mao Lixiang said, "We must first point the direction for the third generation. These children will find themselves in trouble if they can't follow the right direction. First of all, we must guide them and inspire them to garner self-awareness. The guidance from middle school to high school is highly important. When they enter the university, their ways of thinking have already formed. At this point, the priority is to advise them on their future career development and the direction for their future cause."

To become a family business that lasts for hundreds or even thousands of years, an entrepreneurial spirit and a family culture are most essential. Be bold to shoulder responsibilities is a key element of family culture. I have witnessed the transmission of culture, the persistence of the spirit, and the undertaking of social responsibility in the inheritance of the Mao family business. The breakthrough and transformation of traditional enterprises and the sublimation of ancient culture have been perfectly integrated in Fotile.

Instead of becoming one of the world's top 500 companies, it is better to become a 500-year enterprise. Mao Lixiang always hopes that his family business will last forever. Although Yu Xinyuan is still studying in school and Mao Zhongqun's child is only 10 years old, the Mao family has begun to think about how to cultivate the third generation. How to explore a way of passing the family business from one generation to the next? How to make Fotile a world's renowned brand of high-end kitchen electrical appliance that lasts for 100 years and beyond?

Fotile's development and inheritance is a typical case. Mao Lixiang is open-minded — he is willing to relegate power to his children and take heed of opinions from the second generation. After his retirement, he is focusing on the education of family business succession. This spirit of withdrawal after succession is a worthy act that other entrepreneurs can emulate.

5

The Common Agreement of
the Xu Family

In the Mao family, the transition of Fotile from father to son can be described as pushing the boat along with the current. The first-generation entrepreneur was considering recommencing his pioneering work when the old business reached its bottleneck, and the second generation showed the vision for business transformation and upgrading. Supported by the common belief of the father and son, the family business succession took place smoothly as they co-established a new business. However, the handover between father and son of Huamao Group, from Ningbo, Zhejiang Province, did not receive the same luck. This particular succession was comparable to pushing a boat against the current. Unlike Mao Zhongqun — who received support and guidance from his father, Xu Lixun, the successor of Huamao and who had just returned to China after graduating from university abroad, had to take over the business from his father amid a family business crisis. Hence, his path of growth was filled with hardships. After their sons took over the business, the two first-generation leaders differed completely in the distribution of the business' property rights. Mao Lixiang chose active division and devised the "pocket theory" to help distribute assets and equity to his children. In the process, he clarified Mao Zhongqun's core position as the successor,

hoping to avoid the possibility of "wealth never survives three generations" caused by the dispersion of property rights. In the Xu family, Xu
Wanmao formulated the family "charter" with provisions on "separating
the family without dividing the property", ensuring that the wealth of
Huamao would pass on in the Xu family from generation to generation.
His son Xu Lixun was the second-generation leader of the family business. The two family businesses, both based in Ningbo, Zhejiang Province,
had distinctly different choices on the road to succession. Let us take a
look at the characteristics of Huamao's succession.

In 2000, Ningbo Huamao Group was involved in a lawsuit in the
United States because the secretary of the group's US-based company,
Huayuan Holdings Co., Ltd., transferred the company's assets and brought
Xu Wanmao, chairman of the Group, to court. Thus, he had to go to the
US a dozen times to deal with the lawsuit. Xu Wanmao started his business in 1978. After three strategic transformations and institutional
reforms, he transformed the enterprise from a collective-run enterprise to
a family business and went through the hardships experienced by the
entrepreneurs of his generation. The lawsuit was the biggest crisis to hit
Xu Wanmao since he first founded the business. After careful consideration, he decided to appoint his 26-year-old son Xu Lixun as the deputy
general manager to take care of the family business. Xu Lixun, who had
returned to China only one year before, was entrusted with the mission at
this critical moment and embarked on the road of succession.

The first time I met Xu Lixun, he was but an ordinary second-
generation successor who had just secured his place in the family business. Now, he is a charismatic leader of the family business. Normally, in
the course of family business succession, the first generation will have the
prospective successor work his way up the ladder in the family business,
familiarizing himself with the business operation along the way. Several
years later, the parents will relegate power to the child (children).
However, in the case of Xu Lixun, he did not go through such a process.
When his father Xu Wanmao was caught up in the lawsuit in the United
States, succession was literally forced upon him. Xu Lixun was more
inclined to finance. Perhaps he had imagined many times that he would
lead a life as free as a bird flying in the sky. Obligated to shoulder the
heavy family responsibility, he experienced painful struggles for six years

after the succession. Eventually, he came out as the veritable president of Huamao Group.

On August 10, 2008, all members of the Xu family formally signed the "Common Agreement of the Xu Family", in which the principle of family property disposal was laid out — "separate the family without dividing the property". It became the first family-owned enterprise in China to sign a family agreement. Can this family agreement ensure the perpetuity of Huamao Group under the control of the Xu family? As the Xu family's representative to manage the business, how will Xu Lixun respond to the challenge of the growth of the business as well as himself?

Xu Wanmao's Early Business Venture

Huamao Group was founded in June 1971 in Ningbo, a well-known cultural city at the economic center south of the Yangtze River Delta. Over the past 40-plus years, with its foundation in education, Huamao has developed into a comprehensive industrial group focusing on the research and production of teaching tools, basic educational equipment, and popular science products, as well as the running of private schools. It is concurrently engaged in other industries, such as international trade, real estate, financial investment, hotels, tourism, energy technology, railway equipment, and environmental protection. It has more than 2,300 staff members, with altogether 30 wholly-owned and holding subsidiaries, including Huamao Group Co., Ltd., Ningbo Huamao Culture and Education Co., Ltd., Ningbo Huamao Foreign Languages School, and Huayuan Holdings Co., Ltd. in the US. It ranks among China's top 500 industrial enterprises.

Becoming a Farmer Entrepreneur in 1978

In 1971, Yunzhou Commune in Yin County of Ningbo established the Yunzhou Township Bamboo Crafts Factory by relying on local resources. This was the predecessor of Huamao, and it was called a "commune-run enterprise" at that time. Xu Wanmao was a worker/designer/salesman in this small factory. With his innovative products, he gradually stood out in the factory. In 1978, he began to take over this handicraft factory and embarked on his road to business venture.

It should be said that Xu Wanmao was very much alike a bold eagle with clear goals. Just as the bamboo knitting business was flourishing, Xu Wanmao read an article comparing Chinese and foreign students. The article advocated the development of labor skill education in primary and secondary schools. He quickly realized the future prospects of the education industry. As a result, Huamao carried out its first transformation, shifting from handicraft production to the making of teaching tools. In 1981, he began to consider transforming the handicraft factory into one that produced labor skill education products, and presently established Yunzhou Culture and Education Technology Equipment Factory. Its trademark was "Seven Color Flower", which implied that children were the flowers of the motherland. The main business of the factory was to design and produce labor skill teaching tools and teaching materials for primary and middle school students. The eight years from 1982 to 1989 was the most difficult period in Huamao's development. The factory suffered losses from educational products, so it relied solely on the bamboo crafts for survival. In 1985, at the invitation of Zhejiang Arts & Crafts Import and Export Co., Ltd., Xu Wanmao joined a business delegation on a visit to Australia. He became the first farmer entrepreneur in Ningbo who went abroad for his studies. He was deeply impressed by the wide variety of educational equipment in Australia. This visit was quite an eye-opener and he knew what he was going to do next. After returning to China, Xu Wanmao and his men went to the State Education Commission (SEC) six times to request for support. Not until 1989, when Huamao moved from the mountainous area of Simingshan to Wangchun in the western suburb of Ningbo, did it finally receive the support of the SEC. The handcraft materials produced by Huamao were recognized by the SEC and its trademark "Seven Color Flower" got the permission to be used nationwide. In 1991, Huamao Group's "Seven Color Flower" teaching tools were sold all over China, bringing in about 200 million yuan with a market share of 70%.

In 1992, "Seven Color Flower" teaching tools made its first profit in the process of its development. Xu Wanmao began to build an enterprise group for teaching tools, an attempt to make industrial extension in both depth and breadth. In the same year, he invested more than 800,000 yuan to build the Ningbo Labor Skills Education Equipment Research Institute. He then successively established Beijing Seven Color Flower Education

Technology Development Center, Beijing Huamao Education Software Co., Ltd., Shanghai Huamao Culture and Education Products Co., Ltd. and other branches. He also invested in an energy-saving lamp project and a cooperation project with Kaidu Hotel, engaging in R&D and sales of various products.

The second transformation was an industrial transformation. Xu Wanmao's intention was to turn the enterprise into an industrial group of "diversified development while maintaining the depth of its main business", but his effort was not a success. After analysis, Xu Wanmao concluded that the main reason for his failure was lacking a talent pool that matched the strategic transformation. He paid dearly as a result.

The failure of the second transformation made Xu Wanmao realize that the education industry was a market with broad prospects that could be developed in depth. Utilizing the principle of "1+1>2" to generate economic benefits, Xu Wanmao started the third transformation in 1998. He founded Ningbo Huamao Foreign Languages School, and successively established Quzhou Huamao Foreign Languages School and Longyou Huamao Foreign Languages School, gradually achieving industry-university-research integration and what was known as thematic diversification with in-depth development of its main business. Its diversified development was centered on the theme of education. Derived from this theme were education-based real estate, import and export of education products, education-based tourism and other industries. Huamao Education Group was established in August 1999 with an initial fund of 100 million yuan. As a second-level group, Huamao Education Group was exclusively invested by Huamao Group. Adopting the management model of a business division, it was engaged in the study and formulation of the overall plan for Huamao's education industry, so as to guide and supervise the implementation of education management in all types of educational institutions under the group.

The Huamao American Crisis in 2000

In 1996, Huamao Group set up Huayuan Holdings Co., Ltd. in Los Angeles to invest in assets. In 1997, Mr. Ha the company secretary used Xu Wanmao's signature to forge documents and slowly transferred the company's assets to himself. In 2000, Xu Wanmao found out the problem and sent financial personnel to the US to investigate. The company secretary filed a lawsuit in the Los Angeles court to charge Xu Wanmao with the forgery of stock share evidence. As the key witness, Xu Wanmao needed to go abroad to testify in court. He presumed that he would return home within 20 days, but the situation was more complicated than he had thought. At the beginning, in an attempt to disrupt the progress of the lawsuit in the US, Mr. Ha reported to a relevant Chinese government department that Xu Wanmao was illegally transferring assets overseas, hoping to create difficulties that would prevent Xu Wanmao from appearing in court. Later, with Xu Wanmao's constant effort, he finally testified in court in the US. However, due to a lack of knowledge of US laws and regulations as well as someone's deliberate interference, he had to travel between China and the United States frequently to appear in court.

In China, rumors were widespread that Xu Wanmao took away all the money and absconded abroad, Huamao's cash flow was broken, and its bankruptcy was just around the corner. Huamao was leaderless and the situation was critical. At such a time of crisis, who would step forward to shoulder the responsibility and preside over the overall situation? Were they Huamao's senior executives who had been following Xu Wanmao for many years and made notable contributions, or Xu Wanmao's elder son-in-law Zhang Guomin and younger son-in-law Wang Leping who engaged in the business along with Xu Wanmao in the 1970s and 1980s, or Xu Lixun, Xu Wanmao's son, a young man who had just returned to China upon completion of studies abroad a year before?

When Xu Lixun Took over Huamao at a Critical Moment

In 1999, Xu Lixun graduated from Rice University and returned to China. At the very start, he hadn't decided to work at the Huamao headquarters. Like a free-flying bird, he was planning on dedicating himself to his favorite financial industry. However, Xu Wanmao wished that his son would be able to prepare to share the burden with him at this difficult moment. Perhaps Xu Lixun could be compared to a fledgling at this point, and the upcoming six years of trials and tribulations was really a tough test.

Xu Lixun said, "Making a decision was very hard at that time. I don't like running a business and I don't like this industry. I am introverted and not good at communication. People may think I am too proud. If I have to beg for somebody's help to get something done, I would rather not do it."

After returning to China, Xu Lixun was first in charge of the bankruptcy asset management of a Beijing company under Huamao Group. With the outbreak of the Huamao American crisis, Xu Wanmao had to appear in court in the US. The 26-year-old Xu Lixun became the authorized representative of his father.

"At that time, the government made the decision to hold a board meeting at Huamao. Having just returned to China, I had nothing to compare with Huamao's senior managers in terms of qualification and background. Everyone wanted power. Ultimately, because of the government support, I officially entered Huamao on April 30, 2000." Xu Lixun pointed at the conference room he was sitting in, which was also his private office now, and said, "It was in this room that we convened the meeting."

At that time, the Xu family had 12 members working in Huamao, and the equity they held accounted for 79.63% of the company's total. The company's senior staff members were concentrated in the sectors that Huamao developed in the early years, namely the culture and education sector. In this sector, Xu Wanmao's son-in-law Zhang Guomin served as the general manager, and several distant relatives held middle-level posts.

Mao Zenghui, the younger brother of Mao Suzhen, Xu Lixun's aunt in-law, was the purchasing agent in the teaching tools branch of the Culture and Education Company. When recalling the situation at that time, he said, "When the business was just started, we were very united. Yet, after the company gained certain financial strength, people began to have their own ideas. This was especially when Junior Xu came, they were feeling uncomfortable. After all, the old staff members had followed Senior Xu and strived for the company's development over the previous 20 or 30 years. They revered and supported him because he was a charismatic leader. Things were different with Junior Xu as president. It was not that they refused to follow his instructions, but they just had doubts about his management ability. After all, Huamao is a huge group corporation, you must show exceptional ability or achieve remarkable results before you can convince the staff."

Transferring the leadership from a father to his son seemed to be the most natural thing. However, because Xu Lixun had just returned from abroad, everyone was doubtful about his ability to lead Huamao.

Considering the overall interests of the company, many senior managers of Huamao had the mentality of "as long as you don't move my cheese". They were just waiting to see whether the young president was able to survive the crisis and prove himself a strong leader.

The First Six Years of Succession That Tempered Xu Lixun's Spirit

In 2000, Xu Wanmao was caught up in the lawsuit in the US, so he let his son gradually take over the company. Xu Lixun experienced the hardest time in his life. "The entire six years were a period of unbearable suffering. It felt like I was in hell," he said.

When Xu Lixun took over the business, he felt pressure from all ends. First, the industry suffered a downturn. At that time, Huamao's main educational product, the teaching tools, was discontinued after the Ministry of Education introduced a policy to relieve the burden on students. The company's sales were on a decline year after year. By the end of 2005, Huamao faced a deficit for the first time in its history of more than 30 years. Secondly, there was infighting between different cliques in the company. Xu Lixun knew the cause of the problem, "The reason for the internal discord was that I was not able to make them stick together. I did not have enough power in the company; I was not in control of many of its resources. The employees did not listen to me." Meanwhile, there were many tricky moments between Xu Wanmao and his son. Conflicts in Huamao Group were often reported to Xu Wanmao, who liked to serve as a judge. For a period of a year and a half, the senior managers and employees were unhappy with Junior Xu and complained to Senior Xu. For once, Xu Wanmao seriously considered taking back the power he had delegated to his son.

The Friction Between Father and Son

In Huamao Group, everyone called Xu Lixun "young president Xu" and his father "old president Xu."

Xu Wanmao said, "I use the method of slowly delegating power to the next generation. For example, I would slowly relegate power in finance and personnel to my son. The more mature my son becomes, the more power he will get from me. When he is a real mature leader, he will receive all of my power. Perhaps he regards me as a reliable mentor and will turn to me for help from time to time. If my son is really mature, I will let him do as he wishes."

The relationship between Xu Wanmao and Xu Lixun was once strained. In Xu Lixun's memory, once he and his father did not speak to each other for three months. "We have a habit — we don't discuss business at home. For personal reasons, I didn't have good communication with my father. On one or two occasions, I made a decision that he thought to be wrong, he would let the subordinates make adjustments to improve it."

However, as a father, Xu Wanmao was fully aware that if he wanted his son to act independently, he should give him the chance to confront the challenges all by himself. Xu Wanmao realized that his presence in the company was the main obstacle to Xu Lixun truly implementing his decisions. Therefore, he deliberately avoided going to his office, keeping a distance from Huamao Culture and Education Company and spending more time on his business in the US. After a while, Xu Wanmao noted that Xu Lixun started reading the company documents quietly every night.

In 2002, Xu Lixun officially took over the business as president of the group. Even though Xu Wanmao adopted the attitude of letting it go, his son's succession was not smooth.

"After taking charge of Huamao, I would argue with my father every six months. Sometimes when I talked to my father, I hoped he would say something positive about me, just one sentence would be good. But what he saw were all problems. I felt really frustrated."

For example, Xu Lixun always liked the financial industry and was sensitive about the financial market. In 2004, he was planning on investing in the stock market. Xu Wanmao, who started from an industrial enterprise, was averse to the virtual economy. To him, Xu Lixun's investment in the education industry was far from enough. This caused a major difference and conflict between father and son. Mao Zenghui said that Xu Wanmao and his son both had a strong personality; each of them had different ways of thinking, work practices, and concepts. In handling major issues in the company, father and son were both effective, only differing from each other in their styles and manners. Xu Wanmao hadn't received much education, so he tended to rely on his rich experience; Xu Lixun, who graduated from Rice University and Fudan University, was well-versed in advanced management.

Xu Lixun was aware of his father's position in Huamao. "My father was like 'God' in Huamao Group. After all, he started the company single-handedly. But during my six-year succession, my father stayed in the US most of the time. He did not want me to be dependent on him so that I could grow to maturity in practice as soon as possible. In order to develop my abilities and rejuvenate Huamao in those six years, my father made great effort in financial and human resources. The costs we paid for were enormous. However, you can't make an omelet without breaking eggs. It takes huge costs to train a qualified leader. At that time, the education industry had just entered a period of big market adjustment. If my father were in the company, our transformation would have been faster. But with me in the company, it was a bit slow."

Performance: The Only Criterion

Xu Lixun found that the traditional industries were declining. As the new leader of Huamao, it was imperative of him to establish his credibility through outstanding performance.

The method Xu Lixun adopted was straightforward. "I didn't do anything unusual. It was very simple — making money. I earned money and distributed it to them. Just like a soldier whose troops had won a battle, his outstanding military exploits depended on the number of enemies he had killed. This is also true for a businessman. Action speaks louder than words. You have to make money to convince them completely."

In 2004, Xu Lixun got involved in the capital market. Seizing the opportunity of the restructuring of Bank of Ningbo Co., Ltd., he invested 161 million yuan to increase his equities, holding 162 million shares and 2.5-billion-yuan credit lines. In 2005, he received an additional 17 million shares. In July 2007, Bank of Ningbo went public, which brought in lucrative profits for Huamao. In 2007, the investment division of Huamao created 80% profit for the company. "The listing of Bank of Ningbo brought Huamao more money than the amount it had made over the past 30 years," Xu Lixun stated proudly. Many of the senior managers who had followed old president Xu all along were doubtful and concerned about Xu Lixun's decision in the beginning because they did not know a thing about financial investment. Thereafter, Xu Lixun's successes in the investment field won their recognition. Xu Lixun also invested frequently in the capital market, becoming the shareholder of Ningbo Construction and the Ningbo branch of China United Network Communications.

Establishing the System to Attract Talents

With the huge profits to back him up, Xu Lixun began to adjust the company's human resources structure. Many of Huamao's founding members were farmers who had received little education. Their hard work laid a good foundation for Huamao. After Xu Lixun took over the business, he began to recruit new types of professionals.

"Nowadays, enterprise management cannot be carried out through being loyalty to my father only. We need a team that consists of people who have management expertise and possess all kinds of abilities to govern and manage the company."

Therefore, a group of highly educated management personnel joined Huamao. For example, Xu Lixun recruited two vice presidents for the group headquarters, Li Jiangchun and Fu Zhengji, to take charge of the group's finance and marketing. Li Jiangchun graduated from Fudan University with a master's degree, and Fu Zhengji graduated from King's College London with a doctor's degree.

Xu Lixun said, "I am like a helmsman and Huamao is like a big ship. To steer it in the right direction requires the support of many people. It is my responsibility to unite this team and maximize its effectiveness. I am the middleman between various departments. What I have done in recent years is to provide a platform and create a good environment for the managers and employees. When I make a promotion, I never look at their personal relationship and work experience. The only criterion for promotion is their abilities."

At the same time, according to the department setup of the group headquarters, Xu Lixun appointed Huang Yifeng, who graduated from the Department of National Economic Management of Zhejiang University, as the head of Investment Supervision Department. Qin Gao, who graduated from the Department of Software Engineering of Zhejiang University, was hired as the leader of Information Management Department. Xu Lixun not only recruited talents for the group headquarters, but also expressed concern about the group's subsidiaries. In 2003, he recruited Xin Guoli, a college graduate and professional manager, and made him the general manager of the Huamao Dongqianhu Hotel, which was acquired by the Group in 2002.

Besides reviewing and improving the enterprise system, Xu Lixun also implemented the delicacy management featuring "rules more important than the group's president" in the company, including liquidating the company's assets and clearing up equity ownership as well as addressing the problem that some assets had not been accounted for.

Xu Lixun said, "Huamao's development is too fast. In the course of the development of Chinese private enterprises, irregularities are inevitable. The rapid development of enterprises can conceal many problems, just like the neon lights at night covered the dark corners of the street. The 10-year sprint has caused serious internal injuries to Huamao. I need to cure these internal injuries one by one."

The Departure of Brothers-in-Law, Uncles and Senior Managers

The biggest challenge encountered in the process of his reform was the accustomed way of thinking and working methods of the senior managers. They had a genuine love for Huamao Group, which made Xu Lixun hesitant about implementing the reform measures. Furthermore, many of them were his relatives. Xu Lixun's second brother-in-law, Wang Leping, joined Huamao after graduating from high school. In 2002, he left Huamao headquarters to establish Zhejiang Huamao Real Estate Development Co., Ltd., leading Huamao's real estate sector. Zhang Guomin, Xu Lixun's first brother-in-law, followed Senior Xu to start the business in 1984, and later became the general manager of Huamao Culture and Education Company. In 2005, he set up Huaxin Education Development Co., Ltd. in Guangdong to create new projects and develop new markets. Later, uncle Weng Guomin also established Shanghai Mingzhou Education Products Co., Ltd.

In the view of some old employees, "Zhang Guomin looked at things from the perspective of the culture and education sector, while Xu Lixun took the entire group into consideration. Hence, they had disagreements regarding the enterprise development. Either one or the other had to give in. Eventually, Zhang Guomin made the concession, which helped consolidate Junior Xu's position as group president."

Xu Lixun's uncle was among those who left the company. Xu Wanmao had sold a company to him at a relatively low price. Xu Lixun's aunt stayed in the Culture and Education Company doing financial work. Mao Zenghui said, "Our old president Xu always tells me that if I go out to be my own boss, he will support me. This is the style of old president Xu. Instead of giving you money, he offers you a development platform, so Wang Leping and others are quite successful. Old president Xu is always far-sighted, so Xu Lixun will encounter less difficulty in company management. Family business should have some restrictions; otherwise it will lead to chaos in the family. A family that lives in harmony will prosper. Old president Xu and I are from the same village. We gather to drink and dine every year during the Mid-Autumn Festival. Everyone is happy. None of us would like to see our good relationships get ruined because of something happening in the company." Some of the old employees joined Huamao only after they retired. As they were advanced in age, they naturally left. Other old employees were transferred to new positions. For example, Chen Jilun, the former manager of the Financial Department in the group headquarters, was transferred to serve as the financial director of Dongqianhu Hotel. Mao Zenghui worked in Huamao for 19 years. There were many old employees like him who joined Huamao 20 or even 30 years ago. He said, "When the company developed to a certain stage, it was difficult for old employees — including me — to adapt to the company's new management methods. This was because the education we received and other personal conditions limited our further development. Young president Xu addressed the issue of old employees properly, taking into consideration the company's overall interests. For example, some old employees flaunted their seniority, thinking that they had made great contributions to the company, hence no one could do anything to them. Young president Xu knew how to deal with them; he fired two old employees."

After six years of trials and tribulations, Xu Lixun finally established his position as the second-generation leader of Huamao and began to take charge of the company in the true sense. "In the past, general managers of different sectors under the group adopted double-faced tactics against me. But since 2006, our company has become more cohesive and more powerful, which is the best outcome of the price we paid over the past six years."

At the same time, Xu Lixun made it very clear to the board of directors, "The members of the board of directors should not interfere with the general managers of the subsidiaries. Come to me if you have any problems."

Now, Xu Lixun's communication with his father is smooth. "We have a very good relationship and are frank with each other. My father will ask for my opinions before he makes major decisions. Nowadays, I need not report to him unless it is important. However, whenever we are going to take a major reform measure in the company, I will ask my father for his advice. My father will respect my decisions. If he insists on doing something, even if I don't want to do it, I will obey him. This is because I know that a company can only have one prevailing voice. After all, my father and I have the same objective."

With all these experiences behind him, Xu Lixun, once the little eagle, had finally become fully fledged, flying high in the vast sky. Later, at an economic work conference of Huamao Group, Xu Lixun bowed deeply to Xu Wanmao in front of all the attendees to express his gratitude to his father's cultivation and care. Xu Wanmao flashed a contented smile in return.

Huamao's Strategic Development

The Promotion of Huamao's "Three Three One" Strategy

In January 2006, Huamao Group reviewed its 35-year development. Xu Lixun proposed the "Three Three One" development strategy and the supporting documents — *The Outline of Three Projects Development Plan* and *System Guidelines* to the board of directors.

After 35 years of development, Huamao formed a "Three Unique Features" enterprise culture, launched and undertook the "Three Projects" strategic task, and set the goal of building Huamao into a hundred-year-old corporation.

- "Three" unique features: The unique business philosophy with the core of "driving operation benefits with social benefits"; the unique industrial structure with the core of "mutual promotion of education industry and education cause"; the unique management mechanism with the core of "rules more important than the group's president".
- "Three" projects: Construct China's strongest teaching equipment production base, build China's most distinctive private schools, and establish China's most influential international education forum.
- "One" goal: A hundred-year Huamao.

To accomplish this goal, *The Outline of Three Projects Development Plan* was formulated for the work in the coming five years. Approved at the first meeting of the board of directors on February 8, 2007, the outline was then promulgated and implemented.

Huamao Business School

In 2008, Huamao Group established Huamao Business School with Xu Lixun serving as principal of the school. The school provided training to the group's employees, following the model of Whampoa Military Academy. It aimed to discover and develop the talents who were loyal to Huamao and who were highly motivated and capable of promoting the development of the company. The business school transformed the disorganized "training to meet demands" model and integrated Huamao's internal training. It established a regular training platform, making studying a regular rather than a one-time event, which was beneficial to the accumulation, management, and spreading of Huamao internal knowledge and quickly shaping the trainees into the "Huamao people" needed by the company. Outstanding students from the training programs were promoted to different positions, and many trainees grew to become the mainstay of the departments in which they worked.

Huamao's Diversified Development

The diversified development of Huamao Group started since 2002, which included real estate, investment, trade, and other industries. Its real estate sector consisted of Zhejiang Huamao Real Estate Development Co., Ltd. and Ningbo Huamao Real Estate Development Co., Ltd. Founded in 2005,

Zhejiang Huamao International Trade Co., Ltd. focused on being a subordinate line and an enterprise providing supporting service in the field of education, including import and export of goods and domestic trade. Its key products included teaching instruments and equipment, mechanical and electrical products, chemical raw materials and products, metal materials, and building materials. In 2006, it acquired Ningbo Shuxiang Railway Equipment Manufacturing Co., Ltd. which produced rail fasteners. Its products were used on lines such as Shanghai-Kunming line, Beijing-Guangzhou line, Guizhou-Guangxi line and Xiangyang-Chongqing line.

In 2008, Huamao Group invested 20 million yuan to receive 10 million shares assigned by Ningbo Construction Group Co., Ltd., accounting for 3.326% of its total. In December 2010, Ningbo Construction Group was listed. In January 2008, Huamao Group set up Shanghai Aorun Investment Co., Ltd. along with previously-established Shanghai Huayuan Investment Co., Ltd. and Zhejiang Zhonghao Investment Co., Ltd., all three constituted Huamao's investment sector. By the end of 2010, the net revenue of these investment companies reached 311 million yuan. By then, Huamao Group had already formed an investment industry chain which focused on equity investment and secondary market securities.

As an international education forum with a theme of education and culture, construction of the project "Dongqianhu International Education Forum" began in 2010. Following the model of the Boao Forum, Dongqianhu Forum was comprised of a conference center, an education museum, and a five-star hotel. By integrating educational and cultural resources, it would promote the common development of various peripheral industries such as recreation and tourism, and become the venue for large-scale education and culture forums at home and overseas. Through creating a first-class international education forum, the "Dongqianhu International Education Forum" constituted one pillar of the "Three Projects" and supported the "Three Three One Strategy".

In 2010, Huamao Group cooperated with China Forestry Exchange and China Beijing Environment Exchange to establish East China Forestry Exchange Co., Ltd. and Ningbo Environmental Energy Exchange Co., Ltd., participated in the UN Climate Conference, and worked out an initial plan for exploratory development in low-carbon economy. In the next three to five years, Huamao Group will selectively seek energy-saving, emission reduction technologies, and industrialization projects with good market prospects, as well as talents, projects, and resource reserves.

In 2012, Huamao Group launched the popular science museum project. In February 2014, Huamao Science Museum located in Ningbo Huamao Foreign Languages School opened, consisting of the Prehistoric Biology Museum, the Science and Technology Progress Museum, the Earthquake and Firefighting Popularization Museum, and the Science Laboratory. The purpose was to create a standard popular science education base for students. Xu Lixun attached great importance to this new project and hoped to learn from the successful model of foreign countries. The Science Museum was in a field where Xu Lixun was seeking breakthroughs in industrial development. He believed that Huamao Group was stuck in a bottleneck and hoped to shift away from the previous model whereby the company only relied on tendering and bidding in the education field. However, due to the lack of qualified professionals and management team, the progress of this project had slowed down.

Mao Zenghui recalled, "We have taken a complicated and tortuous road. Owing to the concerted efforts over the past ten years and more, the company is prospering. Although I am older than young president Xu, I admire his personality and his way of doing things. Nowadays, many of the wealthy second generation splurge their money on luxurious cars and enjoy their time with friends all day. However, in this respect, he is very self-disciplined. Since he does not act this way, we are also too embarrassed to do so. As one of the wealthy second generation, he has dedicated himself to the family business; he is the one who gets off work the latest."

The "Common Agreement"

The Origin of the "Common Agreement"

Over the years, Xu Wanmao came to be known as a collector. Huamao Art Museum housed treasures collected by Xu Wanmao over more than 20 years. They were part of Huamao's assets and would never be sold. At first, these treasures were kept at home, and Mrs. Xu and the children did not appreciate them very much. When Xu Wanmao decided to put them in the museum, his children said, "They are our property, but dad wants to take them to somewhere else." Mrs. Xu also objected, "If you want to donate these things, I don't mind. But you'd better leave some of them for your children and the family." This caused Xu Wanmao to think about the issue of family wealth. He went to law firms, but the lawyers all said that they had never handled a case like this before. After two years of discussions, he hired Huang Dongli, a member of the WTO Law Committee, lawyer of international law, and professional lawyer of the Chinese Academy of Social Sciences, to draft the "Common Agreement of the Xu Family."

Xu Wanmao has two younger brothers, one younger sister, three daughters and one son. His son Xu Lixun is the principal successor of Huamao, and the two sons-in-law are in charge of Huamao Company in Guangdong and Huamao Real Estate Company respectively. In the common agreement, Xu Wanmao clearly and specifically defined the three core issues in family business, i.e., family intervention in business, split of assets, and the ability of the successor. In 2007, Xu Wanmao said at a group management reading session, "What I worry most is that my family members will rest on our laurels and become profligate playboys. If the proverb 'wealth never survives three generations' became a reality in our family, that would be the greatest failure, sin, and retribution in my life. As both a father and the eldest brother, I have the opportunity to spend my entire life on creating the business of Huamao. If my brothers, sisters, and children can sincerely support this undertaking and continue its sustained development, you are showing the highest level of filial piety to me. We should correctly handle the relationship between our family and Huamao so that no one harbors improper desires. Then we will not repeat past tragedies in which members of wealthy families fight each other brutally. As harmony reigns in our family, everything we do prospers."

As a family-owned enterprise, Huamao is based on the group president responsibility system with the board of shareholders as the highest authority and the board of directors as the leader and set up the Strategic Management Committee as the consultancy body for major business decision-making. The board of supervisors audit and supervise the operation and management of Huamao enterprises. The general managers from various functional departments at Huamao Group level and from companies in different industry sectors are directly led by the group president.

The "Common Agreement of the Xu Family" stipulates, "Xu Wanmao's ownership of all assets of Huamao Group will always belong to the Huamao Group Trust Fund which is to be established. In China, when a sound trust system is not in place, or when the existing trust system is not conducive to enterprise development, then the Huamao Group Trust Fund will not be established soon. In that case, Xu Lixun, the second-generation legitimate successor of the legal representative right and business management right of Huamao Group and the legitimate Xu family successor of each generation after him must guarantee and establish that Xu Wanmao's ownership of all assets of Huamao Group will permanently belong to the Huamao Group Trust Fund. Before the establishment of the trust fund, these shares can be temporarily registered to the eldest son Xu Lixun when necessary. After the Huamao Group Trust Fund is set up, they will be transferred to the fund."

According to the "Common Agreement of the Xu Family", children of the Xu family can inherit the right of management and the right to receive dividends, but they do not have property ownership. If the successor's competence is questioned, a professional manager will be hired instead. The dividends can be distributed, but the enterprise equity cannot be split, and the enterprise assets cannot be disposed. The "Common Agreement of the Xu Family" also has clear provisions on the requirements for descendants of Xu family to take over Huamao Group. Xu Wanmao defined this agreement as the third institutional reform in which the system of Xu family supplements and completes the enterprise system. The first reform took place in 1993 when the company was transformed into a cooperative enterprise. The second reform took place in 1995 when the company was reorganized into a group company limited, turning into a family-owned enterprise mainly controlled by Xu Wanmao.

"I am absolutely responsible for Huamao's long-lasting stability and prosperity. I will ensure my son's succession is smooth and keep working diligently till my last day in Huamao. The Xu family makes this drastic decision for the purpose of building Huamao into a hundred-year-old corporation."

Main Points of the "Common Agreement of the Xu Family"

On August 10, 2008, in accordance with the family property disposal principle of "separating the family without dividing the property", all Xu family members formally signed the "Common Agreement of the Xu Family".

The agreement mainly focuses on the three key issues of family businesses:

First, shareholders from the family may become members of the management or intervene in company management. Will their business activities put family interests first and lack impartiality?

Second, due to marriage and childbirth, will the family-owned shares dilute the enterprise assets?

Third, if the selection of successors is only limited to family members, will this hinder the recruitment and development of talented people?

The main points of the agreement include:

I. Huamao is a family-owned enterprise with a strong sense of social responsibility. The Xu family has unlimited responsibility for Huamao's development and prosperity, but their rights in Huamao are conditional and limited. Huamao's assets are owned by Huamao Group, and the Xu family, as representative of Huamao Group, takes care of these assets. Members of the Xu family "separate the family without dividing the property of Huamao".

II. Except the right to distribute Huamao's dividends, the Xu family has no other privileges. If a family member does not work in Huamao, he or she shall not interfere with the management of Huamao. Family members who work in Huamao must strictly abide by the rules of the Huamao Group, set a good example within their scope of responsibilities, and must not overstep their bounds or seek privileges.

III. Huamao's successor inherits only the asset management right and the enterprise management right, which means the successor serves as the company's legal person and president. The successor cannot inherit Huamao's assets personally. If the successor's qualification and ability to manage the enterprise is questioned, then they should hire a professional manager to preside over the enterprise and exercise the management right under the supervision of the board of directors and the legal representative.

IV. As a corresponding condition, Huamao employees have no right to interfere in and comment on the internal affairs of the Xu family. In particular, senior management personnel should strictly implement the rules of Huamao and follow the Xu family's collective will represented by the board of directors, rather than fulfil the non-organizational requirements from individual members of the Xu family. Otherwise, they will be punished for violating this principle.

V. All Huamao people shoulder the common responsibility to create a harmonious atmosphere, establish the enterprise integrity, counter unhealthy practices and evil influences, and build a Hundred Year Huamao; they should all make their own efforts and contributions to the new development of Huamao.

VI. Huamao's industry sectors and business sectors should support each other. It is Huamao's responsibility to promote the development of both sectors. Provided that Huamao's assets must go through bankruptcy liquidation due to irresistible causes, the remaining assets after the liquidation will be owned by Ningbo Huamao Foreign Languages School. Irresistible causes contain the following two situations:

(1) It is certain that Huamao Group does not have the successor who meets the requirements of this common agreement.

(2) Huamao Group declares bankruptcy due to force majeure, and there are still assets remaining after its bankruptcy liquidation.

The members of the Xu family who have signed the family agreement included: Xu Wanmao's children and their family members, Xu Wanmao's two younger brothers and their family members, Xu Wanmao's younger sister and her family members. The "Common Agreement of the Xu Family" is notarized, and every family got its copy. Another copy is archived in Ningbo Huamao Foreign Languages School.

Family members who work in Huamao are:

Zhang Guomin, Vice Chairman of the board of directors of Huamao Group, President of Guangdong Huaxin Company (Xu Wanmao's first son-in-law);

Wang Leping, member of Huamao Group's board of directors, President of Zhejiang Huamao Real Estate Development Co., Ltd. (Xu Wanmao's second son-in-law);

Weng Guomin, member of Huamao Group's board of supervisors, General Manager of Shanghai Mingzhou Education Products Co., Ltd. (Xu Wanmao's brother-in-law);

Mao Suzhen, Finance Director of Huamao Culture and Education Company (Xu Wanmao's second sister-in-law).

The Future Road of Xu Family's Third Generation

With Xu Wanmao's relentless efforts, the family reached a consensus. Xu Wanmao said, "Through the hard work of two generations, we have amassed considerable wealth. But wealth is a double-edged sword. Wealth management is also a complex activity requiring wisdom. Adopting a correct attitude and dealing with wealth properly is the key to one's life and the next generation's blessings. The Xu family can be likened to the sailors on the ship of Huamao Group, meaning that the Xu family and Huamao Group are interdependent. When the ship is safe, the sailors are safe; and when the sailors operate the ship correctly, the ship will head towards the right direction." Since Xu Wanmao started considering drafting a family agreement, he had been instilling these ideas in his children and his grandchildren's mind.

Xu Wanmao appointed his son Xu Lixun as the sailor of this ship. Xu Wanmao said to her daughters and sons-in-law, "When you work in Huamao, you are just an administrator of the company. Besides, you will not necessarily stay in Huamao. I have no objection even if you start a business by yourself. The better you do on your own, the more we can complement each other. My only requirement is that you must not harm Huamao's interests and you must conduct the business in an open and transparent way. If you work in Huamao, you can participate in the decision-making, but you don't have any privilege. As Huamao is positioned as a family business, the Xu family and the enterprise must build a synergy."

Initially, family members had differing views regarding this common agreement, and Xu Wanmao's wife opposed it strongly. She said, "I don't

want the trust fund to have my equity. I would like to manage it myself."
But in the end, because of her husband and son's persuasion, she acqui-
esced out of consideration of the overall interests of the group. The daughters also accepted the agreement, saying that "in our family, only one male
heir carries the surname Xu".

What Xu Wanmao is thinking about is: "What legacies will I leave to
the next generation? They should not only inherit the wealth. Giving them
the existing wealth will lead to various problems. Therefore, I have formulated the principle — 'separate the Xu family without dividing the property of Huamao'. This common agreement eliminates the possibilities of
their dependence on the existing wealth, making them more independent.
It also reduces conflicts in the family. This agreement will not actually
function until I pass away. If I am still alive or conscious, it does not have
real effect. It involves the next few generations because I don't want to be
a muddle-headed forefather of this family business."

As the only son of Xu Wanmao, Xu Lixun believes that his father "has
done the most correct and wisest thing". "To be honest, I really don't care
about the wealth. First, because of my personality, too much money is no
use for me. Excessive amounts of money will breed corruption and moral
degradation. Second, I only care about whether I am the decision maker
in the company and whether the company is advancing on the road I have
envisaged. I don't care about equity distribution of Huamao. Honestly
speaking, if I leave Huamao someday, I will be more at ease. So, I don't
feel sorry for myself."

In Xu Lixun's view, such a family agreement could only be formulated
by his father and at the right time. He said, "Only my father can do this,
because he is so prestigious that he is able to win every family member's
support for this agreement. I also realize that the breakdown of many family businesses is caused by infighting. My father has nipped the infighting
in the bud. My father's wisest decision is to draw up this agreement, which
fundamentally and institutionally guarantees 'separating the Xu family
without dividing the property of Huamao'. Huamao will always have only
one leader and one voice, regardless of who the leader is. Huamao will
remain unchanged, which is the most important point of this agreement."

The nurturing of the third generation has become one of Xu Wanmao's
top priorities. Encouraged by him, his grandson has been admitted to

Harvard University studying business administration. He is always inculcating his offspring with this philosophy, "The wealth is not yours. Too much money will only put pressure on you. If you are not competent to manage them, the wealth will be useless to you."

Xu Lixun's only son is now 13 years old. He has not considered whether to let his son take over the company in the future. "My son lives in a different era, so I will definitely adopt a different way to handle the succession issue. I haven't thought about it yet. But one thing is clear. I will not let him join Huamao immediately; instead I want him to toughen up by working outside Huamao group. Unless I am too weak, tired or old, I will not pass the family business to him. I can spend 15 to 20 years implementing a plan for his all-round development and only then will the succession take place."

In today's context, Xu Lixun has not put the third generation's succession on his agenda. Will the Common Agreement and the Family Trust help the Xu family maintain their wealth for three generations and more? Are they a driving force or a constraint for Huamao's future development? These are questions that only time will answer.

6

Family Managing Family Business

Since the reform and opening up more than three decades ago, China's economy has taken off rapidly. As one of the important pillars of China's economic development, private enterprises have made considerable contributions. They not only employ more than 60% of the labor force, but also create huge amounts of material wealth for the society. Family businesses are the better ones among the private sector. The rapid accumulation of social material wealth has also led to the increase of the personal wealth of entrepreneurs. The number and scale of people who create wealth in the Chinese society also witness a rapid growth. Family wealth owners who are facing the issues of inheritance and succession have entered the stage of wealth management and planning after wealth accumulation. They have started to realize that they must clarify the value of wealth in order to utilize it in an effective way and let it benefit the future generations. When an individual has amassed far more wealth for consumption and enjoyment than what he would have only needed, the way to distribute it becomes a more difficult problem than the way to create it.

Most of China's family businesses are still in an early stage of development. In the context of drastic economic and social transformations and the implementation of the one-child policy in China over the past three decades, how does China's first generation entrepreneurs choose and develop their future successors, and pass on wealth to future generations? The path of family business inheritance they follow shows distinctive Chinese characteristics. The succession process of both Fotile and Huamao focused on the key issue of the second generation creating their own business and inheriting their parents' business. The Mao family (Fotile Kitchenware) and the Xu family (Huamao) are natives of Zhejiang Province, where private economy is thriving. The two families face similar challenges in laws and regulations, institutional development, and cultural norms. Both families followed the normal practice of traditional Chinese families: The son inheriting the family business from the father. One other thing they have in common: Neither of their companies are listed. In today's society, only few people can restrain from chasing profits through the use of capital, and the two families are precisely the representatives of this minority. This is significantly different from many companies that aim to use the capital market to make a big difference. In the final analysis, as family businesses, the two owners are not willing to lose control of the company because of the introduction of capital. Excessive requirements for financial returns will only disrupt the strategic direction of the company. Moreover, the reason why family businesses can last longer than listed companies is because the former's institutions are more conducive to the inheritance of corporate culture than those of listed companies. Kongo Gumi, the oldest family business in Japan, has a history of more than 1,000 years.

However, in aspects such as helping the family business to nurture and develop a successor, passing on wealth to the next generation, and improving the governance of family and business, the two families have taken different paths. There is especially a large difference in the distribution of family wealth among the children, selection of the family business successor, and the accumulation and dispersion of family wealth — issues which we are about to examine.

The Distribution of Family Wealth

Fotile Group was jointly created and developed by the two generations of Mao family. Mao Lixiang, father and first-generation entrepreneur, devised a tailor-made succession plan for his son Mao Zhongqun and daughter Mao Xuefei, leading them onto the road of entrepreneurial career. All family members dedicated themselves to the expansion and inheritance of the family business. Amity and good communication between family members created a positive impact on the succession of their businesses. In 1992, Mao Lixiang arranged for his daughter Mao Xuefei to work in Feixiang Group, a company manufacturing gas igniters, and supported her to start her own business that provided supporting parts to Feixiang Group. In 1996, with the suggestion from the 27-year-old Mao Zhongqun, Mao Lixiang and his son founded Fotile, China's first high-end brand of range hood. In 2014, Mao Zhongqun took full control of the profitable Fotile that was growing in high speed and eventually became a major shareholder of the company. Mao Lixiang made a lot of suggestions on how to hand over the wealth to Mao Zhongqun's only son and Mao Xuefei's only son. In order to be able to "pass on family business from generation to generation", Mao Lixiang and Mao Zhongqun meticulously worked out plans to pave the way for their successors. The brand of Fotile, to which the Mao family's father and son devoted all their energy, was committed to becoming an international high-end brand that would last forever. This was the common decision and mission of their family.

Huamao Group's succession was not as smooth as that of Fotile. Xu Wanmao, also being a Zhejiang-based entrepreneur, turned a crisis into a "leadership training camp" tailor-made for Xu Lixun, his only son. In the purgatory-like six years, Xu Wanmao himself was also exploring how to let go of power so as to temper his son. Huamao's greatest contribution to the inheritance of Chinese family businesses was the drafting of the "Common Agreement of the Xu Family", which was an attempt to study and standardize practices that would help increase family cohesiveness, conduct smooth succession, and how they would affect the future development of the company. In this respect, the Xu family was leading other family businesses in China.

The "Common Agreement of the Xu Family" signed in 2008 established the principle of "separating the family without dividing the property". In 2014, Xu Wanmao taught the grandchildren about the mindset behind the agreement: "These properties are not yours. They will only put pressure on you. If you are not competent enough to manage them, they will be meaningless." Xu Lixun will soon send his 13-year-old only son to the United States to study, with the assumption that one day in the future, he will pass on his mantle to his son and choose a suitable way for his inheritance. Hence, the "Common Agreement of the Xu Family" provided important guiding principles.

The inheritance of family businesses usually refers to the transfer of ownership and management right of family businesses from the older generation to the younger generation. In a broad sense, it also includes the inheritance of other elements, such as family values and commitments (family motivation), entrepreneurship, social capital and knowledge (social and economic impact), as well as wealth of social affection (performance).

Mao Zhongqun never encountered much difficulty in this regard, because he was eager to "inherit the mantle of the family business from his father" and was willing to embark on a business venture. More importantly, he was very clear about what he wanted and had confidence in the future. However, it was because of this that Mao Lixiang faced a dilemma between where the company would develop and what he really felt. On the one hand, Mao Lixiang knew that the glory of the igniter business had already passed, and he needed to open up a new field. On the other hand, Mao Zhongqun proposed to develop a range hood, which was contrary to the will of the local government. All this put Mao Lixiang in an awkward predicament when he was starting his business venture for the second time. In addition, he had a deep attachment to Feixiang, his first company, such that it was very difficult for him to give it up. He was also concerned about finding appropriate positions for his daughter, relatives, and the company's senior employees. As Mao Zhongqun's concept of "developing high-end range hoods" was extremely challenging, Mao Lixiang was initially unsure whether he would be able to get the support of the local government and whether he could convince the employees to align themselves with Mao Zhongqun's goals. Moreover, as Chinese culture held that "the father is a revered figure in the family", Mao Lixiang hoped that Mao Zhongqun would acquiesce to his wishes in front of relatives, company veterans, and friends. However, Mao Zhongqun insisted that Mao Lixiang take his advice, which made things difficult for Mao Lixiang. In the past, Mao Lixiang had the final say, but now, when running the business with his son, he needed to change his mindset from "I" to "us".

Father and son finally reached an agreement, owing mostly to their sense of responsibility to the family and the role of the family business. Mao Lixiang, being an open-minded father, was very different from old-fashioned Chinese parents. He got off his high horse and gave his son the freedom and independence he asked for. He never thought that in doing so meant the loss of power, identity, and face; instead, father and son shared a lot of in-depth talks. Mao Lixiang's wife played the role of the family's chief emotional officer, being responsible for promoting communication between family members and maintaining the harmony and stability of the entire family.

"Pocket Theory"

Let us use the "three-dimension" model to analyze the shift of business from Mao Lixiang to Mao Zhongqun (see Figure 6.1). From the first day of 1996, Mao Lixiang placed Mao Zhongqun in "Zone 7" and placed his daughter Mao Xuefei in "Zone 4." This was intended to make room for Mao Zhongqun to take over the business so as to ensure a glitch-free handover and a harmonious family atmosphere. Mao Zhongqun and his father reached an agreement that minimized the number of relatives and old employees in the new company, who stayed in the 5th, 6th and 7th zones in Feixiang Group. In order to create a professional management

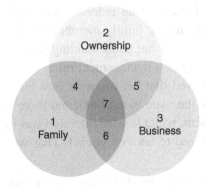

Figure 6.1 Three Dimension Model of Family Business

team, Mao Lixiang's wife moved from Zone 7 to Zone 4. When Mao Lixiang co-founded Fotile with Mao Zhongqun, he was in Zone 7. In 2002, Mao Lixiang withdrew from the management of Fotile and moved to Zone 4, making Mao Zhongqun the only family member in the top management in Zone 7. In 2010, Mao Lixiang transferred his shares to Mao Zhongqun and moved further away to Zone 1. Mao Zhongqun then became a major shareholder and took full control of the Group, minimizing the possibility of equity dilution in the future. Although Fotile has a profit-sharing mechanism, employees do not hold shares. Just as what Mao Lixiang has observed in the case example, empowering Mao Zhongqun also has another purpose of spurring and encouraging him to further the family business into a longer-term development.

Mao Lixiang uses the "pocket theory[1]" to distinguish and define the family's control power and governance rights. The first pocket is the clear separation of the family business and the external equity, with the family control power ensured at the same time; the second pocket is the clear separation of the family's internal shareholding so as to avoid family disputes; and the third pocket is the separation of the family's internal operations. It should be said that the focus of the "pocket theory" lies in the division of family wealth.

At the beginning of the establishment of the company, Mao Lixiang and his wife reached an agreement on this rule: Their brothers, sisters, and relatives could work in Fotile but they should not hold any positions above the director of workshops. When the fourth younger brother of Mao Lixiang was laid off, he asked his brother for permission to work in Fotile as a manager. Mao Lixiang, who placed extremely high importance on emotional attachment among family members, declined the request. He pleaded with his mother for her understanding because he did not want to compromise the enterprise's management rules.

Mao Lixiang believed that he, his wife, and his son belonged to the same pocket (that is, the main blood line), and there would be no conflict of interest among them, while his daughter and son-in-law (known as the collateral line) belonged to another pocket. That was why Mao Lixiang

---

[1] Mao, Lixiang. (2008). Evergreen Family Business: Build a Modern Family Management Model with Chinese Characteristics. Zhejiang People's Publishing House.

separated his son and daughter and allocated funds to help his daughter start her own business. Mao Lixiang explained that this was not due to the influence of traditional concepts, but instead the consideration of the property rights issues that family businesses could encounter in their development. Family members could hold shares of the family business, but it was more desirable for them to engage in separate and independent business operations. Mao Lixiang's intention was to remove the hurdles on the road of his children's business development so that both his son and daughter could capitalize on their strengths and manage their business independently. Mao Lixiang believed that even if it was a family-owned enterprise, the property rights should be clearly clarified. In Mao Lixiang's view, both the pocket of his son and that of his daughter were in fact the pockets of the Mao family.

Today, Mao Lixiang has transferred all his shares to Mao Zhongqun, his son. From his perspective, the successor must hold the majority of shares and the family shares should not be dispersed because of intergenerational inheritance. Otherwise, the family's controlling power will gradually be weakened. Ultimately, the family's influence on the company will be greatly reduced.

Yet, the "pocket theory" also has its defects. Family members who serve in the enterprise may not be motivated to maximize the interests of family members who do not hold positions in the enterprise. Therefore, it is necessary to adopt a sound governance structure to help the latter sit on the management committee (consisting of independent directors of non-family members), who can play a supervisory role and exert influence.

For many Chinese families, harmonious coexistence is an important goal. Just as mentioned above, Mao Lixiang and his son Mao Zhongqun had many frank and sincere talks in the course of succession. His wife acted as an observer and reconciled the emotional conflicts between father and son. In addition, Mao Lixiang organized family meetings and gatherings frequently to strengthen communication between family members. The entire family recognized the importance of cohesiveness (family motivation) and applied the same approach to the family businesses (family business roles). Finally, Mao Lixiang chose to retire from the group to devote himself to social undertakings, and founded the Ningbo Evergreen Family Business Successors School.

From the perspective of the second generation, Mao Zhongqun performed excellently in succeeding his father's business, transforming his father's declining industry into a rising industry with greater potential for growth. Pursuing one's own dreams was very important; more importantly, he created a very favorable environment for himself, and excluded those who may be recalcitrant such as relatives and older employees from working in the new company. Mao Lixiang and his son were very satisfied with the new company, and Fotile products sold very well on the market, proving their method's effectiveness.

When it comes to succession of business, Mao Lixiang prioritizes the guideline based on harmony. Besides this, Mao Zhongqun should also consider the external environment (social and economic impacts), the company's current status (strategy and performance), interpersonal issues (family business roles and family motivation), and his son's dreams and capabilities. In addition to nurturing and training his son and sharing his dreams with him, Mao Zhongqun should also consider cultivating more non-family members as reserve forces for senior executive positions.

"Separating the Family Without Dividing the Property" Theory

Let's take a look at how Xu Lixun inherited the family business. Being entrusted with taking over the family business — particularly at a critical moment — is a rather common succession mode in China, largely because most of China's "first generation entrepreneurs" rarely plan and think about the inheritance of family businesses at an early stage. Most of them are still struggling with the transformation and expansion of the business, resulting in the second generation having to take over the business completely unprepared in many cases. This poses real challenges not only for the overall development of the business but also for the relations between the parent and successor and those between the successor and the older employees. For Xu Lixun, at the beginning of his succession, in addition to worrying about the disagreements between his father and him in terms of business operation, his relations with his brothers-in-law and other company veterans were also extremely complicated. These people had witnessed the growth of Xu Lixun, and totally differed from him in their experience and perspectives. Therefore, it was not easy to establish his own prestige and become a good leader of the enterprise. In addition, he realized that it was necessary to create a professional management team and introduce his modern Western management concept to this old-fashioned enterprise. Difficulties and setbacks were inevitable in this process. Therefore, he took many measures and successfully turned the table. He purposefully relinquished the leadership of the core education business to avoid direct conflicts with his brothers-in-law and company veterans; he studied business management and made every effort to build his own management team; he also told his father that interference from relatives and company veterans had made it very challenging for him to lead the company's development, and he needed absolute control of the company. Finally, he proved his ability and worth with excellent investment results.

In a speech delivered in 2014, he explained that the real reason he was promoted to the company's president in 2002 was that his son was born that year. In Chinese culture, the older generation believes that their children have truly grown up when they finally become a parent, and this event seemed to have affected his brothers-in-law and the veterans' views of him.

In a television interview in 2014, Xu Lixun also noted that in the first few years of taking over Huamao, he did not get along well with his father. This was until he became a father himself later that relations between the two gradually improved. Therefore, he suggested that the younger generation should learn to respect their parents and try to engage in good communication with them.

Again, let us use the "three dimension" model to analyze the transformation of Huamao. Xu Wanmao's planning for wealth can be summarized as "separating the family without dividing the property". Before the crisis, Xu Wanmao was a major shareholder of Huamao Group and was located in Zone 7. After Xu Lixun took over the business, Xu Wanmao gradually moved to Zone 4. Xu Lixun pointed out in his speech that Xu Wanmao had not transferred the company's shares to him at that time. Although Xu Wanmao was in Zone 6 at the time, he hoped he could move to Zone 7. If Xu Wanmao's work in schools is not counted, he will move to Zone 1 when he officially transfers his shares to Xu Lixun. As far as we know, members of the Xu family rarely hold shares of Huamao.

Xu Lixun points out that he is planning to separate the operation of his two brothers-in-law's companies from that of the group. Once the trust fund is established, Xu Lixun will receive dividends, which will be distributed among other family members. Family members are not allowed to divide and sell their property for personal gains.

One of the advantages of "separating the family without dividing the property" is that it can maintain both harmony and stability of the family. Another advantage is that it can ensure that the ownership of the enterprise is in the hands of the family, and can be passed down from generation to generation without deviating as a result of any individual's actions. Family ownership will also not weaken due to conflicts and struggles between people of the same generation or of different generations, or because of the increase of family members, divorce, or improper wealth management.

The drawback of "separating the family without dividing the property" is reflected in lacking incentives to family members and employees. With the exception of the legal heir who inherited management rights (Zone 7), other family members may lack a strong sense of identity and responsibility for the company. This is particularly so for non-family professional managers who will probably replace the legal heirs but who will not get any company shares (Zone 3). Today, Xu Lixun shoulders the burden of Huamao, which, in his words, is out of the love for his parents and a sense of responsibility to the family (this is the result of family motivation). However, the third generation may not be interested in running the family business. Therefore, Xu Lixun does not only need to develop his son's management ability, but he also needs to raise his interest in managing Huamao. In addition, if a professional manager hired from outside serves as the president, the Xu family needs to come up with a method other than granting him company shares to make him feel that he is a member of the family, thus sharing the family's dreams and heritage.

There are two fundamental principles in Huamao's family business philosophy: First, Huamao Group will never go public — the consensus reached in Xu Wanmao's time; the second is the "Common Agreement of the Xu Family" signed by all members of the Xu family. Xu Wanmao had insisted on drafting a unique agreement and made every attempt to persuade other family members to accept the agreement, even though it was not a common practice in China at the time. Xu Lixun also actively promoted the drafting and signing of this family agreement. In his eyes, Xu Wanmao was undeniably the visionary leader of the Xu family business. He believed that while Xu Wanmao remained as Huamao's president, he had adequate time to clarify the tasks and responsibility of each family member so as to ensure the leader of the family business would never steer off course. Xu Lixun was active in urging his father to draft the "Common Agreement of the Xu Family" simply because he had three elder sisters. All of them loathed the prospect of potential infighting between family members because of the division of family assets. They also did not want to see Huamao fail in the hands of the third generation due to the splitting of ownership right.

In 2008, members of the Xu family signed the "Common Agreement of the Xu Family". The agreement makes it clear that a trust fund will be formed to manage family members' stock in Huamao[2]. According to the agreement, Xu Wanmao holds nearly 80% of the total shares, and Xu Lixun and his three elder sisters, as well as other family members, each holds 10% or less of Huamao's shares. The agreement establishes the principle of "separating the family without dividing the property", guaranteeing that nearly 80% of the shares of the Xu family will never be split by the descendants. The family members have the right to receive dividends, which are paid to each family every year. On one hand, this mechanism guarantees that several generations of family members are financially secure. On the other hand, it fundamentally solves the disputes over the inheritance of family property, and removes all concerns of the family losing control of their business due to excessive dispersion of shares after inheritance over several generations. In addition, the agreement also establishes the inheritance system by the eldest son and eldest grandson, and has provisions on the distribution of remaining property once the company declares bankruptcy because of risks.

The "Common Agreement of the Xu Family" is clearly written and all-encompassing. It has specific provisions on the family and business's vision and the relationship between the two, the decision-making power

---

[2] Wang, Feng. (2015). Xu Lixun, the CEO of Huamao Group: From Passive Succession to Active Transformation. *Harvard Business Review* (Chinese version), 10.

of family members, the contribution and expectations of family members, the ownership right of assets, and the selection of successors. We may need some time to see the implementation and effectiveness of the "Common Agreement of the Xu Family". After the intergenerational inheritance is completed, we will find out whether most family members (if not all of them) agree to and strictly abide by this agreement. Does this agreement enhance the family's cohesiveness? Does this agreement enhance the trust between family members and in the enterprise? Can this agreement ensure the sustainable development of the company?

In fact, the process of drafting the agreement is also very important. Consultation and negotiation before signing the agreement is a good opportunity for communication between family members. They can discuss the family values, the core business of the company, and the relationship between the family and the company. Signing the agreement is actually a gesture to explicate or strengthen family solidarity. This family agreement has achieved full coverage of the "family, business management, and ownership", and broken new grounds in the inheritance of Chinese family businesses. The principle of "separating the family without dividing the property" is a promise after balancing the two aspects of enterprise development and family inheritance. The Xu family hopes that, through this agreement, the dream of building an enterprise that lasts for centuries can be achieved.

Of course, this family agreement needs to be constantly improved. Although the agreement is unprecedented in China, there is still a contradiction between the legal and moral binding force of the agreement. All family members who have reached the age of 18 signed the "Common Agreement of the Xu Family", but this agreement does not bind on Xu Lixun's son, who is not of age then. Therefore, the Xu family needs to deal with circumstances not discussed in the agreement or make plans for unexpected things.

In China, the selection of successors of family businesses is usually in this order: son, daughter or son-in-law, professional manager from outside the family. Xu Wanmao and Xu Lixun can pass on the family values to Xu Lixun's son and develop his interest in the education industry. However, whether his son will eventually inherit the enterprise will ultimately depend on his own ambition and ability. Xu Lixun once said that he has noticed his son's potential and is proud of his progress. He also said he could accept it if his son refuses to serve as the president of Huamao. However, Xu Wanmao hopes that the legal heir can defend the family property and pass it on from generation to generation. Xu Lixun also stated that he hopes that his son will at least be the chairman of the group after he retires.

Family members and professional managers from outside the family may have different attitudes toward family businesses. For example, they may differ in their desire for preserving and promoting the social and emotional wealth of the family. Xu Lixun will probably consider the possibility of hiring an external professional manager, but he must simultaneously be careful in handling various issues including motivation and retention of professional managers. Due to the failure to provide shares as an incentive, Xu Lixun has to consider other ways to motivate and retain external executives, so that they can have more opportunities to contribute to Huamao's development.

While the succession between Mao Lixiang and his son Mao Zhongqun proceeded smoothly, Huamao Group's succession was more complex and they faced more challenges. While Xu Lixun faced conflicts from people of the same generation and those of different generations, Mao Zhongqun was spared from dealing with conflicts within the family. While Mao Lixiang and Mao Zhongqun were master and apprentice, Xu Wanmao completely delegated the power to Xu Lixun. Obviously, both fathers were willing to give their sons a free hand by not clinging to power; they were very different from the domineering parents who made their successors' lives miserable. In addition, Mao Lixiang and Xu Wanmao, like many Chinese people, put the harmony of the family above everything else.

Family Wealth: Two Different Approaches

Due to the big difference in the situation of their family and business, Mao Lixiang and Xu Wanmao adopted different approaches in managing and distributing family assets based on factors such as family values, the number and structure of family members, as well as the respective contributions of family members to the business development. Although the methods adopted by the two families for inheriting wealth are different, their purpose is the same: To achieve harmony and stability of the family and the safe inheritance of family wealth. Both families regard family harmony as a top priority.

Company values explain the elements that the organization holds dear. They can play the role as a compass, defining the organization's position and the route it should take. They also have the function of a sieve, retaining ideas and actions that may cause the deviation of the organization or undermine the organization at bay. As a part of the organizational culture, company values are created and reshaped by owners, founders, top management, and employees based on changes in the business environment. The same is true of the organization's vision, mission, goals, and strategy, which arise along with the development of the company.

Over the past three-plus decades, China's economy and society have undergone tremendous transformation, which results in different experiences and values among the people of different generations. Due to the "cultural revolution", the first generation of Chinese family business leaders generally receive little education. Although the Chinese economy has gradually transformed from a planned economy to a market economy, the management concepts and practices of Chinese entrepreneurs are still less standardized and advanced than their Western counterparts. In addition, the first generation of entrepreneurs are concerned most about bringing bread and butter to the family. Therefore, almost all of them start their business in order to improve the quality of life of their families rather than out of their own interest. They advocate collectivism in their interaction with the government, employees, and society at large. In addition, very few of the first generation of entrepreneurs have the experience of working and living aboard, but many of them choose to send their children abroad to embrace a broader and deeper international experience. Therefore, the second generation of successors are inclined to individualism (focusing on their own interest), and often come up with new ideas in business models, management concepts, and practical measures. For example, Mao Zhongqun favors high-end market, product research and development, and brand building while Xu Lixun enjoys financial investment and low-carbon economy.

Fotile's Mao Zhongqun did not have the experience of studying or working abroad, while Xu Lixun of Huamao, although having studied in the United States for four years, did not stay there to work. Hence, in these two families, the influence of overseas experience on the second generation's thinking, vision, and values is minimal. This is contrasting from those families whose children have studied abroad and stayed and worked for more than five years. These children, with long-term study-abroad experience, often encounter serious culture shock upon returning to China. They will find it difficult to re-adapt to the Chinese society, and the communication with their parents in work also becomes a problem.

Both first generation leaders of Fotile and Huamao have passed on entrepreneurship to their children. Mao Lixiang and his son uphold the principle of humility and kindness, enjoy sharing knowledge with others, and engage in social welfare activities. They are steadfast and persevering. Xu Wanmao and his son are hard-workers who are eager to win. As Xu Wanmao's life experience is full of twists and turns, he hopes that his son will remain calm and dignified in the face of adversity. In the first six years of Xu Lixun's takeover of Huamao, Xu Wanmao adopted a laissez-faire attitude, giving his son complete freedom to explore. The education business and Ningbo Huamao Foreign Languages School are particularly important to Xu Wanmao, who wants to continue this cause for a long time. Xu Lixun showed little interest in education at the beginning, but after Xu Wanmao's persuasion, he finally realized that education is not only the core industry of the family, but also the manifestation of family ethos. Xu Lixun later said that the core industry of the first generation matters a lot, so he urged everyone to protect it rather than resist it.

In the early years, Mao Lixiang worked hard to survive in the market, and later transformed into a social entrepreneur, establishing the Ningbo Evergreen Family Business Successors School. Mao Zhongqun advocates a management approach based on Confucianism and Taoism, and is committed to the mission of "pursuing the physical and intellectual happiness for all employees," which showcases the function of a social entrepreneur. Some people assert that Fotile is a social enterprise. Indeed, as Mao Zhongqun said in a case we discussed earlier: "Fotile is a mission-driven enterprise rather than simply a profit-oriented business." However, in

China's fiercely competitive home appliance market, an industry observer criticizes Fotile of "lacking the pioneering spirit".

Xu Wanmao and his son do not think that money is the most important asset. Xu Wanmao said that he is so passionate about education because he has an unrealized dream: To receive formal education. Moreover, Xu Wanmao's father told him to continuously dedicate himself to the education industry just before his death. Therefore, although the group's education division makes limited contribution to its total profits, Xu Wanmao still considers the education industry to be a pillar of Huamao. He is convinced that social wellbeing will promote economic efficiency without emphasizing performance assessment criteria of conventional capitalism. He also believes that enterprises are the wealth of society, and the wealth of the family should eventually return to society. Through the establishment of the Ningbo Huamao Foreign Languages School, Xu Wanmao wished to ensure that "education and its spirit will last forever". Obviously, Xu Wanmao has become a paragon of social entrepreneurs.

As Xu Lixun matures, he gradually understands the importance of education to his father. He is also involved in public welfare projects of the low-carbon economy. In 2013, he launched the "Rainbow Action" with the aim of narrowing the gap between the rich and the poor. This is a 7-day summer camp organized by the Huamao Education Foundation. Eighty children from wealthy families in Ningbo pair up with children of migrant workers and gather at the Ningbo Huamao Foreign Languages School for a summer vacation together. The children of migrant workers stay with their grandparents in their hometowns during the school semesters and come to visit their parents who work in the city during the summer vacation. Xu Lixun plans to launch this initiative in other cities in Zhejiang and even the rest of China. Xu Lixun, following in his father's footsteps, has also become a social entrepreneur himself.

The owners of family wealth are often leaders of the first generation, and they are now facing the challenge of how family wealth can be safely passed on to their children and how family businesses can be built to last. By looking at the approaches chosen by the Mao family at Fotile and the Xu family at Huamao, we find that, regardless of the family wealth and whether it is "concentrated" or "scattered out", the key is to ensure control by the family successor, even if the two families have different ways to divide and share their wealth. Vision is vital in order to make long-term plans for the inheritance of wealth. They should make it clear what is going to be passed on to whom, and when and how the succession is taking place. The ultimate goal is to guarantee the security of family wealth, long-term success of family business, and happiness of family members. The fundamental issue is to whom they are going to pass on the family wealth, because this bears on the perpetual security of wealth and long-lasting amity in the family.

In managing family property, which approach do you prefer, Mao Lixiang's or Xu Wanmao's? The choice depends on factors such as family values. Mao Lixiang and Xu Wanmao's families and businesses face completely different situations. Mao Lixiang has only two children, while Xu Wanmao has four. It is reasonable for Mao Lixiang to give the majority shares and full control power of the company to his son, because Mao Zhongqun founded Fotile together with his father. Mao Lixiang also took care of his daughter Mao Xuefei by rewarding her for her contribution to Feixiang Group. In contrast, Huamao was founded by Xu Wanmao and his two sons-in-law. If the family members did not sign "Common Agreement of the Xu Family", there would inevitably be grave struggles within the family. Moreover, the business of education service and the Ningbo Huamao Foreign Languages School are particularly important to Xu Wanmao, who wants to keep this business for a long time. The approaches of the two families are both adopted to achieve harmony and stability of the family.

Of course, there is no perfect family agreement in this world. The shortcomings of the "Common Agreement of the Xu Family", apart from the fact that the trust fund was not established at the time, also included the contradiction between the legal and moral binding force of the agreement, such as the possible conflicts between rules and family values. All family members who reached the age of 18 — including Xu Lixun's wife but not his son (the future legal heir who was then a minor), signed the agreement. Therefore, this agreement is not binding on Xu Lixun's son right now. What the future holds for this family business will hence depend on the Xu family's determination and ability to deal with issues not covered by this agreement. Therefore, the Xu family should ask Xu Lixun's son and other members of the younger generation to accept and sign the agreement after they reach the age of 18. Prior to that, the Xu family should share the family values and the principles of the family agreement with the younger generation. In Chinese society today, most young people deem the property of their parents as their own. In addition, Xu Lixun or his legal heir should be supervised by other family members to ensure the establishment of the trust fund, and after the formulation and implementation of relevant laws in China, the assets of Huamao — temporarily registered under the name of Xu Lixun — shall be transferred to the trust fund.

The wealth of family businesses is often closely related to the distribution of the company's shareholdings. The model of wealth inheritance, to some extent, is the choice of how to distribute the shareholdings of family business. Following are the three most common methods to decide whether to decentralize powers or to divide assets:

1. Decentralizing power through shareholder contract (see Figure 6.2)
   • Individual members are not allowed to sell shares independently.
   • Vote unanimously at the shareholder meeting.
   • Others.
2. Family-controlled companies (see Figure 6.3)
   Family-controlled companies need to create a clearly-defined "charter":
   • Individual members are not allowed to sell shares by themselves.

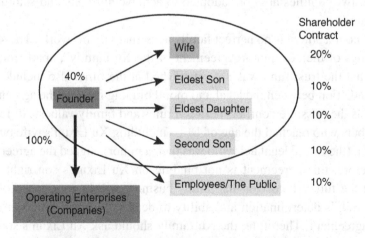

Figure 6.2 Decentralizing Power Through Shareholder Contract

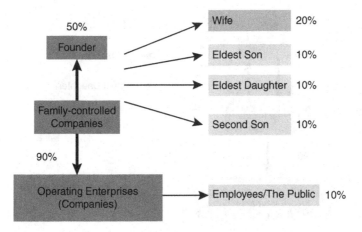

Figure 6.3 Family-controlled Companies

- All differences shall be resolved within the family-controlled companies, which is subject to the majority rule of voting rights, and then shall be decided by unanimous voting at the shareholder meeting of the operating companies.
- Others.
3. Family trust fund (see Figure 6.4)

From wealth creation to wealth accumulation, China's wealthiest families have shifted their attention to wealth management — the key of which is the security and inheritance of wealth. Legal tools that can be used for this purpose are receiving heightened attention, and this includes testament, family trusts, family foundations, and life insurance.

- The founder completely transfers the equity to the trust fund and no longer owns any company shares nominally. Family members receive only dividends, not equity.
- Family representatives will form a trust group, following the principle of one person one vote versus the actual equity of the holding company.

The family trust is a comprehensive structure arranging for wealth inheritance based on the *Trust Law*; it is a special property rights structure and needs supporting laws and regulations that are compatible with its functions. China's current trust property registration system and taxation

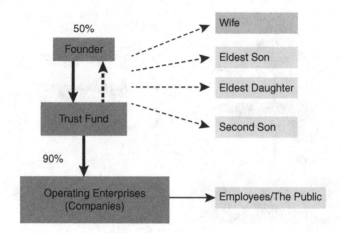

Figure. 6.4   Family Trust Fund

system will lead to the taxation of non-transactional transfers, thus limiting the scope of the subject matter assets under the trust. Family trusts are not omnipotent. Regardless of the countries practicing civil law system or those abiding by the Anglo-American law system, the establishment of family trusts should not be used for the purpose of tax avoidance and debt avoidance but they are only a possible outcome. This possible outcome is based on a highly professional trust design and management for the purpose of goodwill inheritance. The design and management of family trusts must be reasonable and legal, and at the same time require that the family trust stakeholders (including principals, trustees, beneficiaries, protectors, etc.,) reach a full understanding and consensus on their respective responsibilities, obligations, rights, and benefits.

"Succession of an enterprise" includes the following two: One is to receive equity and become a shareholder and the other is to take over the power of the enterprise and become a decision maker and manager. The key however lies in choosing the right successor, because although wealth itself can be passed on easily, the capability to manifest wealth and keep it cannot be physically passed down. At the same time, how to take account of family ties, balancing capability and ethics to benefit all parties, and maintain stability and harmony of the family needs to be considered in a comprehensive and prudent manner. How does one effectively nurture the "wealthy second generation" so that future generations can better take over the power of enterprises and become excellent corporate decision-makers and managers? How do they ensure the wealth in their hands is steadily transferred to the next generation? How to provide longevity to the enterprises with a more suitable family wealth blueprint? All these questions asked by China's "first-generation entrepreneurs" are waiting for their answers.

In addition to the inheritance of equity and management rights, the inheritance of family and family business values is also very important in the succession of enterprises. Organizations need values, and so do families. The level of commonly shared values within an organization and a family differs from company to company. In addition to functioning as a guide and sieve, shared values are a source of competitive edge for family businesses. Upholding consistent family values is essential because it is part of the common family motivation that determines the rise and fall of the intersection between family and business. Confucius once said, "While water can bear a boat, it also can overturn it." Compared with other countries' century-old family-owned enterprises, the development of Chinese family-owned enterprises is less than 40 years, and not many successions have taken place. Members of family businesses should take this theme seriously and lay the foundation for future development.

7

From "De-familization" to "Building a Family-based Culture"

Family-run management has played a major role in the course of the development of private enterprises from their commencement to the present day. Without the devotion of the families, there will not be Chinese private enterprises today. However, with the expansion of the enterprise, deviation in the value orientation of the two systems (the family and the enterprise) has caused dilemma to both the development and management of private enterprises. For Chinese family businesses standing at the crossroads of intergenerational succession as well as the transformation of enterprises, is "de-familization" really an inevitable choice for the family business inheritance that will help the businesses extricate themselves from the current predicament? The influence of a long-standing family culture in Chinese civilization on the family business inheritance should not simply be rejected. Chinese family culture should still be preserved and carried forward, although we admit that "de-familization" must be considered seriously after the family business has grown considerably. How to strike a balance between the two requires serious consideration by family leaders. Nowadays, the transference of leadership from father to son entails many possible choices and practical restrictions. It is not easy to pass the family business to either a son or a professional manager.

How to solve the problem of supervision over professional managers and give them the trust they need? Trustworthiness of professional managers is a key step in the standardization of management after "de-familization". Between trust and ability, which takes precedence? This is not an easy question to answer.

Most of the two generations in China undergoing business succession now have a relatively simple family structure, although I have also come across some big families. They grew and prospered in the good era of reform and opening up and the families stayed together through thick and thin. The second generation who were brought up in such families will have a strong sense of honor and commitment to their family and business. Here I would like to relate the story of an interesting family — Neoglory Group's Yu and Zhou family, who has more than 30 family members living under the same roof. Let's take a look at how the "de-familization" management is proceeding in an environment of strong "family culture". After several ups and downs of professional managers, how do the second generation in the family shoulder the heavy responsibility of establishing a team and accelerating the development of the family group?

In the past four decades, Zhou Xiaoguang and her husband Yu Yunxin have turned from street peddlers to the founders of Neoglory (China) Holdings Group. By 2015, the total assets of Neoglory Group exceeded 30 billion yuan. In 2008, their 23-year-old eldest son, Yu Jiangbo, returned to China after studying seven years in London. Zhou Xiaoguang was worried about the main business of jewelry as it underwent transformation and upgrading and not satisfied with the professional manager team. The "Chinese Jewelry Queen" wanted her son to resign from the bank and join Neoglory Jewelry Co., Ltd. In order to share the burden of parents, Yu Jiangbo finally decided to return to the family business. He started as the assistant to the vice president of marketing and was appointed the general manager of Neoglory Jewelry in 2011. He then began a series of drastic reforms, such as outsourcing non-core production processes and establishing high-end multi-brand strategies. The reform measures achieved good results. He not only expanded the company's existing business, but also made breakthroughs in the new e-commerce business and opened up three vertical integration businesses: Taoqu Network establishes online stores, Warehouse Technology engages in logistics, warehousing and diversified services, while Taoci Network Technology is positioned as an e-commerce software provider.

Yu Jiangbo also shouldered the heavy burden of uniting more than 30 family members. Together with his parents, he established the family committee and worked out a family "charter". Time is a crucial essence. His younger brother Yu Jiangming and other siblings are studying abroad. The family will face new choices before long and it needs to work out the details of the family committee as soon as possible. Zhou Xiaoguang announced at the staff meeting in February 2014 that Neoglory would quadruple the sales in ten years to become a 100 billion-yuan-worth company, and Neoglory would embrace the future amidst intergenerational succession.

The Origin of Neoglory

Xinguang, the Chinese name of Neoglory, is obviously formed by taking "Xin" from Yu Yunxin and "Guang" from Zhou Xiaoguang. Neoglory is the result of the joint effort of this couple, epitomizing their happy married life as well as harmonious big family. Neoglory is a leading private enterprise group that integrates investment, real estate, and trade with its main business in fashion accessories. It has more than 20 wholly-owned and controlled subsidiaries and more than 4,000 employees. Among them, Neoglory Jewelry has been a top producer of fashion in the domestic market for many years. Its products boast original design and various styles, with production and sales volume ranking first in the industry. It now has a base with a building area of 168,000 square meters for the production of fashion jewelry, and a sales network spreading across the globe. The real estate division with Wansha as the mainstay has become a leading enterprise in the industry locally. With a development area of more than 8 million square meters already completed, the real estate division is developing another 7 million square meters of land for construction. In addition, Neoglory, in cooperation with other leading companies in their respective industries, has systematically built commercial, industrial, and capital platforms through the integration of regional and industrial advantages, and carried out several major projects that have immense influence on the industry, such as the acquisition of Shanghai Miramar, reorganization of

Xinjiang Xintian Group, purchasing shares from Dalian's Aeon Life and so on.

1978: Leaving the Mountainous Hometown to Make a Living Across the Country

In 1962, Zhou Xiaoguang, whose parents were both farmers, was born in a remote mountain village in Zhuji, Zhejiang Province. At that time, farming could hardly yield any profits, and the family's livelihood relied on a pig it raised throughout a year. Although her parents worked very hard, they found it extremely challenging to make ends meet. Her childhood was filled with starvation. As the eldest child of seven children, she knew that she needed to help her parents share the burden of the family. Even on rainy days, she seldom stayed at home. Instead, she was thinking of getting some grass to feed the pig or finding some firewood after school. Although she was only a little child, she knew how to take care of her brother and sisters. She was always thinking of what she could do to help the family.

In 1978, China launched reform and opening up. Out of a woman's natural sense of responsibility, the 16-year-old Zhou Xiaoguang shouldered the burden of supporting the family by embarking on a trip to Northeast China to sell embroidery. She was the only person in the village of more than 3,000 people to venture out into the world. At that time, the standard of living in the northeastern region was higher than other areas of China. The train trip took her three days and four nights. When talking about the decision she made many years ago, she showed no resentment. "There were so many younger siblings in the family that the basic material needs of the family could not be met. At that time, even if there were a mountain of swords or a sea of flames in front of you, you had to forge ahead rather than turn back. There was no other choice. If you were brave enough to face the challenge, it was possible to bring a drastic change to the family's life."

Zhou Xiaoguang said with a smile that when she arrived at Dongyang Railway Station after walking for more than four hours and when she got on the train for the first time in her life, she was so overwhelmed by excitement that she did not feel much the sense of bewilderment that she was earning a living away from home for the first time. Many years later, air travel has become a routine for Zhou Xiaoguang, but you can still feel her excitement when she talks about her first experience on a train.

At that time, all she had on her was less than 100 yuan she had borrowed from her mother. In order not to waste time, she peddled her ware during the day and journeyed by train at night. Holding a *Map of China* and carrying goods that were as heavy as her own weight, Zhou Xiaoguang traveled the better part of China within a few years. She journeyed northward in spring and southward in autumn. Although it was hard work, selling goods for a few hours would earn her the money equivalent to one month's salary in the factory. Zhou Xiaoguang knew she must stick it out. The wealth she amassed over the years of selling her goods all over the country laid the foundation for future business development. She said, "I learned a lot and accumulated much experience in those years. I traveled extensively to Yunnan, Guangdong, Guizhou, the three provinces of the northeast and the northwest. I came to understand that culture and customs were different from place to place, and I learned the different ways of communicating with people in different regions and thus had a better understanding of their cultural backgrounds. I started my business at a time when few people in China were engaged in private business — a process in which I learned a lot."

1986: Doing Business in Yiwu

In 1985, Zhou Xiaoguang married Yu Yunxin, a merchant from Zhejiang Dongyang who also sold embroidery products. Shortly after giving birth to her eldest son, Yu Jiangbo, Zhou Xiaoguang told her husband that she wanted to settle down. Thus, in 1986, the two used all their savings to buy a booth in a first generation small commodities wholesale market in Yiwu. At that time, the small commodities market was just established, with only 700 booths. When selling embroidery in the northeast, Zhou Xiaoguang also tried to sell accessories. When she noticed that the northeastern women liked to wear colorful headwear, she made the decision to engage in accessories business. Therefore, her husband went to Guangdong and other places to purchase goods, while she and her family members processed them before selling them in Yiwu. Her potential as a shrewd businesswoman was tapped. In a few years' time, the couple bought a new apartment in the best residential area in Yiwu and bought a shop in downtown Chaoyangmen. Her sound judgment paid off before long, as Chaoyangmen became the best commercial section in the center of Yiwu. Their wealth increased exponentially. She had achieved almost all the goals when she embarked on the adventure away from home. Besides, she had a child. It seemed that she should be satisfied and relax a little bit. However, Zhou Xiaoguang remained as ambitious as ever.

In 1992, Zhou Xiaoguang was selected as an agent by a well-known accessories company in Taiwan, and opened the first accessories store in Yiwu, selling imported and homemade products. Sales were good and Zhou Xiaoguang got to know her consumers and their buying habits. When they found that supply often fell short of demand and that the local government was taking measures to encourage private enterprises, Zhou Xiaoguang and her husband came up with the idea of setting up their own factory.

1995: Investment and Construction of Factories — From Small Business to a Large Enterprise

In July 1995, the couple invested 7 million yuan to build an accessories factory, and named it Xinguang (Neoglory) by using the last character of each person's name. This was a difficult decision, as the investment was all the couple had amassed over the years. Failure would mean they had lost everything. At that point, Yu Yunxin offered Zhou Xiaoguang great support. He said, "In the very beginning, we had nothing. If the worst comes to the worst, we can start it all over again." Zhou Xiaoguang said, "When we first went to Yiwu in 1986, we only had 15,000 yuan. We created all the assets through hard work. By the time we were planning to establish our own company in 1995, we had already bought a lot of shops in residential areas, so there was no need to open a factory. Moreover, I was not versed in operating a factory because I just knew the market very well. So, I told my husband, if we built a factory and failed, what should we do? He just said that, considering the personality and experience of both of us, we could start up all over again if we failed. He was sure our friends would lend us a hand. Having said that, we began to build the factory."

In October 1995, the Neoglory accessories factory was up and running. Some 450 skilled workers were recruited from accessories companies in Guangzhou, and more than 40 technicians and managers were senior staff who had worked in accessories companies in Taiwan. In addition, Zhou Xiaoguang also asked the team to speed up the launch of more than 8,000 styles of accessories. Known for their latest style and variety, Neoglory occupied the market quickly.

1996–2008: Channels Matter — Expanding and Improving Wholesale and Retail Networks

Soon, Zhou Xiaoguang opened a branch in Guangzhou's Accessories Street. At that time, women in Guangzhou loved to wear scarf buckles, and the branch immediately reported this information back to the head office. In just three days, the company designed and produced dozens of scarf buckles of different colors and shapes and launched on the market. As a result, Neoglory accessories became an instant success in Guangzhou. During the Spring Festival of the following year, Zhou Xiaoguang opened a market subsidiary next to the Yiwu Small Commodities Market, and took the lead in launching the scarf buckles, which were also well received by local customers. Later, she sent salespeople to north China to set up a branch in Shenyang in order to open up the northeast market and gather information on the latest trend there.

In the following two years, Zhou Xiaoguang adopted the general agent system and found distributors who became general agents in 13 cities across the country including Shanghai, Beijing, and Xi'an, and quickly opened up the domestic market with annual sales of tens of millions of yuan. However, with the expansion of the market, this model showed its drawbacks. The conservative general agents refused to expand further, impeding the development of Neoglory. In 1998, Zhou Xiaoguang revoked the permits to the general agents and set up direct-sale stores, leading sales to multiply within a year to reach 100 million yuan. Meanwhile, the direct-sale stores could also collect sales information for the head office to make market analysis. Inventory, however, also increased, leading to higher operating costs and constrained cash flow, so a sound management was required to maintain turnover and profits. Moreover, the revoke of the general agent rights practically turned those distributors into competitors. For Neoglory Accessories, competing with local dealers in places that it was not familiar with put it in a disadvantaged position.

Zhou Xiaoguang began to transform the wholesale-centered sales model to the terminal retail model in 2000. The decision was made because she found that the retail price of Neoglory accessories was five to ten times the wholesale price, with most of the profits going to the distributors. Her attempt to open chain retail stores was initially not a success because the wholesale channels in the past did not establish the Neoglory brand. In October 2005, Zhou Xiaoguang reiterated at the Neoglory Strategy Meeting that Neoglory Accessories would transform from manufacturers and wholesalers to retailers and brand operators. From then on, Neoglory Accessories encouraged distributors to cooperate with Neoglory to open direct-sale stores to maintain wholesale channels; in the meantime, they also established a franchise store system and launched brands like Neoglory Boutique, Neoglory MI, Tofü, Tiannü Zhiai, Xibao High-end Specialty Store, all aiming at high-end customers. As of 2008, Neoglory had nearly 400 retail stores in cities across the country.

1997–2007: Ten Years of Expansion to the International Market

In 1997, Zhou Xiaoguang and her designer team began to participate in accessories fairs around the world, expanding their knowledge of the world's latest accessories styles and materials and simultaneously mastering the new techniques. In 1998, Zhou Xiaoguang took her own jewelry to Hong Kong to participate in the jewelry exhibition there. This is the first time that Neoglory Jewelry embraced the world market. While communicating with Hong Kong customers, she felt that she had a good understanding of the industry after so many years working in the industry and was ready for further expansion of Neoglory Accessories in the world.

When recalling this trip to Hong Kong, Zhou Xiaoguang said, "I took my products for the first time to international exhibitions and their unprecedented success greatly enhanced my confidence. I feel that I am fully capable of selling our products on the international market. I will not only make Neoglory number one in China, but also establish a Chinese brand in the world."

In early 1999, Zhou Xiaoguang went to Europe for the first time to look for business partners. In the same year, because she wanted to relegate powers to the first professional manager, she went on a one-month visit to the United States to get to know the needs of overseas customers. In 2000, Zhou Xiaoguang went to Hong Kong to participate in the jewelry exhibition with confidence. At that time, because China was on the eve of joining the World Trade Organization, Neoglory Accessories attracted more than 70 customers from more than 50 countries in Asia, Europe, and America. It was the first factory in the Chinese mainland that broke up the monopoly of the accessories market by South Korea and Hong Kong. Because of the greatly increased number of orders after the exhibition, Zhou Xiaoguang began to think of ways to ease the bottleneck of the company's production and operations.

In April 2001, with the efforts of Zhou Xiaoguang, Neoglory Accessories established official cooperation with Swarovski, the Austria-based jewelry giant. Neoglory would purchase Swarovski's crystal raw materials and other materials, and both companies would jointly organize jewelry launch and open stores for selling crystal ornaments.

In 2005, Zhou Xiaoguang adjusted her overseas market strategy and appointed Zhou Yuxia, fourth daughter in her family, to be in charge of the development of Neoglory Jewelry in emerging markets around the world as well as the establishment of overseas branches. As of 2008, Neoglory had established a total of 7 branches and direct-sale stores in Hong Kong, UAE, Moscow, Spain, and other places. Soon after that, Neoglory Jewelry cooperated with Czech-based Preciosa Group, and Neoglory Jewelry's Hong Kong Branch became Preciosa's exclusive agent in China.

The development of emerging markets and the adjustment of domestic retail channels enabled Neoglory Jewelry to achieve increases of 50% and 30% in annual sales in 2006 and 2007 respectively. Even during the financial crisis of 2008, its sales grew by 15%. In 2008, sales in emerging markets accounted for 80% of the total amount of exports, while sales in Europe and the United States fell from 80% to 20%.

Introduction of Professional Managers

In 1998, when Zhou Xiaoguang began to establish direct-sale stores and make a foray into the international market, she felt that her management knowledge could not keep up with the development of the company. For example, the company did not have an Enterprise Resource Planning (ERP) internal information system. Recognizing the importance of talents in business operations, she hired a professional management and consulting team to carry out a comprehensive management transformation, initiating a transition from family-oriented management to a modern corporate system. In the following ten years, she recruited three professional managers.

The first professional manager was Jiang Xingzhong from Taiwan. In 1999, he was appointed as the general manager of the company, the first professional manager in Yiwu. Two months after he took office, Jiang Xingzhong proposed a set of reforms covering organizational structure, management system, and corporate culture, which, however, encountered resistance from the company's veterans. Therefore, Zhou Xiaoguang told Jiang Xingzhong, "Go ahead with your bold reform. I will give you three months for the 'bleeding.' The bottom line is that sales must not fall by more than 40%. You don't need to worry about any problems other than this."

She added, "Then I decided to go on a one-month visit to the United States, and during this period I relegate all the management powers to the professional manager and I will not keep in touch with others but him. By doing this, he can have room to remove all obstacles that interfere with his authority."

Jiang Xingzhong indeed achieved a lot, including the creation of specialized management systems, standardized production processes, opening of direct-sale stores and increasing sales, as well as the establishment of ERP internal information system to help companies manage production and sales. With the completion of the company's basic management framework, Neoglory witnessed a period of rapid development. After three years in charge of management and operation in Neoglory, Jiang Xingzhong was unable to add anything new to the management model because he lacked in-depth understanding of the jewelry industry. His judgment of market trends was not precise enough to adapt to the rapidly growing Neoglory at that period.

At the end of 2002, Zhou Xiaoguang hired the second professional manager Liu Qingkun. After graduating from Tsinghua University, he went to study in the United States. He then served as the general manager of Delphi Auto Parts (Guangzhou) and had good experience in the management of foreign invested companies. Although he was not familiar with the jewelry industry beforehand, he did thorough research into the industry after taking up the job. He was also good at coordinating the relations between various departments and he was very effective in standardizing the company's business operations. During his tenure, a large number of direct-sale stores and retail stores were opened, hiring more than 6,500 employees at its peak.

The rapid increase in the number of stores brought about substantial market expansion. At the same time, inventory also increased a lot. This kind of over-zealous expansion — when the general manager was under pressure to pursue quick success — had negative effects on Neoglory's long-term development. In the early days of Neoglory, it worked in close cooperation with local dealers in selling the products. As Liu Qingkun adopted a different strategy by opening self-operated stores on a large scale, they virtually replaced the local dealers and turned them all into Neoglory's competitors in the local market. Competing with local distributors in places where culture, consumers, and markets were unfamiliar put Neoglory in a disadvantaged position. The resulting increase in inventory also greatly increased Neoglory's operating cost. The increase in store cost and inventory cost squeezed Neoglory's profit margin and reduced the company's working capital and turnover rate. Despite rapid expansion, pressure of a sharp decline in market competitiveness was mounting in Neoglory.

During his tenure, Liu Qingkun achieved 30%–50% increase in annual sales, but cost also increased significantly: The employment of an additional 6,500 staff members, 4 to 5 times increase in inventory, and higher operational costs after increased numbers of stores. When Liu Qingkun departed at the end of his four-year term, he left a heavy burden on Neoglory.

Lu Xiaozhong, the third professional manager, was promoted from within Neoglory in 2006. Lu joined Neoglory in 1998 and was responsible for production for many years before he was promoted to the factory director. He paid much attention to production efficiency. But he was not sensitive about the market, clients, and consumers. His indecisive decision-making led to the imbalance between production and sales. These shortcomings not only limited the development of the market, such as forging brands and developing e-commerce, but also caused dissatisfaction of employees due to the unsmooth coordination between departments. During the time when Lu Xiaozhong assumed the post of general manager, Neoglory Jewelry was suffering from weak production capacity, high costs, and declining market competitiveness. At the same time, there was widespread dissatisfaction among the employees about the rapidly decreasing rate of efficiency and bad coordination within and among the departments. Many of Lu Xiaozhong's production-oriented concepts severely constrained the development of Neoglory. At that time, marketing, production, and the entire supply chain were not working smoothly, leading to the stagnation of marketing strategies and performance.

During the tenure of the first professional manager, Zhou Xiaoguang and Yu Yunxin paid much attention to the jewelry business, while the professional manager spent his time and energy on standardizing company management. Most of the decisions concerning industrial operation were made by the couple. During the tenure of the second professional manager, after a short break-in period, Zhou Xiaoguang showed great trust in the professional manager and gave him all the powers he needed. Thus, the professional manager's decision to expand the business was carried out unimpeded. The last professional manager was a senior employee of Neoglory, who was highly trusted by Zhou Xiaoguang. But perhaps because of this, she was imperious in her communication with the general manager. Of course, Neoglory's fast declining sales was also a factor contributing to her way of communication.

Zhou Xiaoguang summed up her experience, "As long as the professional manager devotes himself wholeheartedly to his duties, Neoglory will give him all the power he needs. Professional managers possess the expertise that is beneficial to enterprises. But I noted that professional managers are not fully committed. Some professional managers have the ability but not the integrity we expected. Other professional managers are trustworthy but they lack the ability, consciousness, and the right attitude."

At that time, it was not only the fashion accessories industry, but the whole of China was short of home-grown professional managers of moral integrity and professional competence to support the rapid economic development of the country. And there were no effective laws to restrict the unethical behaviors of professional managers. This caused uneasiness in entrepreneurs. Zhou Xiaoguang believed that the best way to employ professional managers was to let professional managers have full play of their own strengths within the range of their management system rather than have the professional managers run a system or set up a platform.

Yu Jiangbo Is the Choice in Crisis

Before the financial crisis of 2008, the prospect of a crisis loomed large in Zhou Xiaoguang's mind. By adopting a strategy of selling more products at lower prices, Neoglory had maintained steady exports to developed countries in Europe and America. Orders for Christmas gifts in foreign countries usually reach their climax in August and September every year and the annual amount is worth about 8 million US dollars. In 2007, however, the orders that came in were worth no more than 3 million US dollars. Therefore, Zhou Xiaoguang went to the United States to find out the reasons for the declining demand. She found that the US market was sluggish, that the number of customers had been reduced by half, and each customer's amount of purchase was also cut by half. The total market volume was less than 1/4 of regular demand. Since 40% of Neoglory's products were sold on the overseas market, Zhou Xiaoguang began to feel the pressure. Neoglory's sales fell 10% from September 2007 to March 2008 compared to the same period the previous year. Besides, the pressure brought about by the higher costs from the domestic wholesale and retail network and the instability of the entire management team made Zhou realize the limitations of professional managers.

Additionally, Neoglory was already a diversified enterprise at the time, but Yu Yunxin and Zhou Xiaoguang were especially fond of the jewelry sector. Falling sales in the jewelry division caused them much anxiety.

In October 2008, 23-year-old Yu Jiangbo, the couple's eldest son, returned to China and served his internship in the Beijing office of Union Bank of Switzerland (UBS). At the age of 16, he was sent by his parents to the UK to study at Imperial College London and obtained a bachelor's degree in mathematics and applied mathematics. He continued to obtain a master's degree in human resources management from the London School of Economics and Political Science as an honors student. Soon he received a UBS offer thanks to his good performance as an intern at the company and was ready for work in this Fortune Global 500 company. His plan was to accumulate some work experience in this multinational company before returning to Neoglory to take over the family business. Neoglory, which was enshrouded by the financial crisis at that time, had begun to show signs of danger. Zhou Xiaoguang wanted her son to take over the family business as soon as possible to help it get out of trouble. Yu Jiangbo had to make a decision between two choices: One was to stay in UBS and worked in his favorite field of investment; the other was to return to the family business and be involved in corporate management. After thorough consideration, Yu Jiangbo decided to join Neoglory as the assistant to the vice president of marketing for Neoglory Jewelry. He said, "It was during the financial crisis and I believed there would be many opportunities in times of crisis. As China's economy was developing rapidly, we might be experiencing an economic cycle. In the course of events, I'd rather test my abilities in a Chinese enterprise than work as an ordinary employee in a foreign company. It would take a long time to climb up the ladder in a foreign company, and then if I want to come back and work at a local enterprise, the adaptation would be very difficult. To be honest, my academic background and personal interest incline toward investment. But in order to be a good investor, one has to acquaint himself with the industry and get a good grasp of how to run a business. Challenging as it may be, managing a business is the best way to tap my potential. Hence, I welcome the opportunity to test myself in the family business."

Two Years of Experience Has Gradually Gained Ground

In the first two years after joining Neoglory, Yu Jiangbo focused on acquainting himself with the market and production. He would pay visits to all Neoglory customers, from the provincial capital cities, first-tier cities to the fourth- and fifth-tier cities, and overseas. While he was familiarizing himself with the market, Yu paid special attention to the demands of dealers and consumers and thought of how to provide better service to them. By doing so, he also had a grasp of the market distribution of the industry. Yu also worked in every workshop to get a better understanding of jewelry production processes and technologies.

Yu said, "I think we have to know the market first. Another important point is that I've engaged in some strategic thinking during these two years, including how the company should be positioned and what we are going to do in the next step. I've put some of my ideas into practice to see how effective they are."

During a jewelry show in Las Vegas, USA, Yu Jiangbo discovered that Neoglory's line of products fell short of the expectations of overseas consumers. These consumers — because of their education and information from an objective media — know what styles they prefer and what brands can meet their demands. In China, there are some difference in consumers' brand preferences between downtown Shanghai and Xinzhuang on the city's suburb. The difference is greater between first-tier cities and third-tier cities and the difference is even greater between first-tier cities and fifth-tier cities. This made Yu think about redeveloping the brand strategy of Neoglory Jewelry. He said, "We basically adopt a multi-brand strategy now, with two brands now mainly catering to first-tier cities, and you can find them in Shanghai's Jiuguang, Super Brand Mall, Xintiandi, for example, while other brands are catering to second- and third-tier cities. Besides, we are going to open a jewelry collection store."

After serving as an assistant to the vice president of marketing for a year, Yu took over the job from his boss after the latter resigned. The former vice president of marketing, who had been working in the home appliances industry previously, was not familiar with the jewelry industry but had a good working relationship with Yu Jiangbo during his tenure. As a senior executive recruited from outside the company, he found it difficult to do things as he wished in an enterprise like Neoglory with accumulation of more than ten years. The then general manager Lu Xiaozhong paid more attention to production, leading to conflicts between market-oriented and production-oriented management. When Yu assumed the post of vice president of marketing, he started thinking about how to address the problems between production and marketing.

As head of the marketing division, Yu Jiangbo began putting his own management ideas into practice. Gradually he assembled a contingent of employees who supported his management ideas and style. Also, they were eager to promote the company's reform and development to achieve the goals under Yu's leadership, thus they set up specific three-month or six-month goals.

By that point, Neoglory Jewelry was on the list of enterprises that would participate in the 2010 World Expo and Yu Jiangbo was appointed by his mother as the head of Neoglory's working group to accumulate experience and display his talent. They erected a "Sparkling Matrix" crystal wall 18.5 meters long and 2.6 meters high at an area leading to the exit of the main exhibition hall of the United Pavilion of China Private Enterprise during the World Expo. It was the world's largest crystal wall, made up of 35,000 crystals. Each crystal was engraved with the name of a private enterprise. Apart from that, the two major events organized by Yu Jiangbo and his team during the World Expo — Launch of Popular Jewelry Trends and Neoglory Day — were also very successful. The products they designed specially for the World Expo and the brand name Neoglory became the focus of attention.

Which Comes First? Personal Relationship or Rules?

In 2009, Neoglory planned to go public. Considering that the investors would wish to see stability of the management and further development of the company, Zhou Xiaoguang decided at the end of 2010 to let Yu Jiangbo replace the general manager. It could be said that the strategy to have the company go public sooner rather than later and the increasing dissatisfaction of the board of directors with the performance of the general manager Lu Xiaozhong accelerated Yu Jiangbo's succession. Zhou Xiaoguang said, "The problem is that professional managers always regard themselves as professional managers, not masters of the enterprise. Yet, Jiangbo always considers himself to be the owner of this enterprise, regardless of his abilities. What is more valuable is that he is not afraid of taking on the responsibility. This is something that professional managers lack, so I have full confidence in him. In the process, if Jiangbo has the support of our entire team of senior employees, even if he starts from a lower position such as the assistant to the vice-general manager, he will play his role well because he is a down-to-earth person, not pretentious at all."

Considering that there might be disagreement in the company, Zhou Xiaoguang convened a meeting of middle-level managers and above before announcing the appointment. At the meeting, she said, "In the process of handover, whether you are middle- or senior-level managers or veterans of the company, you will realize that only by nurturing our next generation can our company develop further and have greater prospects. Just like the first time when we started our business, I hope that everyone will give him full support and cooperation so that he can develop his potential to the full. Everyone must be mentally prepared and show your magnanimity."

At the beginning of 2011, Yu Jiangbo became the general manager of Neoglory Jewelry. Although he had achieved some positive results in marketing in more than two years after joining the company, he was still under great pressure as he officially took over the whole company. He felt that many problems were caused by the leaders because of their unsound ideas. The original team upheld his parent's management concepts firmly, so Yu Jiangbo needed not only to change their minds but also develop a new team of his own and new mechanisms and culture, which would be a long process.

The change in personnel was where Yu Jiangbo had the most of disagreement with his mother during the succession. Yu Jiangbo felt that her management was based on the order of "personal relationship and rules", but he prefers "regulation, reason, and relationship". However, the employees at middle level and above who had been working in Neoglory for ten or more years were not used to his management style. They felt unhappy working under him, so they continued complaining to Zhou Xiaoguang and asked for her help. However, Yu Jiangbo continued with his adjustment and refused to compromise in terms of principle. He believed that the general manager's decision-making power should be clear and communication be conducted on the basis of mutual respect. Whenever he realized there was disagreement between him and the staff, Yu Jiangbo would resort to active communication. One year later, a balance was achieved between relationship and company regulation. Xiao Ruidong, the vice president of Neoglory's marketing, said, "Chairwoman

Zhou's biggest feature in her management is that it is extremely inclusive, and the management is achieved through the rule of the leader as a person. Jiangbo still has room to improve in this regard. He is a person who abides by the rules and hopes that the business will be done by following regulations. This is probably the biggest difference between an entrepreneur returning from overseas and a locally grown one. Jiangbo started from scratch and needs more experience. People can notice obvious changes in the leader's management style. His management style has gradually shifted from a learning-oriented style to a reflection of some of his personal opinions and finally to extremely unequivocal personal views. From the perspective of managing the whole team, Jiangbo is more versed in listening what others have to say. His identity as the son of Chairwoman Zhou exerts no influence on his personnel management. What matters is his charisma and leadership style."

In Neoglory Jewelry, Yu Jiangbo's reform was known as recommencement of pioneering work. How to start in some emerging fields? Because whether it was to be traditional retail or e-commerce, these changes meant the original team had to do many things differently. Yang Yunxiong, vice-general manager in charge of R&D and production, said, "Jiangbo has brought in a pragmatic management and working style and established his own management system. As he is the boss and owner the company, he will not gang up with any faction or clique. He is both the general manager and a member of the board of directors. He must consider both the current situation and the long-term development of the company. Therefore, he looks at problems from a perspective different than that of others. In those two years, we shut down departments, dismissed employees, and canceled projects, which met with strong opposition and resulted in great difficulties. Sometimes, even his mother was dragged in. Despite the pressure, we continued to streamline the organization, in a really big way. We probably dismissed 1/3 of the managers, merged many departments, and removed what needed to be removed. For example, some departments created just for some relatives of a certain leader must be removed".

Take the production and R&D departments for example. From the end of 2010, through merger and cancelation of departments and step-by-step assessment, the number of officials at the deputy section chief level or above were reduced from nearly 100 to 28 within less than one year.

For the placement of some senior employees, as long as there were good openings made available in the company, Yu Jiangbo would give priority to the senior employees. At the same time, he also provided many opportunities for senior employees at the middle level and above to continue studying. Yu Jiangbo wanted the senior employees to be ready to embrace changes. If they were reluctant to accept change, then Yu Jiangbo would make appropriate adjustments.

Zhou Xiaoguang granted full authority to Yu Jiangbo, who had total independence to do things as he wished. She believed that the less intervention the better, and she could make her presence felt through other means. At the same time, Zhou Xiaoguang was trying to adjust her own mindset to relegate power to her son. She knew clearly that people born in the 1980s and 1990s were the dominant force in the market and she knew little about them. But Yu Jiangbo, who was born in the 1980s, knew much more about their needs. A year later, Yu Jiangbo's performance was approved by his mother. "He is sober-minded, very mature, and is a person of vision. Most important is that he does things in a down-to-earth manner, not pretentious nor impulsive. He is good at self-control and is immune to outside disruptions and temptations. His team's performance over the past year speaks volumes for itself, and the team has taken on a new look. In addition, he has a mild temperament, showing respect to the elders and people of the older generation. In fact, after he became the general manager, there are fewer conflicts between us than before he assumed the position."

Reform, Transformation, and Upgrade

Believing that the economic recession brought about by the financial crisis presented a good opportunity for industry integration, Yu Jiangbo began to carry out comprehensive reforms.

Changing Production and Management Mode and Conducting Production Outsourcing

Yu Jiangbo made the strategic shift from production orientation to brand orientation. From 2011, Neoglory Jewelry carried out reforms in the production R&D and supply chain management to strengthen the research and development of key technologies and processes. Non-key production processes were outsourced to small factories in Yiwu to support their development and to factories in Guangzhou, Shenzhen, and even Vietnam, where labor costs were lower and recruitment easier than in Zhejiang. By early 2014, about 30% of Neoglory Jewelry's products were outsourced.

Other changes included improvement of standardization of production procedures and tightening quality control, establishment of a performance evaluation system, and an improved incentive scheme. As Neoglory Jewelry was manual-labor intensive, it consisted of more than ten production processes. Although each process required a 99% acceptance rate, the total acceptance rate was only a little more than 80% after a dozen processes. For example, electroplating consisted of five or six small processes. Shoddy work by some of the workers resulted in quality problems, but it was hard to identify the process where the problem first occurred. Yu Jiangbo thus adopted a team-based production plan under which work completed every day within each team was counted and publicized and any problem in quality could be traced and the responsible person held accountable. Meanwhile, Yu also established different incentive schemes for different groups of people. For example, he replaced the previous method of paying workers fixed salary with full-piecework-based method, which means that the more one produces, the more one gets.

In the past, Neoglory Jewelry made all their products before selling them. Since the quantities were huge, the large stock of jewelry items led to extremely high cost. As the assembly process accounted for 60% of total production cost, Yu tried out the semi-finished product inventory model. Processes prior to the assembly process will be completed first. The assembly process will not start until there is clear market demand for the products. What's more, the semi-finished products can be recycled and reused. This model saves more than 60% of the production cost and can keep inventory at a relatively low level. These reforms proved to be a success one year after he took over as general manager. Neoglory Jewelry cut its employees from a high of 6,500 to 2,000 while its production capacity increased by 40% and sales increased by 35%–40%.

Adjustment of Brand Marketing Strategy

Yu Jiangbo established two important centers, which are also incubators. The Strategic Development Center, established in 2011 aims to break new ground in business models and channels; the Brand Center, established in 2012, aims at brand innovation. In the same year, the new company logo was officially released, and the Brand Center, planning and design department were moved to Shanghai. Xiao Ruidong, vice president of marketing of Neoglory Jewelry, said, "Jiangbo is never a traditional manager, but a person who embraces innovation. The biggest change in brand strategy is the discussion of the brand lineup. The strategic transformation of Neoglory Jewelry is also supported by the two incubators."

There are four changes to the brand marketing strategy:

The first is to optimize the multi-brand strategy. Neoglory Jewelry expanded and strengthened its brand system by launching nearly ten brands to cater to different customers, including some high-end and original Chinese brands. For example, Neoglory Jewelry acquired the original Chinese brand "SU live" in 2011, making it the number one high-end silver jewelry brand of Neoglory. Besides, in 2013, Neoglory Jewelry cooperated with Yin Yi, a compere of Zhejiang Satellite TV and founder and designer of "Eve Silver Jewelry" to support brand repositioning. In the same year, Neoglory Jewelry cooperated with the internationally renowned Belgian cartoon brand "THE SMURFS" to develop jewelry based on the animation of the Smurfs and distribute it globally.

The second is a multi-channel strategy. In addition to the wholesale and OEM model as well as retail segments such as counters in department stores, integrated stores, and online stores, Neoglory Jewelry also expanded to new channels such as TV shopping and bespoke gifts for companies. In 2011, Neoglory Jewelry sold its products on 21 large-scale TV shopping stations across the country, which achieved a three-fold growth in 2012. In 2012, through cooperation with bespoke gift websites such as Kadang.com, Neoglory Jewelry gave companies and individual consumers the choice to buy customized gifts online. In 2013, the Tofü Store officially opened in Shanghai. This is a store integrating many of the brands in fashion accessories. It is not only a one-stop shopping store, but also a platform to try out the products, coordinating offline and online shops. By the beginning of 2014, Neoglory Jewelry had opened six Tofü Stores. Emerging channels accounted for about 30% of Neoglory Jewelry's total sales in 2013.

The third is to conduct cooperation with domestic and foreign fashion brands. For example, Neoglory Jewelry has established strategic partnerships with international crystal brands such as Swarovski and Ireland-based Tipperary and provides accessories for apparel companies such as H&M and Meters/bonwe, providing an integrated solution from the draft of fashion design so as to increase the added value of the products.

The fourth is to make better plans for overseas sales channels, including opening direct-sales retail stores in shopping centers in the United Kingdom, Russia, United Arab Emirates, the United States, and Mexico, and working with retailers such as H&M, Zara, J.C. Penney, and Walmart. In 2013, Neoglory Jewelry acquired the American jewelry brand Fashion Accents, the global top selling brand of hypoallergenic earrings, facilitating Neoglory Jewelry's expansion of business in the US and South America. Yu Jiangbo said, "Relations with these customers have improved through cooperation over the past few years. Our purpose of partnering with them is not for making profits, but to learn how they manage the supply chain, how to do retail business, and how to bring Neoglory in line with these international fashion trends. We consider it a major breakthrough in our international business."

E-commerce in Transformation

In 2009, promoted by Yu Jiangbo, Neoglory Jewelry opened an official flagship store on Taobao.com, QQ Mall, and other online platforms. In 2010, Yu Jiangbo initiated the establishment of the first e-commerce association in Yiwu, namely the E-Commerce Association of Jiangdong Sub-district, and served as the first president of the association. By stepping into the e-commerce sector, Yu Jiangbo ushered in a new marketing and development model for the future of Neoglory Jewelry to help its upgrading and transformation. He explained, "Merchants from Zhejiang are the most active in the entire private economy. In addition to inheriting enterprises, it is more important to inherit the entrepreneurial spirit of the older generation. During this process, they are confronted with the transformation and upgrading of enterprises through the help of Internet. For this purpose, we have made explorations in many areas."

Yu Jiangbo's strategy can be divided into three stages:

The first stage is the creation of an industrial chain for e-commerce. At this stage, three companies are established under Yu Jiangbo's instructions. The first company, namely Zhejiang Taoqu Network Technology Co., Ltd., is established as a one-stop marketing service company focusing on marketing. In addition to helping Neoglory Jewelry to carry out online sales, the company also provides e-commerce operation services for some well-known brands of Zhejiang merchants. The second one is Shanghai Taoci Network Technology Co., Ltd., an extension of e-commerce sales to third-party marketing and advertising services. In cooperation with a Japanese R&D team, it has developed software for sales data collection and analysis such as "Jyohoutsu" and "Shinkansen". The third company is a breakthrough in the e-commerce industry chain. At a time when the domestic warehouse and distribution service for third-party e-commerce was still in its infancy, Yu Jiangbo invested 20 million yuan in establishing Zhejiang Wwwarehouse Technology Co., Ltd. to provide fully digitalized back-end (warehouse, logistics, and information system) services for e-commerce. In 2012, Warehouse Technology was voted the Top Ten Global E-commerce Service Providers in the Ninth Netrepreneur Summit. In 2014, it was officially approved as a national high-tech enterprise with a market valuation estimated at 400 million to 500 million yuan.

The second stage is the planning of cross-border e-commerce. At present, Neoglory's cross-border e-commerce business has a team of nearly 30 professionals speaking the languages of English, Russian, Portuguese, and Spanish, and has opened over 20 stores in AliExpress, Amazon (US site and UK site), Ebay (US site and UK site), DHGate.com, and other platforms, and has its own independent e-commerce website. It also plans to set up warehouses of Wwwarehouse (to undertake logistics and distribution of cross-border e-commerce) and to acquire an e-commerce company from Brazil.

The third stage is the establishment of platforms for enterprises. In 2014, Yu Jiangbo launched the Optimization Project of China Fashion

Jewelry Supply Chain, which, with the help of the mobile Internet, turned components purchasing from a labor-intensive, inefficient, and irregular transaction to a simpler, efficient, and transparent transaction. In the process, it benefited the distribution structure comprised of the components manufacturers. Finished products manufacturers, distributors, foreign trade companies, and retail stores were smashed and the value chain was reshaped to remove intermediaries to achieve lower cost and higher efficiency. Yu Jiangbo hopes to reshape the ecosystem of China's fashion jewelry, by changing the current abnormal pattern of the jewelry industry in which "bad money drives out good money". This is so that a large share of the profits will go to the components manufacturers with high-quality, cost-effective products and to good finished-products manufacturers. Yu Jiangbo has a large budget for this new project and is eager to see its success, thus maintaining Neoglory Jewelry's leading position in China's fashion jewelry industry and helping the industry to develop.

Big Family System

There is an office building at the group headquarters, with the first to fifth floors being offices while the sixth and seventh floors being the living areas of the Neoglory family. This is where Zhou Xiaoguang's family — her parents, the families of her sisters and brother — live. The three generations consist of over 30 members. There is a long-standing friendship between the Zhou family and Yu family. When Zhou Xiaoguang's mother was young, she learned embroidery from Yu Yunxin's father. Zhou Xiaoguang has five sisters and one younger brother while there are six brothers in Yu Yunxin's family. In addition to the couple Yu Yunxin and Zhou Xiaoguang, there is another couple formed between the two families: Zhou Xiaoguang's third sister married Yu Yunxin's sixth brother and has a son named Yu Jiangwei. In recent years, Zhou Xiaoguang would organize a summer vacation for all family members. In 2012, the whole family went to the northeast to go through again their entrepreneurial experience. Zhou Xiaoguang said, "I was deeply moved by a remark by my son. He says that our big family is a piggy bank where everyone shows love for others and makes much dedication. When everyone contributes his/her bit to this family, there will be more and more positive energy in this piggy bank. Everyone saves a penny, and over time the accumulation will fill up the piggy bank."

Most of the Zhou family members hold senior posts in the group. Zhou Xiaoguang is the chairwoman of the group, responsible for formulating the company's macro strategy and participating in social activities and investment inspection. Yu Yunxin is the vice chairman and president of the group. Since 2003, he has focused on real estate business. Their son Yu Jiangbo is on the group's board of director, vice president, and general manager of Neoglory Jewelry. Zhou Xiaoguang's father had previously been in charge of finance; her fourth younger sister Zhou Yuxia was responsible for the expansion of Neoglory Jewelry's overseas business before she was in charge of jewelry selling at the International Trade City. She is the vice chairwoman of Neoglory Jewelry. Zhou Xiaoguang's younger brother Zhou Yisheng is on Neoglory's board of directors and is the executive vice president of the Strategic Investment Center responsible for investment. Her sixth younger sister Zhou Liping is responsible for raw materials trade in China. Third younger sister Zhou Xiaofang and fifth younger sister Zhou Huiping also work in the group.

The group's shareholding structure at present is that Zhou Xiaoguang and Yu Yunxin hold more than 70% of the shares, and the remaining shares are owned by other family members. In 2012, Neoglory Jewelry carried out a shareholding transformation before it began to go public, with the group possessing 76.73% of the shares, and employees possessing about 8% of the shares as an incentive scheme. Yu Jiangbo's shares are also a part of the 8%.

Neoglory also set up a special fund for the senior employees who have worked hard for many years in the group. The fund aims to help their children get a decent education, find a job in Neoglory, or help the senior employees to pursue further study, making them feel that they are part of the big family. Furthermore, Neoglory also established a Lifetime Achievement Award and other awards so that these non-blood-connected people can also get involved as part of the family.

From "De-familization" to "Family Culture"

Soon after the employment of professional managers, Zhou Xiaoguang would discuss business inheritance with her counterparts whenever she visited well-known foreign family companies. In 2006, Zhou Xiaoguang led the Neoglory delegation on a visit to the headquarters of Swarovski, their important business partner. One of the important issues they discussed was the inheritance of family business. Zhou Xiaoguang learned that the Swarovski family had formulated family rules and corporate vision at the very beginning of the business, and the later generations only made minor adjustments to the established rules. Swarovski also had a strong independent team of directors to help with business management. The team's function was to balance the choices of family business leaders and business inheritance as well as to identify the strengths of every family member. Zhou Xiaoguang said, "I led a team of family members and company executives on a visit to Swarovski in 2006 to learn from their practices. Our visit coincided with their inheritance from the fourth generation to the fifth generation. Even though the fifth generation boss was already in office, we were received by the fourth generation boss instead. The succession in Swarovski lasted five to eight years, and they needed time to develop new successors. Moreover, they did not think that only sons could inherit family business. Instead, they would select the most suitable person from the family business as successor. The fifth generation boss was a son-in-law of the family."

What Zhou Xiaoguang achieved from this visit can be summarized as the following three points: First, they have a very good plan in the family. The founder of Swarovski has three sons, with each of them being in charge of a division of the business. All of them are good at cooperation and execution. Secondly, the inheritance process is well-planned and smooth. The process of handover has a transition period of several years. Thirdly, the family business hires independent directors who have no blood relations. They take an objective position and have played a positive role in the business. She added, "Of the world's top 500 companies, 175 are family-owned enterprises. These family-owned enterprises have been able to maintain their prosperity through family holding and outsider participation rather than inheritance through blood ties. Swarovski is a good example. After discussions with the Swarovski family, I am delighted to discover that the 'family culture' of our family has been deeply rooted in the hearts of the next generation, which represented the 'gene' of family business inheritance. The third generation of the family understands the importance of teamwork from childhood and you can find in them the family's sense of responsibility, courage, love, and dedication."

The Yu-Zhou Family Committee and the Family "Charter"

Zhou Xiaoguang thus hit upon the idea of establishing a family committee. She hired Professor Joseph P.H. Fan from the Chinese University of Hong Kong who studies family business as a consultant to design such a committee from a neutral third-party perspective. From 2010, Yu Jiangbo began to push forward the establishment of the committee. He said, "My parents had this idea before, but the idea did not materialize. I realize that people of my generation have matured over the years. I really don't want to see problems of the previous generation being carried over to our generation. I hope that we can solve these problems as early as possible, while people of the older generation are still alive. So, this is why I am appointed to promote this matter."

"All members of the family are involved in discussing the rules of the family committee and every item must be agreed unanimously. The details of the organizational structure and tasks of the Neoglory Family Committee are still under discussion and we may end up with a family council and a family committee." The family council will be comprised of all the members while the family committee is initially composed of seven family members, which means one representative from the families of each of Zhou Xiaoguang's seven siblings will discuss family affairs and development issues. Meanwhile, the problems of enterprises will be discussed at the shareholders' meeting and by the board of directors instead.

In 2013, Zhou Xiaoguang began to draft a family "charter". It originated from an attempt to facilitate communication between the first and second generations, especially at the enterprise level. She hopes to clarify the rules of procedures through the family "charter", including provision of assistance to the second generation in formulating personal development plans, as well as the establishment of venture development fund for the second generation. Zhou Xiaoguang knows that the individuals of the second generation have their own ideas. They can pursue personal interests such as art and do not necessarily have to start a business or enter the family business. However, the venture development fund shall not be granted unconditionally. Family members must use their corporate equity as a guarantee. If the business fails, it is possible their corporate equity will be confiscated. For family members who wish to enter the family business to develop themselves, the family "charter" has laid out clear procedures and rules. For example, the second generation should start from the lower-level posts and will only be promoted after they prove themselves to be competent.

Another important task of Yu Jiangbo is to develop study and employment plans for the second generation. There are 13 children in the second generation of the family and Jiangbo is the eldest one. He has taken care of his younger siblings since he was a child. He was the first to study in the UK, so he devised plans for his sisters and brothers to study abroad, and provided help to seven of them who also studied in the UK. In addition to Yu Jiangbo, three younger brothers have returned to Neoglory to serve their internship. His cousin Yu Jiangwei is in the real estate department of the group, and another cousin Jin Jiangtao is in the finance department of the group while his younger brother Yu Jiangming is studying in the United States and comes back for internship during the summer vacation.

When formulating the family "charter", Zhou Xiaoguang also invites people without blood ties to join the family of Neoglory. Yu Jiangbo is aware that the employment of professional managers has its problems. For example, professional managers normally are unwilling to make decisions; they want the chairman to make the decisions and frequently ask for instructions because they are trying to shirk their responsibilities. They are afraid of making wrong decisions and tend to play safe. They hope only to play the role of an executor, always trying to go along with the wishes of their boss. They are not very enthusiastic about promoting the development of the company, and shirk breaking new ground or making breakthroughs. Of course, professional managers know that they must do well to pass the performance assessment at the end of the day, so in decision-making they pay more attention to quick results than long-term development. That is why Yu Jiangbo hopes to establish a lifetime honorary award for outstanding professional managers, including granting them equity. He hopes to find a way to better integrate "personal relationship and rules" or "rules and personal relationship", and establish a better system so that outstanding professional managers with a strong sense of responsibility enjoy similar financial rewards as family members and take up more responsibilities.

The gradual separation of ownership and management rights has always been a goal which Yu Jiangbo has been striving to achieve, as neither side can develop healthily once the family's sentiments are mixed up with business affairs. Regarding the wealth planning of the family, Yu Jiangbo remarked, "Basically, they spend as much as they need; of course, it is within a reasonable range. Everyone gets paid, and there will be a small amount of bonus at the end of the year, but no dividends in the strictest sense have been paid so far. The same is true for buying housing and cars. Every household has a house and two or three cars which can meet the basic needs of everyone. The decision is made by my parents. We have made clearer and more specific provisions in this area, including the payment of dividends, the venture development fund for the second generation, and the allocation of assets around the world."

Yu Jiangbo's dream is to make Neoglory "the most harmonious large-family business in China and an epitome of family business in the world" while Zhou Xiaoguang's dream is to "quadruple the sales of Neoglory in ten years and turn it into a 100 billion-yuan-worth enterprise". Nowadays, Yu Jiangbo has become the head of the second generation of the family. The experience in Neoglory Jewelry has mellowed him and he is demonstrating excellent management ability. He is more and more involved in decision-making to ease the burdens of his parents. In 2015, Yu Jiangbo got married and had a son. His mother-in-law and Zhou Xiaoguang have been good friends for many years. His marriage has injected new vitality to this big family. The four generations of the Yu and Zhou family live in blissful harmony, and the younger generation has begun to show their talent. As the leader of the family, Zhou Xiaoguang and Yu Yunxin start thinking about how to keep the balance among the families. How should they attract and select other people of the second generation and professional managers to support the development of the group? How should

Yu Jiangbo promote the establishment and operation of the family committee?

From the hope of "de-familization" to professional management, Neoglory finally turned back to "rebuilding the family culture" after witnessing the tenures of three professional managers. Aiming to become a new generation family business in China, Neoglory tries its best to build the group on the foundation of a strong "family culture". In the end, the discourse whether a family business should hire a family CEO or a professional CEO remains to be a matter of constant debate in the academic world.

8

Family CEO or Professional CEO?

Some scholars maintain that the two systems of business and family should be separated. Enterprises need specialized management by professional managers, and family members should not get involved. Specialized business system that favors professional managers is based on the separation of ownership and management right. Through specialized division of labor and principal-agent relationship, improvement in professional ability and breakthrough in talent selection are achieved within the corporation. The drawback of this model is that professional managers may disagree with family values, leading to risks such as differences in the direction of pursuit of interests, asymmetrical information reception, lack of trust, and representation problems.

In China, many family firms have tried the path of professionalized management, but ultimately failed. The main reason is that China does not have a mature professional managers market. In order to maintain long-lasting prosperity, family businesses must face up to the severe challenges brought by inheritance. There are pros and cons appointing the successor from within the family or selecting a professional manager from outside the family, which has been a topic of endless debate in academia. The earlier literature review advocated the separation of ownership and management right. But as the business prospers, it is natural that professional management will replace family-based management. Some family business researchers propose that the development of family companies is divided into different stages. They find that with the expansion of a family firm, the possibility and necessity of hiring a professional manager from outside the family increase continuously. The increase in the size and growth of the company are the main factors that encourage family businesses to turn to professionalized management. Firms that fail to do so will eventually lose in the competition, and this explains why so many family businesses have been eliminated from the market.

Several studies have compared family inheritors with non-family ones and discover that the latter performed better on performance excellence indicators.[1,2] Employing a professional CEO with outstanding management skills indeed assists a company in improving its performance. However, some scholars discuss the risks of introducing external professional managers because they may take speculative actions which will endanger family control. In view of the merits and drawbacks of either choice, family firms usually find themselves in a dilemma of choosing their own children or professional managers as successors to the business.

Family CEO vs. Professional CEO

Should family firms appoint their own descendants or professional managers? Let's take a look at the risks and benefits analyzed by various theories. Agency Theory[3] is a mainstream theory that explains the relationship between enterprise ownership and management rights. Some Agency Theory researchers point out that there is innate conflict of interests between shareholders and professional managers. If professional managers take over the business, they will be presented with lots of opportunities

---

[1] Smith, B. F., & Amoako-Adu, B. (1999). Management Succession and Financial Performance of Family Controlled Firms. *Journal of Corporate Finance*, 5(4), 341–368.

[2] Morck, R., & Stangeland, D. B. Yeung. (2000). Inherited Wealth, Corporate Control, and Economic Growth. In Concentrated Corporate Ownership. NBER Conference Volume. University of Chicago Press, Chicago, IL.

[3] Klapper, L. F., & Love, I. (2004). Corporate Governance, Investor Protection, and Performance in Emerging Markets. *Journal of Corporate Finance*, 10(5), 703–728.

to seek personal gain and very often they will take advantage of the opportunities, which may result in a negative impact on the performance of corporations. On the contrary, appointing family members to succeed can effectively reduce agency costs, as it is unlikely that they will jeopardize family interests. At the same time, Transaction Costs Theory[4] also indicates that many intangible assets in the succession are difficult to transfer. Heirs within the family can share some of the "unique wealth creation"[5] in family firms, such as family names, social relations, reputation of the family, etc. These intangible assets can hardly be inherited by external successors. Similarly, researchers of Resource-Based View[6] believe that the motivation for using family inheritors is that they can provide the company with key strategic resources and unique social and political networks to assist enterprises in identifying opportunities and promoting business development.

However, critics say that this unique family bond has its downside. Hitchhiking or evading responsibilities on the part of family members will lead to moral risks and speculation. What's more, family successors may also cause principal-agent problems within the family. Even on the bright side of family bond, sometimes family CEO will not hesitate to sacrifice the economic performance of the company so as to preserve family "socioemotional wealth"[7] as well as to maintain family control over the business.

Speaking of family heirs, two varied views exist. Some researchers find strengths in a family CEO such as extreme dedication, in-depth understanding of the unique tacit knowledge of the firm, advantages in

---

[4] Williamson, O. E. (1989). Transaction Cost Economics. *Handbook of Industrial Organization*, 1, 135–182.

[5] Sirmon, D. G., & Hitt, M. A. (2003). Managing Resources: Linking Unique Resources, Management, and Wealth Creation in Family Firms. *Entrepreneurship Theory and Practice*, 27(4), 339–358.

[6] Habbershon, T. G., Williams, M., & MacMillan, I. C. (2003). A unified Systems Perspective of Family Firm Performance. *Journal of Business Venturing*, 18(4), 451–465.

[7] Gómez-Mejía, L. R., Haynes, K. T., Núñez-Nickel, M., Jacobson, K. J., & Moyano-Fuentes, J. (2007). Socioemotional Wealth and Business Risks in Family-controlled Firms: Evidence from Spanish Olive Oil Mills. *Administrative Science Quarterly*, 52(1), 106–137.

governance, staunch protector of family socioemotional wealth, etc. Employing family members is an effective way to avoid principal-agent problems, which is strongly supported by Agency Theory. Thus, heritage by family descendants is a wise choice for family businesses. The resource-based view also stands on the side of the family CEO. From a perspective that transcends economic interests, this view maintains that through a series of core resources at their own disposal, family businesses can have a long-term edge in competition. With the help of these distinctive and precious intangible assets, such as family prestige, political relations, and socioemotional wealth, family corporations can adopt and implement strategies that others cannot emulate. Therefore, the appointment of family CEO can better protect and carry on this kind of intangible resources, retaining the competitive edge and the control of the business for generations.

On the other hand, some scholars[8] put forward a diametrically opposed point of view, focusing on the dark side of the offspring succession. Based on the Agency Theory, their research discovered the decision-making mechanism of family business requires high degree of personal autonomy and lacks self-discipline, which often results in a variety of internal obstacles. Altruism is apt to induce perceptual bias, self-interest behavior, hitchhiking, and the difficulty of contract execution, thus bringing internal agency costs to family corporations. They maintain that this special family bond will entice family members to abuse opportunities. Therefore, intra-family agency relations are also at stake. Studies indicate that family members can take advantage of privileges to reap various additional benefits, such as special allowances, jobbery, or non-property benefits. Moreover, those recruited through nepotism, even if unqualified and incompetent, cannot be dismissed, which poses serious challenges to human resources management (HRM). Lots of highly competent professional managers are often reluctant to work for family businesses when they realize that they have little room for a promotion or raise. In addition, because performance and talents are not used as the criteria for promotion

---

[8] La Porta, R., F. Lopez-de-Silanes, and A. Shleifer. (1999). Corporate Ownership Around the World. *Journal of Finance*, 54, 471–517.

assessment, it is more likely to trigger and exacerbate differences and conflicts in the management team.

There are two different views on the appointment of professional managers. Family companies are unwilling to employ external talents because it brings high risks and threats, one of which is the well-known agency problem.[9,10,11] Some studies have concluded that employing professional managers may cause serious consequences of "creative destruction", meaning that professional managers' power may expand sharply in the process of the rapid business growth. Eventually, the family loses control over management and finance. Because of the fear of losing control, family shareholders often prohibited professional managers from adopting innovative measures, which effectively stifles business growth. Literature on family business culture also indicates that they are more concerned about the survival of the family business than its financial performance.[12] For the owners of family corporations, family values and unity are most important and should not be undermined or challenged. Professional CEOs are often criticized for ignoring family culture; namely they often unwittingly deviate from the core family values.

Yet, employing professional managers also has its positive side. Speaking of talents sources, family successors are selected from a limited pool of family talents. On the contrary, professional managers can be selected from a vast pool of excellent talents outside the family. As a result, family inheritors may not be as efficient and capable as professional managers. The latter usually have received better education with more experience in the industry. Some scholars[13] think that the employment of professional managers is a rational choice for

---

[9] Berle, A., & Means, G. (1932). The Modern Corporate and Private Property. McMillian, New York, NY.

[10] Anderson, R. C., & Reeb, D. M. (2003). Founding-family Ownership and Firm Performance: Evidence from the S&P 500. *The Journal of Finance*, 58(3), 1301–1328.

[11] Demsetz, H., & Lehn, K. (1985). The Structure of Corporate Ownership: Causes and Consequences. *Journal of Political Economy*, 93(6), 1155–1177.

[12] Astrachan, J. H., Klein, S. B., & Smyrnios, K. X. (2002). The F-PEC Scale of Family Influence: A Proposal for Solving the Family Business Definition Problem. *Family Business Review*, 15(1), 45–58.

[13] Dyer, W. G. (1986). Cultural Change in Family Firms. Jossey-Bass.

family businesses to solve the problems of nepotism and family conflicts. Generally professional managers are formally trained and well educated, and they can bring new management norms and strategies to promote the development and expansion of businesses. Compared with those who inherit their father's business, professional managers are disposed to act objectively and rationally. Researches show that professional managers usually have good command of management skills, which is conducive to achieving better financial performance. Bertrand and Schoara[14] deem that the performance of family inheritors is not as good as that of external professionals due to the destructive effect of nepotism. On the other hand, Caselli and Gennaiolib[15] believe the reason is that meritocracy has not been effectively implemented by family businesses. Figure 8.1 shows the pros and cons of family CEO and professional CEO.[16]

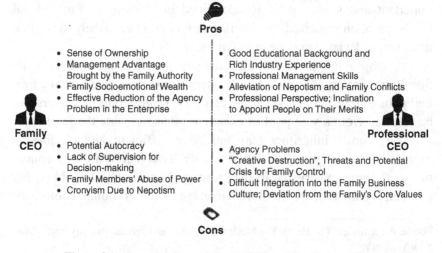

Figure 8.1   Pros and Cons of Family CEO and Professional CEO

[14] Bertrand, M., & Schoar, A. (2006). The Role of Family in Family Firms. *The Journal of Economic Perspectives*, 20(2), 73–96.

[15] Caselli, F., & Gennaioli, N. (2013). Dynastic Management. *Economic Inquiry*, 51(1), 971–996.

[16] Lee, Siew Kim Jean (2015). The "Silver-spoon Generation", No Longer Be the Main Force for Inheritance. *Harvard Business Review* (Chinese Version), 7–8, 110–112.

More Professional CEOs Are Needed in the Future

In the previous research[17], I have found that the vast majority of the founding generation expect their companies to be passed on, with only 5% of them accepting shareholding reduction, transfer or closure of the corporation after retirement when there exist no competent heirs. Nevertheless, not all or the majority of them expressed the wish that businesses should be inherited by the second generation; a little more than half of them (55%) said they would consider having professional managers take over the family business. This trend coincides with the family business survey of Forbes in 2014[18]. According to the data, more than 400 of the 747 family companies listed on the A-share market in China have brought in the second generation, numbering 700-odd people; the second generation serving as executives or board members account for 56% of all second generation members, and 41% hold shares but do not have any positions; another 3% work as lower-level employees and do not hold shares. More than half (54.4%) of family firms have family members serving as CEOs, while the remaining 45.6% hire professional managers. It can be seen that the proportion of professional managers who take over family businesses has been on the increase, and their number is almost equivalent to that of family members. Professional managers have become a new tendency and emerging force for the inheritance of family management rights.

The first generation entrepreneurs who wish to see their businesses succeeded by their offspring all believe that the second generation should inherit the equity. However, nearly two-thirds (62%) of them have a more flexible attitude when they were asked if they think the heirs should inherit and exercise management rights at the same time. If the second generation serves as major shareholders and therefore has ownership of the firm, then it is ok if they employ professional managers to administrate the enterprise. If the corporation encounters a major crisis or the professional manager is incompetent, the second generation will personally

---

[17] Lee, Siew Kim Jean, Rui Meng, Lu Yunting, Cui Zhiyu. (2014). White Paper on the Inheritance of Chinese Family Business: The Willingness and Promise of the Successor. CEIBS Center for Family Heritage.

[18] Mao, Jingjing. (2014). Solving the Deadlock of Inheritance: An Investigation Report of Family Businesses. *Forbes* (Chinese version), 9, 50–57.

manage the company. This is another indicator that, on the whole, the founding generation has no clear preferences over who inherit the family business — family members or professional managers.

Entrepreneurs of different age groups hold differing views on who will take over the business. The older generation is more persistent on the heritage of the second generation; business founders of the younger generation (those under 50) are more open-minded as to who will manage the company in the future. Similarly, they also take a more open attitude on whether the second generation should exercise management rights (see Figure 8.2). A clear majority of them think that the second generation may not have to exercise management rights and may run the firm depending on the actual situation or simply act as a shareholder to control the ownership.

Furthermore, the higher the education level of the entrepreneurial generation, the more open their attitude is towards whether the second generation should exercise management rights. In the case of a good educational background, the proportion of the founding generation considering that the second generation should exercise management rights is far lower than the proportion that maintains the idea that the second generation should inherit the equity (see Figure 8.3).

Based on what we have just discussed, we may conclude that in the next decade, as the first generation entrepreneurs reach retirement age, the main force to inherit family businesses will still be the second generation. Meanwhile, however, we will also find that, over time, when the younger

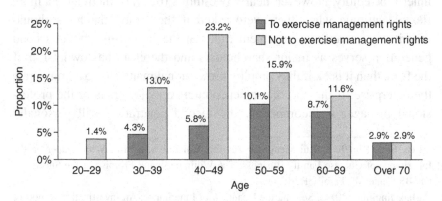

Figure 8.2   The Influence of the Age of the First Generation on the Way of Succession

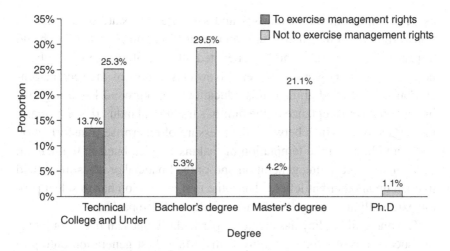

Figure 8.3 The Influence of Academic Degree of the First Generation on the Way of Succession

and better educated first generation gradually approaches the peak of business succession, they may be more inclined to allow the succeeding generation to inherit equity but not management rights, and by then, it will be an irresistible trend for professional managers to run family firms.

Concerns of the Second Generation

Chinese family businesses have just reached its first peak period of succession. The second generation is still the first-choice for the inheritance, but the vast majority of them have just come onto the stage. Due to China's one-child policy, the number of successors is limited. If future successors are selected only from within the family, then qualified candidates are extremely limited.

Likewise, as possibly the only candidate in the family, how will the second generation person handle the conflict between family mission and their own interests? When considering inheritance, the second generation often has three major concerns: Firstly, the senior employees who followed his parents in building up the business are still working in the company, then how will the young successor convince them and win their trust? Secondly, his parents' enterprise is almost in existence for as long as he is, and both the businesses and staff are in a state of decline, so transformation of the enterprise is an urgent task. Thirdly, what will he do to persuade his parents who have devoted all their life to the family business to delegate power completely? Nowadays, most of the second generation have studied abroad; this educational background has a negative impact on their acceptance of the family's traditional industries, especially in the face of conflicts between the pressure of enterprise transformation and upgrading and the temptation of making a quick buck in the market. Many in the succeeding generation opt for the financial or investment field to open up another battlefield. Thus, the first generation has to select people externally to manage the family's industrial companies.

The one-child policy has created a particularly unusual background for the succession of Chinese family firms. Many first generation entrepreneurs worry that their only child will be unable to take over the business due to a lack of interest or ability. If that is the case, then the painstaking efforts of building up a firm for many years may come to naught. At present, since the number of family heirs is limited, the first generation is bound to take into consideration their child's interests, willingness, and abilities, and weigh the dual issues of enterprise development and family inheritance. Instead of having the descendants take over the business against their will, it is better to contemplate how to bring in external talents to strengthen the company's management team. Therefore, the first generation entrepreneurs who are not that old need to ponder over and learn how to cultivate and find suitable professional CEOs for their own firms. These professionals should not only ensure the firm's growth, but also stabilize family control. That is to say, they can balance the relationship between the two in order to achieve everlasting development of family businesses.

The continued development of family firms does not necessarily mean the second generation are meant to inherit both management rights and ownership. It is also a wise choice to train them to be good shareholders. Hence, the selection and cultivation of professional CEOs are especially important to the succession of family businesses. Will future professional managers be willing to enter family firms? How will family firms attract professional CEOs who are compatible with them? These are important questions that must be answered. How to select and train competent professional managers and how to choose CEOs who can carry on the spirit of family businesses is the biggest challenge for family firms if they want to move towards professional management and transform from "family business" to "business based on family".

Whether it is due to the lack of interests or abilities of the second generation, or the needs of corporate development, the employment of professional managers in family businesses is a trend in future. Nevertheless, employing professional managers is still a delicate option for domestic family companies. The experience and management skills of professional managers may enable corporations to avoid family infighting, but whether professional managers regard family businesses as their own is a matter of concern. Meanwhile, the assessment of professional managers in family businesses is often confined to performance indicators. Even if equity incentives are adopted, professional managers tend to pursue the rapid growth of short-term performance which will effectively damage the long-term development capabilities of the enterprises.

Some family companies are beginning to diversify themselves, or to tap into the international market. In order to meet the demands of corporate expansion, using external talents is an irresistible trend for the development of family businesses. However, it is a very long and complex process for family members to regard "outsiders" as "people of their own circle" and to hand over management rights with a peaceful mind. This not only requires patience, planning, and magnanimity on the part of the business founders, but also tests the ability, morality, and wisdom of professional managers. In China, many entrepreneurs do not start to contemplate enterprise succession until they are in their sixties. By then, if they find that their children's ideals are inconsistent with the family businesses, and there are no qualified candidates in the firm to serve as managers, the succession process will become difficult, hindering the firm's continued development.

Furthermore, if something unexpected happens to the business founders, such as death, becoming incapacitated, or having an accident, the hasty succession will inevitably have a negative impact on the development of family businesses. A large number of researchers have discovered that the lack of succession planning is one of the prime reasons for the fall of many first-generation family businesses. Numerous heirs born in the

1980s have to face this difficult problem. For example, after the accidental death of Ruan Jiagen, the former chairman of Zhejiang Runtu Co., Ltd., his only daughter Ruan Jingbo, 27, was appointed as the new chairperson, becoming the youngest chairwoman of the Chinese A-share listed company overnight. In the absence of a well-thought-out plan, if the founder meets with an accident, it is easy for the family to lose ownership and management rights. Moreover, a fierce struggle and conflict may be triggered by the inheritance, leading to the disintegration of the business. For instance, after the accidental death of Li Haicang, founder of Shanxi Haixin Steel Group Co., Ltd., his son Li Zhaohui touched off a family strife in the process of inheritance. The steel kingdom of yore founded by Li Haicang has currently collapsed, which is rather distressing.

Alternative Succession Path

At the moment Chinese family businesses are caught in a dilemma: Namely, "the silver-spoon generation" may lack strong willingness or abilities to take over the business, and the qualities and motivation of professional managers can hardly meet the requirements of "the founding generation". This shortage of satisfactory successors is likely to last for some time. It is hoped that with the accumulation of both time and experience, Chinese family businesses can gradually find a way out in terms of inheritance.

Apart from constantly summing up experience at home, we can also use the experience of other countries for reference.

Path I: Nurturing Successors in the Family

When it comes to selecting successors in the family, we have summarized three ways: First, the traditional father-son succession, as happened in Huamao Group; second, the succession involving father and son creating a new business, as happened in Fotile; third, joint management succession, i.e., an experienced professional CEO and the second generation successor work together to run the business, as happened in the New Hope Group. Through our research, we find that family values and family relationships often play a pivotal role on the willingness of the second generation to take over the business. In other words, if the founding generation expects the second generation to inherit the family business, it is essential to cultivate core family values and maintain harmonious family relations, which should be done when the legal heir is in his childhood. Specifically, they include the following points:

- Foster clear and attractive family goals and directions;
- Increase family gatherings and communication to enjoy good times among family members;
- Create a family atmosphere of openness, trust, and communication;
- Share common visions and goals and work together;
- Share and respect family history and traditions;
- Participate in family-based charity and assume social responsibilities;
- Find a reliable mentor for the second generation successor;
- Set up a family committee and invite respected elders to provide advice to the family.

Path II: Towards Professional Management

As for the second generation who are reluctant to take over the business, the first generation need to plan for the selection and training of successors as early as possible. One method is to either shut down or sell the family firm, and pass on the wealth to the second generation who start up a new business to suit their own interests. Although this practice is not regarded as the family business succession in the traditional sense, family wealth is inherited within the family. Another method is to give equity to the second generation, but let professional managers take over management rights, as in the case of Midea. Midea has built a structure of "owner, board of directors, and management" that functions separately, and other Chinese private enterprises can draw from its experience.

When a family firm decides to recruit a professional CEO, it takes time and patience for the business founder to systematically train the CEO. A professional CEO selected from within the firm is superior to a professional CEO recruited externally because the latter will often find it difficult to integrate into the family business. A senior manager who has worked in the enterprise for years has a better understanding of the various stages of corporate development and its characteristics, which is inductive to internal collaborative management. Meanwhile the internally selected professional CEO has a clearer understanding of his role in the firm as he and the first generation entrepreneur have worked together for many years. Therefore, he can effectively balance the relationship between the firm and the family. Specifically, they include the following points:

• Foster professional managers who share common visions and values with the business founder;
• Establish a de-familization corporate culture;
• Develop clear business decision-making rules and transparent financial management plans;
• Formulate plans for enterprise development and diversification;
• Clarify the distribution of corporate dividends and resources;
• Set the roles, rights, and obligations of each member in order to ensure fair treatment for everyone;
• Ensure the simultaneous growth of talents and enterprise through effective material and spiritual incentives schemes;
• Set up a board of directors which can effectively balance the interests of family, enterprise, and the society, and steer the long-term corporate development to the right direction;
• Make a strategic plan for family wealth and enterprise development.

Succession Planning

No matter which path they opt to complete inheritance of the enterprise and the family wealth, the founding generation must be prepared well in advance. On one hand, China's current law enforcement (established rules) is not forceful enough to deter and punish immoral or illegal acts committed by non-family executives; and the level of public credit (informal system) is relatively low, meaning that leaders of family firms find it hard to have total trust in professional CEOs. Additionally, the shortage of managerial talents in China has constrained these entrepreneurs. On the other hand, non-family executives frequently complain about the lack of trust or excessive expectations from family business owners. They assert that if they wanted to be an entrepreneur like their boss, they would have started up their own business in the first place. They feel that the boundary of work and life should be clearly defined and the two should be balanced. Therefore, in the next decade, the main force that will inherit family businesses may still be the second generation.

However, with the shift of the times, the continuous development of the economy, the sophistication of the talent market, and the need for internationalization, family firms may be more inclined to let the second generation succeed to equity as shareholders and directors, rather than business managers. By then, it will be the trend for qualified and talented professional managers to administer family corporations.

It seems a sure thing that professionalized management of family businesses is a future development tendency. But given the current training and constraints on professional managers at home, and a lack of good incentives schemes, there is still a long way to go before suitably competent professionals can be found to take over the business.

First of all, business founders must be mentally prepared for the succession. They need to work out a systematic plan early; they should not wait until the last minute to think about and select their successors; they should start at least 10 years earlier to develop the future successor to the family business, just like what Midea did. Fostering successors is a relatively long process as future successors must be fully prepared to take over the power to run the business. Family business founders should train the prospective successor in accordance with a proper plan and later strengthen their abilities in practices.

Next, training successors (no matter they are descendants of the family or professional managers) requires time and patience. A professional CEO selected from within the firm is superior to a professional CEO recruited from outside. This is because first a senior manager who has worked in the enterprise for years has a better understanding of the various stages of corporate development and its characteristics, which is inductive to internal collaborative management. Secondly, finding a competent and talented candidate from within the corporation is conducive to the establishment of professional manager's loyalty and enterprise prestige. Thirdly, the internally selected professional CEO has a clearer understanding of his role in the firm as he and the first generation entrepreneur have worked together for many years. Therefore, he can effectively balance the relationship between the business and the family.

Then, we should absolutely build a professionalized management system and corporate culture. He Xiangjian, founder of Midea, proposed a system of delegation of power featuring "methodical centralization of power, orderly separation of power, rule-based delegation of power, and moderate use of power", which can serve as a reference. Such a system is beneficial to the development of professional managers in the family firm. Of course, effective material and spiritual incentive mechanism are fundamental to ensure the simultaneous growth of talents and enterprises.

Finally, the establishment of a board of directors can effectively balance the interests of family, corporation, and the society, which is necessary for enterprise development, because it can steer the firm's long-term development in the right direction.

In the next chapter, we will describe in detail how succession was carried out in Midea from the founder to the professional manager, so as to explain a few questions: How the first generation get ready for the inheritance, how professional managers succeed to the family business and how they can find the right position in family corporations?

9

Succession of Professional Managers

Most of the first generation entrepreneurs prefer to pass on the family business to their children when it comes to succession. But Midea is different. He Xiangjian, the founder of Midea, after years of hard work in the business domain, handed over the group's management right to Fang Hongbo, a professional manager who had followed him for many years. This decision was not a surprise. He Jianfeng, his only son, finally returned to Midea to serve on the board of directors after staying away from the group for many years. Midea's approach is not a common practice in China. After all, the professional manager has no blood ties with the founder, and the difficulties and challenges they faced in the process of taking over are no less than those faced by succession between father and son. The succession in Midea was not an impulsive decision by He Xiangjian, of course. Before the succession took place, He Xiangjian spent many years implementing the Management Buy-Out (MBO) restructuring of the group to make Midea a listed company. He had also improved the enterprise management system and did his best to develop future successors from within the group. More importantly, he gave his son total freedom to develop his abilities and gain experience by working outside the family business. When He Jianfeng eventually returned to Midea, he was as good a director as anyone else. While the family wealth was guaranteed, the enterprise was under the charge of Fang Hongbo, an experienced manager loyal to the family. Therefore, He Xiangjian could enjoy his life after retirement without worries. For Fang Hongbo, from the day he took over the group, he became the center of attention and was under mounting pressure. Everyone was concerned about the development direction of Midea. I waited eagerly to see what Fang Hongbo would do to balance the relationships and continue to develop his own team after He Jianfeng, the second generation of the family, took over the group as a shareholder. How to give incentives to professional managers and whether they will have a share of the family's equity remain great challenges for Midea in the future. The succession story began when He Xiangjian announced that he would step down from the chairman of the board.

The Founder of Midea, He Xiangjian

He Xiangjian is the founder of Midea. Born in 1942, he dropped out after graduating from primary school. He worked as an apprentice, a worker, and a cashier. In 1968, he led some neighborhood residents in raising money to set up a production team to produce vials for medicine and plastic caps. Later, the team made components for enterprises. Traveling extensively in search of markets strengthened He Xiangjian's business sense. In 1980 not long after China launched the reform and opening up policy, he began to produce fan spare parts for a state-owned electrical appliance factory. In the same year he applied what he had learned into practice and started producing his own brand of electric fans. In 1981, He Xiangjian officially registered the trademark Midea and became the director of a factory with more than 250 employees. In 1986, the electric fans produced by the factory were exported to Hong Kong. In 1985, the factory introduced advanced technology from Japan and started to produce window air conditioners. In 1993, Midea Electric Appliances received approval to go public, becoming China's first township enterprise to be listed on the stock market. From 1990 to 1994, Midea ranked third in air conditioning sales in the industry at home.

On August 25, 2012, He Xiangjian, Midea's 70-year-old founder and chairman, announced that he would retire from his post as chairman and take his position in the holding company behind the scenes. This was the second time he stepped down from a chairmanship position following his resignation as chairman of Midea Electric Appliances in 2009. Midea Group is a home appliance giant built up by He Xiangjian through hard work over several decades. In addition to a listed company, Midea Group also owns small household appliances, electrical machinery and logistics businesses. He Xiangjian's successor was Fang Hongbo, a 45-year-old professional manager and former chairman and CEO of Midea Electric Appliances. When he took over the position as the Group's chairman, Fang Hongbo faced a lot of challenges. On the one hand, the company's sales were on the decline, and a business transformation was an urgent requirement. But Fang Hongbo did not know whether he would win the trust and support of the senior employees. Moreover, the Group was overstaffed and it was very difficult for him to implement his strategy to improve the Group's performance. Although his mentor He Xiangjian regarded him highly and had full confidence in him, he knew that the Chinese tradition of passing the family business from father to son would be more acceptable to family members and senior employees, since Mr. He has three children.

From the time when Fang Hongbo learned that he would take over Midea, he had been thinking about how to play his role in the Group. This time the responsibility was much heavier than when he assumed the chairmanship of Midea Electric Appliances three years ago. He knew that he had to sort everything out orderly: Although he would spare no effort to dedicate to the future of Midea, the outcome might be rather counterproductive if he could not win over the trust and support of his colleagues. He was worried that he could not live up to the expectations of He Xiangjian and his colleagues. Thinking of this, he could not help contemplating, "Perhaps only real performance can convince other people; however, we must change our business model to adapt to the Internet era. Changing a company's strategy will surely cause newer problems. Under the dual pressure of 'introducing reforms' and 'keeping the staff stable', how shall I lead Midea to a new future?"

Delegating Power to Business Divisions and Training Managers

In the 1990s, household appliances enterprises entered an era of fierce competition when price wars were frequent in the industry. All parties tried to eliminate their competitors by winning as many market shares as possible through lowering prices, and almost all enterprises in the industry were losing money. In 1996, the sales ranking of Midea air conditioners dropped to the seventh place and the annual output value of the enterprise declined sharply from 2.5 billion yuan to 2 billion yuan. That year's profits mainly came from some of the investment returns. It was widely rumored that the government intended to let Kelon merge with Midea, and the brand of Midea was in serious jeopardy.

He Xiangjian believed that the reason why Midea was heading downward in the fierce competition was that the company suffered from "big company disease". Midea already had five production lines including air conditions, fans, rice cookers, etc., with a total of over a hundred products. The decision about the operation of these production lines was centralized in the headquarters of the group. Because of the large variety of products, both the sales staff and the functional departments of the headquarters needed to be responsible for multiple products. Therefore, the focus of their work was not clear. Meanwhile, as He Xiangjian himself had to pay attention to both sales and production due to the centralized decision-making policy, he was unable to meet the growing demand for the ever increasing product categories. Huang Xiaoming, the former senior vice president of Midea, commented, "In those days, there were more than 10,000 people in the company, and all the departments reported to the boss. Mr. He had endless documents to read and endless signatures to sign every day."

In 1997, He Xiangjian decided to introduce the business division system to Midea and set up five business divisions: Air conditioning, household appliances, compressors, motors, and kitchen utensils, which would be responsible for manufacturing and sales, while the functions of the headquarters would only focus on overall strategic decision-making and control. Business transactions between business divisions adopted a market-oriented mode of operation. At the same time, the company appointed professional managers to take on the important tasks in those units. At this point, Fang Hongbo became the general manager of the air conditioning division of Midea, responsible for domestic sales. In order to clearly define the powers and responsibilities of professional managers, Midea issued *Division of Power Manual*. The headquarters would only be responsible for finance, budget, investment, and management of senior professional managers. The business divisions would be highly autonomous; they could set up their own teams, and manage R D, production, sales, and other processes of the industrial chain independently, with independent right on human resources. He Xiangjian once said, "As long as the incentive mechanism, decentralization mechanism, and accountability mechanism are well established, outstanding people will emerge to help us run the business."

Taking the chance of the organizational restructure and business decentralization, He Xiangjian persuaded some of Midea's founding members to retire and deliberately weakened his family's influence on the company, including asking his wife, one of the 23 founding members, to retire. After the establishment of the business divisions system, He Xiangjian himself also withdrew from the management of daily business activities. While the elders withdrew from the front line of business, young managers came to the forefront. However, the talents market of professional managers had not yet formed in China at a time when the country had just stepped out of the era of planned economy. Nearly all professional managers of Midea were trained internally a few years before, and they became experienced with the development of Midea. Huang Zhiguo, dean of the Midea College and Director of Talent Development, once said, "The reform that brought to Midea the business divisions system in 1997 was an extremely important historical turning point for Midea. On the one hand, the company was divided into several major business divisions, realizing the specialization of management and operation under the background of product diversification, saving the boss from having to deal with daily trifles; on the other hand, a group of elders retired from the front line of operation, and young managers took over their positions. Fang Hongbo was appointed at that time."

Since the establishment of the business divisions in 1997, the organizational structure of Midea was constantly being readjusted. Each time, the reform was related to centralizing and decentralizing power, but they always followed the principles of "methodical centralization of power, orderly separation of power, rule-based delegation of power, and moderate use of power".

Fang Hongbo's Experience in Midea

At a time when Midea was in trouble in 1997, He Xiangjian appointed Fang Hongbo as chairman to be in charge of Midea's most important air conditioning sales business in China. It was a controversial arrangement, but He Xiangjian overrode all objections. In 1992, the 25-year-old Fang Hongbo joined Midea as an editor of an internal newsletter and served in the Office of the President. He Xiangjian was much impressed by his ability. During Fang Hongbo's five years in Midea, he was promoted to the Deputy Chief and then Chief of Public Relations, Advertising Manager, and Marketing Manager. It was him who created the popular advertising slogan "Midea Creates a Better Life" in 1995, and invited the movie star Gong Li to serve as Midea's representative, which popularized the brand to the public. "Although I did not know whether He Xiangjian nurtured someone else, I could tell that he was doing his best to nurture me. He often asked me to go to his office, and he would take out a small piece of paper which he used to take down his daily notes. He would then talk to me at length about when and where I made an inappropriate statement or spoke impulsively." Knowing that he was highly regarded by his boss, Fang Hongbo was determined to devote himself to Midea.

Soon after he took office, Fang Hongbo paid visits to select customers. But he got the cold shoulder because his products did not meet the needs of the customers. In order to be more customer-oriented, Fang Hongbo proposed to "change sales into marketing and make manufacturing satisfy customers' demand". He also suggested to He Xiangjian that the sales channels should be flattened, which meant that they would go directly to the quality customers instead of going through marketing agents.

The Chinese market was based on the mainstream idea that sales were determined by products. After Fang Hongbo's proposals were approved by He Xiangjian, Midea air conditioners quickly got out of the predicament, and its market position rose rapidly. In the second year after Fang Hongbo took office, sales of Midea air conditioners rose to the top three, reaching 900,000 units with a growth rate of 200%. This re-established Midea's status as a top brand in the air conditioning industry. He Xiangjian once said to Fang Hongbo, "Knowing that I selected the right person makes me happier than seeing the increase in sales of our products."[1]

After winning his first victory, Fang Hongbo made another great stride. In 2000, by virtue of his outstanding performance, he became the general manager of the Air Conditioning Business Division of Midea. The Air Conditioning Business Division was the largest of the six major divisions in Midea, accounting for almost 60% of the group's sales that year. Fang Hongbo was therefore known as Midea's most powerful man from outside the He family.[2] After that, he was promoted several times because of his excellent work.

Numerous Midea

Before 2000, a fierce price war was under way. In order to achieve economies of scale, almost all household appliances manufacturers adopted the strategy of rapid expansion. Midea also actively carried out mergers and acquisitions. Almost all household electrical appliances enterprises claimed to "build the country's and even the world's largest production line and continue to hold the banner of diversification high, and to expand to other unrelated industries through capital operation." Fang Hongbo recalled, "In 2004, we did not produce fridges and washing machines, but in five years' time, Midea became the only company that could rival Haier in this field."

With the vertical development and horizontal expansion, Midea's organizational structure became more and more complex. In 2004, the group added a new level — secondary groups — to the structure. As the business became more and more complex, the previous business division structure was considered to be the cause of repeated investment and fragmentation. At that time, He Xiangjian aimed to make Midea an "investment holding group"; his ideas were to strengthen the secondary

---

[1] Zan, Huifang. (2014). An Exclusive Interview with Fang Hongbo: How to Make the Succession and Transformation of Midea Successful. *Chinese Entrepreneur*, 7.

[2] Luo, Tianhao. (2009). Fang Hongbo: How Was a Close Subordinate of the President Appointed to the Highest Position in a Business Division. *Insight China*, October 22.

groups' management and control over business divisions, while transferring some powers of business divisions to the secondary groups. Secondary groups were established on the same ideas that sustained the existence of business divisions system, i.e., professionalization of management and operation of various industries. The new structure manifested improved efficiency through the co-ordination of resources and provided a better platform for the best of the former general managers of the business divisions to play their abilities to the full. Yet, in this process the group structure became more complex. According to the analysis of a senior executives of Midea, "Establishment of the secondary groups simply changed the hitherto operations by separate teams into group operations."

Since then, Midea had formed a four-tier structure comprised of Midea Group, secondary groups (including the listed company Midea Electric Appliances), business divisions, and product companies. Each level had its own operational management, financial management, asset management, and brand management departments. Under the secondary groups were a total of nearly 25 business divisions, all operating independently and signing contracts independently. There was a saying in Midea, "Before coming here, we saw one Midea; however, we found numerous Midea after our entry."

This structure reflected He Xiangjian's philosophy of balancing. He himself served as chairman of the group. Horizontally, He could check and balance the secondary groups; vertically, organizations in the four-level structure could check and balance each other. This philosophy ensured that no one was predominant. The disadvantage was that it gave life to many subcultures that rivaled each other, and the situation worsened with the passage of time.

The First Step of Succession: Midea Electric Appliances

Rumors of the Son Succeeding to the Family Business in 2004

At the end of 2004, there were rumors about the change of the board of directors of Midea Electric Appliances. It was said that He Jianfeng, the son of He Xiangjian, was expected to enter the board of directors in the near future. All rumors ended when He Xiangjian announced the group structure adjustment plan at the group staff meeting on December 25. Midea would divide all industries into two secondary groups: Household Electric Appliances Group and Refrigeration Electric Appliances Group to be headed by Zhang Hechuan and Fang Hongbo respectively. Given the Chinese cultural tradition of "passing on the power from father to son," this move quickly triggered speculation about the real intention. Although the decision gave Zhang and Fang more real power, it could be a move aimed at separating Midea's "family ownership" from "elite management right" and He Jianfeng would very likely assume the chairman of Midea's board of directors. This time, He Xiangjian was paving the way for his son to take over the business at a higher level in the group in the future, rather than in the listed company.[3]

He Xiangjian's Son and Infore Group

He Jianfeng, He Xiangjian's only son, started his own business in 1994, which had always been closely related to Midea. He Jianfeng's enterprise was originally a contract manufacturer for Midea, specializing in the licensing production of small household appliances, and later renamed Infore Group. By 2002, Infore Group had five industrial companies and two trade companies, with more than 5,000 employees. These businesses were considered a platform on which He Xiangjian tested his son's ability. From September 2003, Midea Electric Appliances acquired He Jianfeng's fan business, rice cooker business, kitchen utensils business, and so on, which became the factual basis of the rumors in 2004. Because Chinese laws required board members or executives to avoid same industry competition, which meant that He Jianfeng could not join Midea Electric Appliances' board of directors or management team if he still possessed those businesses.

Moreover, Midea had already put all its business operation under the management of professional managers as early as 1997. If He Jianfeng

---

[3] Su, Dandan. (2015). Conjecture about Midea's Succession Roadmap: He Xiangjian's Imitation after Lenovo. Techweb.com.cn.

wanted to return to Midea, he would work with many senior employees who had contributed a lot to Midea, and his qualifications might not be good enough to win their trust and support. Meanwhile, He Jianfeng did not continue to follow his father's success in manufacturing but turned to the capital market and financial industry.

In September 2008, Infore Group announced that it would officially change its name to Guangdong Infore Investment Holding Group Co., Ltd. in accordance with the company's strategic needs, achieving complete transformation from an industrial company to an investment company. He Xiangjian, He Jianfeng, and He Qianchang (He Xiangjian's eldest daughter) were all major shareholders of Infore Investment. He Qianchang owns Hefei Bainian Molding Technology Co., Ltd. She and her sister He Qianxing (the second daughter of He Xiangjian) were natural person shareholders of Hefei Huitong New Materials Co., Ltd. Both companies were engaged in the upstream industry of Midea. At the same time, He Qianxing was also engaged in the electronic devices industry and once ran Guangdong Xindi Technology Group.

He Xiangjian said earlier, "Midea has never been a family business and does not have to worry about successors. If my son does not want to come back to join Midea, the way out for Midea Electric Appliances in the future may rely on the management of professional managers.[4]" In 2009, He Xiangjian explicitly made the following statement, "Midea's future CEOs will eventually be professional managers. Our family members will just be shareholders."

"Fast Lane" Succession

Things improved greatly in Midea in 2008 from what it was in 2000. Midea's sales revenue in 2000 was less than 10 billion yuan, while in 2008 the figure reached 90 billion yuan. In 2008, after a series of mergers and acquisitions, Midea announced a "new three-year plan" whose objective was to achieve sales revenue of 120 billion yuan in 2010. Since the new

---

[4]Editorial department of this publication. (2012). Taking over the Post to Run Business, Change of the Succession Mode: From "Father to Son" to Employing a Professional Manager. *Business Management Review*, 11.

goal was put forward, Midea began to expand to new fields with new production projects springing up.

By that point, the professional manager culture had prevailed in every corner of the group. Managers in Midea's branches were all professional managers and there was no one from the He family working on the core management positions. On August 26, 2009, He Xiangjian announced his resignation as chairman and director of the board of directors of the listed company Midea Electric Appliances, and Fang Hongbo, former vice chairman of the board of directors and president of Midea Electric Appliances, would assume the position of chairman. He Xiangjian would continue to serve as chairman of the board of directors of Midea Group. With the withdrawal of He Xiangjian, Midea Electric Appliances' board of directors was completely comprised of professional managers, and it was known that Midea entered an "era of professional managers".[5]

Fang Hongbo was not surprised to be chosen to take over the company. As early as ten years before taking over, He Xiangjian said to him, "You need to raise your sights; you will not remain in this position long, because you need to bear greater responsibility." With the passage of time, He altered his remarks, telling him specifically, "I will hand over the power to you in the future." However, He did not say exactly when he would. It was not until 2009 when Fang Hongbo took over the chairmanship of Midea Electric Appliances from He Xiangjian did he realize that He Xiangjian had already made it clear to hundreds of employees at a company meeting, "Our company will be put under the charge of professional managers in the future. Midea will not become a family business."

At the time of the handing over of power, Midea Group was at its peak in development. Guided by the concept of "the bigger the size the better", Midea joined the "100-billion-yuan club" in 2010, with sales revenues exceeding the 100-billion-yuan mark. The beautiful financial results so encouraged the 68-year-old He Xiangjian that he proposed a new five-year plan to "re-create a Midea", with a sales revenue goal of 200 billion yuan by 2015. At that time, the size of the Refrigeration Group increased

---

[5]Tang, Ming. (2012). The New Leader of Midea: Entering the New Era of Professional Managers. www.cnr.cn, August 26.

by 90% in the first quarter of 2011 compared with the same period the previous year; the Home Appliances Group increased by 60% and the Mechanical and Electrical Group increased by 50% compared with the same period the previous year. "We thought that we didn't have to wait until 2015 before we can achieve the 200-billion-yuan target," recalled one executive.

Fluctuation in Sales and Seeking for Transformation

Expansion Blocked

At the end of the second quarter of 2011, the optimistic expectations of the previous year did not turn into reality. The financial returns of Midea fell sharply. Sales of electrical appliances increased by 59% in the first half of the year, but net profit increased by only 13.7% compared with the same period of 2010, which meant that costs increased too fast. Analysis indicated that the market was not expanded significantly. The growth was the combined result of rapidly increased scale, overstock at sales channels, and price reduction, stimulated by the ambitious goal of 200 billion yuan. Over the previous years, Midea adopted a low-cost strategy, but its products were not the best on the market and its profit margin was not big. Its impressive sales figures came largely from huge stock and the ability to replenish stock promptly. In the absence of explosive growth in the market coupled with the company's pursuit of an overly ambitious sales goal, there was overstock at sales channels. In its attempt to increase the size of business rapidly, Midea established many production lines to manufacture small household appliances. The research and production of such products were inexpensive, but some of the finished products had no competitive edge, and others were already operating at a loss. On top of that, the complex structure of the group made internal resources sharing difficult, leading to low operation efficiency.

Midea Electric Appliances Leads Transformation

In Midea Group, the listed company Midea Electric Appliances led by Fang Hongbo was among the first to undergo transformation. In the second half of 2011, Fang Hongbo, the chairman and CEO of Midea Electric Appliances, proposed the "top-quality project", which emphasized the originality and quality of its products in order to increase profit margins and product image. In the past, however, the idea was to cut costs and fight a price war until competitors were "wiped out". This strategy ran counter to the new strategy of paying special attention to improve the overall ability to manufacture quality goods, and the management found it hard to change their mindset. They still stuck to the old familiar approach in their work, making it difficult for the new strategy to be carried out. For example, the old strategy was to keep suppliers' prices as low as possible, build factories everywhere, buy equipment, and expand production capacity, while the new strategy emphasized quality awareness, careful selection of best raw materials, large investments in research and development technology, and the introduction of high-end talent.

As the chairman and CEO of Midea Electric Appliances, Fang Hongbo already had enough power to downsize the company. In the first half of 2012, Midea reduced its electrical product models from 22,000 to 15,000, eliminating products that relied solely on low-cost competition with small profit margins. Fang Hongbo said, "We have to do this. If we do not downscale, we will lose everything." In 2010, the total number of employees in the company was 98,676. By 2011, there were only 66,497. As many as 32,708 employees were laid off, of which 32,317 were from posts in production.

Streamlining was not limited to the production line. In the integration of sales channels, Midea also acted aggressively. In the past, Midea had its agents in every county when the expansion was at its peak. After the ending of Appliances to the Countryside policy[6], both Midea and the agents could not make profits, and there was huge redundancy of agents. Hence, Midea begun to integrate the channels. One agent would be in charge of five big counties or a dozen small counties.

In internal management, the company used to assess the management by sales and profits, with sales as the most important indicator but no

---

[6] From the end of 2008 to the end of 2011, China allocated subsidies for domestic sales of household appliances enterprises whose export declined because of the global financial crisis.

quantitative requirement for profit margins. This meant that although the company was large, it did not create value for shareholders. From 2012, the group demanded that remuneration increase should not surpass profit increase, an attempt to raise profit margins. In operation, the group needed to develop products with high gross margin, reduce product models, improve internal management, and increase the output of per-unit input. This meant that some orders that created low gross margin but entailed higher risks had to be abandoned, something that had been considered "intolerable" by management in the past.

With the efforts in the second half of 2011, although the contraction strategy led to a decline of year-on-year revenue growth rate from 57.7% to 24.9%, the operating profit increased by 96%.

The Second Step of Succession: Midea Group

This massive overhaul was known to and permitted by He Xiangjian. As the chairman and CEO of Midea Electric Appliances, Fang Hongbo was the actual implementer of the transition. Although Midea consisted of separate divisions of business with different corporate sub-cultures, they always shared the same values in the Group's attempt to dominate the market. The problem disturbing Midea was that the overall strategy of the group did not adapt to the new circumstances. However, Fang Hongbo did not have the authorization to carry out similar reform in other business divisions beyond his jurisdiction.

Fang Hongbo was worried that if no drastic measure was taken to reduce the size of Midea, the group would continue on the path of willful expansion that would lead to disastrous consequences. However, job cutting, change of suppliers, reorganizing channels, and adjusting product strategy involved all aspects in and outside the group. Midea was in urgent need of someone who was not afraid to slam on the brakes as the "car" was speeding down the highway. To take up the important task of reinventing Midea, this person must have great courage and determination. He must have the prestige and influence and could stabilize the overall situation after the reinvention. Given these requirements, He Xiangjian was an ideal leader to implement the reform. However, Fang Hongbo knew that people who would be among the first to be laid off were the senior employees, and this would certainly embarrass He Xiangjian.

Transition from the Old to the New

In the summer of 2012, before the time when management executives took their usual leave, the 70-year-old He Xiangjian told Fang Hongbo that he was ready to retire, saying that he wanted to withdraw from the group completely, not even serving as a member of the board of directors. Before that, he met a few top executives of Midea and asked them about their opinions of Fang Hongbo, his intentions being obvious to them all. On August 25, 2012, He Xiangjian told Fang Hongbo clearly that he would make Fang chairman of Midea Group, who would be in charge of all the Group's businesses except for Midea Electric Appliances.

He Xiangjian said in his farewell speech, "Midea is a large international group. A person without enough energy and ability cannot run the group well. Therefore, my responsibility to the enterprise requires me to hand over the management right to a professional manager with more energy and more internationalized management expertise. If I remain the chairman of the group, professional managers would not be able to fulfil their full potential to their abilities. Therefore, I am stepping down to make way for professional managers who can run the company in accordance with their thinking. I am not really retiring, I will work in the Midea Holding Company and devote more energy to strategic research." At the farewell meeting, he also made clear his principle in relation to Midea's affairs, "I will no longer ask about operation of the company, and I will not be involved in the affairs of the company, and I will no longer attend company meetings."[7]

The new members of the board of directors of Midea were Fang Hongbo, Huang Jian, Cai Qiwu, Yuan Liqun, Huang Xiaoming, Li Jianwei, He Jianfeng (son of He Xiangjian), Chen Jinsong (Managing Director of ICBC International's Investment Banking Division), Hu Xiaoling (Managing Director of CDH Investments Fund Management Company), and Li Feide. With the exception of He Jianfeng (who entered Midea for the first time), Chen Jinsong, and Hu Xiaoling, the other seven members joined Midea in the 1990s. They are of about the same age, serving the company for an average of 15–20 years, all promoted by He Xiangjian.

---

[7]Yu, Hua. (2012). The Handover of the Founder He Xiangjian, Midea Has Entered an Era of Professional Managers. *IT Times Weekly,* 9.

He Xiangjian commented, "It is unwise to solely rely on one person for the development of an enterprise. Failure is inevitable if we put the steady and sustainable development of an enterprise on the boss, on relationships, or on material incentives."[8] According to a former executive of Midea, He Xiangjian spent more than ten years observing and examining outstanding professional managers, letting the leaders of various business divisions compete against each other like a "horse race" in order to select the right successor for the business.[9]

Capital Operation of the Group Before Going Public

Before handing the group over to Fang Hongbo, He Xiangjian was planning the overall listing of the group. From November 2011, a number of PE (private equity) institutions bought shares from Midea Holdings, with CDH holding 7.82% and Zhuhai Rongrui and related parties holding 13.33% of Midea shares. A PE institution cannot withdraw and get their returns until the company it invested in is listed or acquired by another one. Therefore, these events were considered to be the prelude to the overall listing of Midea.

On August 24, 2012, the day before the announcement that Fang Hongbo would become the new chairman of Midea, Midea Electric Appliances released its semi-annual report. On August 27, Midea Electric Appliances halted the stock trading, preparing for the overall listing of the group. The new listed company would include the small home appliances business, motor business, and logistics business which were part of the Midea Group but which were not included in the previously listed company Midea Electric Appliances.

Since the day Fang Hongbo became the chairman of the group, he took up the task of reducing staff, increasing efficiency, and planning for transformation. He must also plan the overall listing strategy of the group as soon as possible. On July 30, 2013, a share swap to absorb the merger of Midea Electric Appliances was approved by the China Securities

---

[8] Feng, Yue. (2011). Midea's Mechanism of Professional Managers. *Enterprise Management*, 9.

[9] Chen, Xinyan, Feng Ye. (2012). Midea's Handover of Leadership. *Southern Weekly*, September 19.

Regulatory Commission (CSRC). On September 18, 2013, Midea Electric Appliances was delisted and undertaken by Midea Group. According to the annual revenue ranking, Midea would overtake its competitors Qingdao Haier and Gree Electric Appliances to become the largest household appliances to go public in A shares.

He Xiangjian left Midea Group but remain in Midea Holdings. Founded on August 5, 2002, the registered capital of Midea Holdings was 330 million yuan, with only two natural shareholders: He Xiangjian held 94.55%, and his daughter-in-law Lu Deyan held the remaining shares. The holding was 100% controlled by the He family. He Xiangjian was the executive director of Midea Holdings, his wife Liang Fengchai was the supervisor, and Li Jianwei was the manager. Under Midea Holdings are Midea Group, Midea Real Estate and other secondary industrial groups. In October 2011, Midea Holdings held 84% of the shares of Midea Group, with the figure falling to 59.85% by June 30, 2012. After Midea Group went public, Midea Holdings and Ningbo Kailian Industry and Commerce Development Company together held more than 1/3 of the shares in Midea Group, and the He family was still the controlling shareholder.[10]After cashing out more than 4 billion yuan, He Xiangjian was considered to have turned his attention to real estate industry after retiring.

Paving the Way for the Succession: The Adjustment of Group Structure

In terms of operation, in order to create a more favorable condition for Fang Hongbo to streamline the group and integrate resources, He Xiangjian disintergrated the four secondary groups under Midea Group before handing over the power to Fang Hongbo. Only Midea Real Estate — which had little to do with the group's main business — became part of Midea Holdings. The three other secondary groups, i.e., the Refrigeration Appliance Group (Midea Electric Appliances, Little Swan), Home Appliances Group (microwave oven, rice cooker), and Mechanical and Electrical Group (Hong Kong listed company Weiling Holdings, Midea logistics business) were dissolved. Their original functions were

---

[10] Wu, Aizhuang. (2014). Midea's Internal Power Struggle Escalated, Three of Seven Core Executives Have Left. *MoneyWeek*, July 14.

transferred to the group headquarters and 15 subordinate product divisions, aiming at realizing the coordination of resources in the group in terms of finance, procurement, channels, warehousing, and so on. "There used to be a clear boundary between the business divisions, and there was basically no communication," Fang Hongbo recalled, thinking about how to make full use of all resources.

These cancelled sub-groups used to exist beyond the domain of Midea Electric Appliances. Huang Jian, head of the Home Appliances Group, and Cai Qiwu, head of the Mechanical and Electrical Group, were once on the same level as Fang Hongbo. After Fang Hongbo took office as chairman of Midea Group, the two of them served on the board of directors and were vice chairmen of the group's unified management system, and both had to report to Fang Hongbo.

In view of the new pattern, some insiders made the following observation regarding Midea's structural adjustment. "Mr. He had a high prestige within the company, and all professional managers followed him. As Mr. He is absent from the current structure, the process to coordinate the managing executives poses a problem. After all, this is no longer the structure under which each managing executive was in charge of a secondary platform."

After Fang Hongbo took office as Midea's chairman, he put forward a consensus for the integration of the group in the future. "First, Midea needs to reduce its size but commits to do things big. Secondly, Midea has only one standard. No matter where you come from, you must incorporate yourself in an all-encompassing system." The new group headquarters' structure was very simple, i.e., Fang Hongbo himself led several functional departments.

Implementing the Equity Incentive System for Senior Executives

After Fang Hongbo took office, Midea's situation was grim at the end of 2012, with operating income of 102.651 billion yuan, down by 27%, or nearly 30 billion yuan less than the same period the previous year. Figures in 2011 showed that increase in revenue slowed down, but figures in 2012 represented a real deduction.

Fang Hongbo knew that the performance of the company would be his examination paper handed in to He Xiangjian. The old business model was already lagging behind the requirements of the era and reform was an urgent need. But the reform could not be carried out all by himself; he needed the strength of the senior executives, who must change their mindset quickly and adapt to the future. Moreover, Fang Hongbo knew that an incentive scheme to the management was needed not only for the next few years, but also for the long-term future. "In two years' time, perhaps my innovation capacity and management skills would not be able to keep up with the time. Then people who would succeed me need to be encouraged and selected in advance, and the succession of the next generation may not be the same as in the past."

Equity Incentive for the 7-person Executive Team

Fang Hongbo recalled the company's past incentive scheme for the executives: From 2007, He Xiangjian made great efforts to arrange a scheme under which the earnings of senior executives would match their counterparts in the global market. Taking advantage of stock reform, Midea implemented a virtual equity incentive plan on the advice of a consulting firm, covering only a team of seven executives. When Midea went public in 2013, only five of the original seven-member executive team stayed in Midea, and the personal wealth of the new seven-member executive team soared.[11]

Midea's principle of incentives was always to give employees a low but fixed remuneration and a high but changeable (performance-dependent) remuneration, and the long-term incentive is usually high. However, equity incentive system was not in place. The equity incentive plan in 2007 was only for the original seven-member executive team, of which none was a general manager of the business division. However, as the business division headed by some of these executives was positioned as a secondary industrial group, the executive concerned became eligible for the equity incentive plan, although the combined size of all the operations

---

[11] Wu, Aizhuang. (2014). Midea's Internal Power Struggle Escalated, Three of Seven Core Executives Have Left. *MoneyWeek*, July 14.

of this specific secondary group may not be as large as that of the largest business division. Such an arrangement could create some imbalances. The business divisions were the foundation of the group. If managers in business divisions were not fully motivated, then where would Midea select its future successors?

Equity Incentive for Core Executives (the Meisheng Plan)

In 2012, in lieu of the fact that the management teams of the business divisions of the group still adopted a single short-term cash-based incentive approach, Midea launched the "Meisheng" equity incentive plan, which was extended to 47 people. It was mainly aimed at the level of head of group department, general managers, and deputy general managers of business divisions. These managers set up a limited partnership, Ningbo Meisheng, which held 3% shares of Midea before Midea went public as a whole in 2013. The shares came from Midea Holdings, transferred to them by He Xiangjian. After Midea went public, the executives indirectly held a combined 1.75% of shares. These shares were distributed to them depending on the size of the sales and their contribution to profits. From 2013 to 2015, if the overall performance of the group reached the assessment requirements, and the individual performance met the target, these executives could exercise their power; if they failed to meet the target, they needed to withdraw with net assets. Executives bought the shares at a price lower than the market price at the time. If there was a new round of growth after the group went public, the income from long-term incentives would be substantial.

Equity Incentive Extends to the Middle-level Managers in the Future

Fang Hongbo also planned to launch new equity incentive schemes for middle-level managers after 2014, and they would cover more than 1,000 people. This could turn out to be a double-edged sword because people tended to have different views about the incentive schemes, and this would affect their attitude to work. Fang Hongbo believed that out of the need for cultivating talents, the heads of departments should think about which talents would be the focus of training in the future through the specific decision of how to allocate equity.

Challenges Faced by Fang Hongbo

Although the adjustment of the internal structure finally gave Fang Hongbo the authorization to implement his strategy, he had to face the grave situation of 2012. He knew perfectly that the old business model would be of little help and reform must be carried out immediately. On the one hand, however, it was unclear whether the reform would lead to a rebound in future performance; on the other hand, doubts and rebukes had poured in before the reform was fully implemented. Who could guarantee that the transformation would have an immediate effect? What empowered Fang Hongbo was He Xiangjian's trust in his personality and capability, as well as his good performance in Midea Electric Appliances — which represented a good performance of Midea Group's business — after the transformation under his leadership.

Fang Hongbo felt that in the face of all the problems, he needed to rationally analyze them before making a judgment. "The whole business has been sold and employees are laid off. The whole group is in chaos, and there are all kinds of opinions. I don't have many people around me who I can confer with, so I need to figure out what is going to be done. We need to take action without any hesitation."

Rousing the Management from the Old Rut

Fang Hongbo was well aware that some managers had not only lost the motivation to learn new things, but also resisted changes for the sake of their own interests. He felt that it was their mental sclerosis that hindered the development of Midea. "Managers became director generals, and they began to refuse to learn, to change, and to accept new things. What is Internet? They just resist to change. They have formed their own community of interests, giving priority to themselves and protecting people around them. They protect the interests of their own departments and refuse to cooperate with others." Fang Hongbo felt that the structure, team, and culture of the group must be completely reconstructed in order to rejuvenate Midea.

In order to change the mindset of the management, he frequently talked about the need to transform the company and adapt to the new era, "We used to put more weight to short-term profit. But now we need to know what value the number of users can create for us and what value web traffic can bring to us. In Midea there used to be two types of people with the lowest academic qualifications, one in after sale service and the other in logistics. In the past, they could engage in warehouses and transport, but now times have changed. We are in the era of e-commerce and need to connect with users. In the future, the requirements for human resources will be completely different."

Fang Hongbo expressed his attitude towards transformation very clearly, "You have to change your mindset and your actions. If you can't, we have to let someone else take your place." At an executive meeting, Fang Hongbo even said, "No matter who you are and how many years you have served in the company, as long as you are unable to keep up with the current times, I will dismiss you even if it means I have to step down as chairman." In fact, after the reorganization of the group, Fang Hongbo focused on the group's strategy and investment. The 14 business divisions independently managed production, research, and sales, so the actual powers of several other executives were gradually weakened.

Fang Hongbo knew very well that the decisive measures of streamlining business and dismissing people would ultimately damage the interests of many people. Fang Hongbo surmised that at the moment he took over Midea, many executives who had already gained equity already had the idea of leaving but did not say it out loud. He turned the matter over in his mind and concluded that if he could not prove himself with good sales figures, he might find himself deserted by his followers and colleagues. What's more, the merit of downsizing was difficult to assess in the short term.

Fang Hongbo was aware that there was a huge contrast between his rational and decisive style and He Xiangjian's gentle style with a strong human touch. When He Xiangjian opened his mouth to speak, he made his listeners feel comfortable. But Fang Hongbo was straightforward and direct when he criticized people. In the past, Fang Hongbo was not afraid of sticking to his opinions when talking with He Xiangjian, even in public. Although his leadership style would not be readily accepted by many, Fang Hongbo wanted everyone to know that he was trying to deal with matters on their merits. In order to set a good example in promoting a cultural atmosphere of equality and openness, Fang Hongbo would throw off his airs, take the public elevator, and stand in a queue to get his food in the canteen instead of using the elevator and canteen exclusively reserved for him.

Relationship with He Xiangjian

Fang Hongbo was concerned about He Xiangjian's reaction to such a major reform in Midea. With 20 years of service in the company, Fang Hongbo regarded He Xiangjian's relationship with him as a relationship between father and son. After Midea's succession took place, was the relationship between the two still the same? At a time when Midea's performance was in difficulty, He Xiangjian authorized Fang Hongbo with enough power to implement reform. As a matter of fact, He Xiangjian only attended Fang Hongbo's briefing meetings twice a year. He Jianfeng, who had a seat on the board of directors, rarely expressed his views and almost not involved in the management of Midea. But Fang Hongbo remained modest, believing that he must redefine his relationship with He Xiangjian after the succession. Fang Hongbo's new definition of their relationship was that of agent and owner. Fang Hongbo insisted that he should strictly abide by his role as a professional manager, and even if He Xiangjian did not say it specifically, he would report to him from time to time.

Fang Hongbo pondered the subtleties of the new relationship. "It is based on great trust, which has been developed over the past 20 years. But from the moment I took over the business, I must handle this relationship with great care, or else the trust between us would be lost in an instant; it is rather fragile. After all, it is not a relationship of blood, but a relationship of contractual employment." However, Fang Hongbo felt that he was different from an ordinary agent. "I have been working with my boss for many years. It is a very delicate relationship. I know what he means with a look in his eyes, an expression on his face, and even the way he puts his hands. Coupled with my understanding of the entire growth process of Midea, I possess the strengths no other person from outside the company does, so the succession of Midea cannot be duplicated." Although this feeling was indescribable, Fang Hongbo made a conclusion that "in China, the most effective governance is still the family business".

Successful succession by professional managers is rare in China, not to mention in such a large group like Midea. There were no good examples he could copy or refer to, and no similar friend to confer with. Fang Hongbo felt the overwhelming burden only people in such a high position would feel. In the face of huge external pressure on the company's performance, the internal management whose mindset could not be changed quickly, and an unfathomable boss who was like his father, Fang Hongbo wondered why he took up the heavy task. After taking over as the chairman of Midea, the burden was doubled. If equity was not taken into account, Fang Hongbo's nominal annual income was only half what it used to be. "It must be driven by the inherent impulse from the bottom of my heart; if I am motivated by interests alone, I don't think I can lead this enterprise further. There are many talented people, but those experienced talent scouts who can discover them are few. A favor the size of a drop of water should be repaid with one of the amount of a surging spring." Fang Hongbo defined his role as that of a passer-by, and if his ability was to fall short in three or five years, he would quit like everyone else. But for now, at least, he would withstand the pressure from all sides and live up to the trust of He Xiangjian.

Changes in the Management

After the two previous events related to equity incentive schemes, Huang Jian's resignation in October 2013 caused a shock both inside and outside Midea. It was at a moment when Midea had just been listed on the stock market and was implementing a business transformation after the succession between He Xiangjian and Fang Hongbo took place. In the media it was known as "the infighting of Midea". Shortly after that, Huang Xiaoming and Cai Qiwu also stepped down from their posts in April and July in 2014. Huang Xiaoming took up a new post in Midea Holdings. According to the rules of the securities market, their wealth of more than 1 billion yuan each will not be heightened until September 18, 2016.

Fang Hongbo said the reason why he worked so hard was because he wanted to pay back to He Xiangjian for his trust. However, several colleagues in charge of different sectors who joined the company at the same time as him were not as lucky as him. After He Xiangjian selected Fang Hongbo as the successor, the others left the company one after another. Behind all the stories there was helplessness and a price to be paid, the mixed feeling of bitterness and sweetness known only to those who had gone through the experience.

New Business Direction

He Xiangjian entrusted Fang Hongbo with a very arduous task. "Not only we cannot stop, but we have to speed up. Since there is no road ahead, you have to find a new exit." From the perspective of business strategy, Midea used to be the representative of good manufacturing in China, but in the future, the pressure of rising costs will be huge, the direction of low-cost manufacturing must be changed, and the development speed must not slow down for the sake of innovation in competition.

Midea chose what Fang Hongbo called "the second runway". It implemented the mobile strategy from 2013 to 2015, that is, to have mobile phone-based intelligent home appliances. This pointed to a possible future orientation for Midea, but the simultaneous implementation of the two strategic models could mean that incentive schemes would become more complex or result in conflicts. Fang Hongbo needed to think about how to design a new incentive mechanism to avoid the loss of a large number of senior executives, while at the same time give the old Midea a new lease of life.

From a township enterprise to a listed company, from entrepreneurial management to professional management, from boss culture to manager culture, Midea has undergone one round after another of reforms and transformations, during which Fang Hongbo has also experienced a lot, becoming more and more decisive but always keeping a low profile. The key is that he knows his role in Midea very well. He said that he was only a "passer-by" in Midea and he had his tasks to complete during this particular period. One day, however, he himself will become something of the past.

Since he started the business in 1968, He Xiangjian has experienced several rounds of changes. In 2012, he completely handed over the group to the professional manager Fang Hongbo and he only served as the chairman of Midea Holdings, which marked the separation of ownership and management of a family business. By passing the management right to a professional manager, Midea has set a stellar example in the succession of family businesses in China.

10

Mother-to-daughter Succession in Boosting Brand Internationalization

Female leadership or "she-power"[1] is attracting public attention in recent years. "It is not easy to be a woman, and it is even harder to be a super woman in a family business" is a common saying in China. Women in family businesses are endowed with more role identities (both enterprise managers and family identities). As members of family businesses, women's special identities are often more easily influenced by both systems, so they are typically exposed to double identity conflict or even multiple identity conflict. The role of women should never be ignored whether they are involved in the management of a family business or not. IESE Business School professor Kristin Cappuyns surveyed 200 "inactive" family members from 98 Spanish family businesses[2] and conducted a comparative analysis by gender. He found that even the inactive female family members scored high in "devotion", "loyalty", and "idealism". Women's intuition and sensitivity help to create a sense of commitment. Their strong sense of commitment to the family may trickle down into the family

---

[1] Lee, Siew Kim Jean. (2013). Hard and Soft Leadership: She Rises. *Harvard Business Review* (Chinese version), 9, 52–57.

[2] Cappuyns, K. (2007). Women behind the scenes in family businesses. *Electronic Journal of Family Business Studies*, 1(1), 38–61.

business relationship, and even affect an enterprise's market performance by exerting influence on an entrepreneur's motivation and related business decisions. On top of that, women's enthusiasm for the family can provide pivotal assets for family businesses: A powerful "family cement".

"Being graceful in the drawing room and skillful in the kitchen" is the requirement of the Chinese nation for modern women, but the value and influence of modern women in the family and business has long gone far beyond this domain. Shen Aiqin, founder of the Wensli Group, is undoubtedly a woman of achievement, and her successor, Tu Hongyan, is also a woman who makes a big difference. They are both business managers and mothers/wives. Therefore, the way they juggle their different roles in the family and business is a special topic for female entrepreneurs. Shen Aiqin has dedicated her life to Wensli, creating a diversified corporate kingdom around the silk industry. While she was selecting her own little daughter as her successor, other family members helped mediate and solve the intergenerational conflicts of the inheritance. Tu Hongyan and her husband Li Jianhua — by virtue of their love for the silk industry and their family responsibilities — have realized a total transformation of traditional silk business by a series of bold moves, including acquiring the French silk luxury brand "MARC ROZIER" and hiring the former CEO of Hermes silk, Patrick Bonnefond. Over its development, Wensli Group has witnessed a woman starting up a business, a daughter inheriting from mother, the role of a son-in-law in the inheritance of family businesses, the internationalization of Chinese family businesses, and the management by foreign CEOs in family businesses. When inheritance coincides with transformation, Wensli's second-generation successor, Tu Hongyan, is working closely with her husband to make the company an international company and even a leading company in the world's silk industry. They regard Wensli as a producer of luxury goods in a time when Chinese brands are rarely found in the international luxury market. In the process of succession and transformation, this traditional Chinese family-owned enterprise is beginning to build its own international luxury brand with the aid of a foreign executive. In this process, the role and strength of women and her balanced relationship with the son-in-law have all played an unparalleled part.

Family Passion and Inheritance of Silk

Wensli, the Story of Silk

Sericulture has a history of nearly 5,000 years in Hangzhou, Zhejiang Province, and the city enjoys the reputation of "Silk House". In the Han Dynasty and the Tang Dynasty, the silk products from Hangzhou were not only tributes to the imperial court but were also exported to the Western countries along the "Silk Road". Therefore, Hangzhou is a renowned silk production and trading hub in history.

Shen Aiqin was born in Jianqiao Township, Hangzhou. The family of Shen was a famous sericultural household in the area. The forebears of Shen had established Hangzhou Jianqiao Silk Factory and the products were exported to overseas.[3] Shen Aiqin grew up in the silkworm house and dropped out of school at the age of 14 to help her family with farm work. During the ten-year Cultural Revolution, she worked consecutively as a barefoot doctor, a women's team leader, and head of the local Commune Health Center. In 1975, Jianqiao Commune appointed Shen Aiqin head of the Hangzhou Jianqiao Silk Factory, a township enterprise with only about 20 migrant workers and 10 old ironwood looms that were spared by the state-owned large factories. They were heavily in debt, and short of working capital and raw materials. She borrowed 20,000 yuan from relatives and friends, and travelled to Shanghai, Shaoxing, and other places to hire more than a dozen elderly skillful workers who formerly worked at a state-owned silk factory, thereby solving her technical problems. She also established a set of rules and regulations to tighten management. However, in those years of planned economy, raw silk was allotted by the state. Shen Aiqin mobilized the whole factory staff, while taking the lead to look for raw materials and use the materials discarded by the state-owned factories as their main raw materials. However, since product sales were also under the control of the state, she and her staff suffered many hardships, visiting one department store after another to present their silk products to them. Finally, they succeeded and their silk products were sold in many department stores. Jianqiao Silk Factory slowly paid off its previous debts and

---

[3] Xiao, Shu. (2012). *China's Queen of Silk: Legend of Shen Aiqin*. Zhejiang People's Publishing House.

made a profit. In the spring of 1978, Shen Aiqin became a target of prosecution in the campaign against capitalism and was requested to leave the silk factory. Yet, she would rather work as a cleaner in the canteen than leave. The first generation Chinese private entrepreneurs like Shen Aiqin were most grateful for the opportunity brought about by the reform and opening-up policy at the end of 1978. She was re-appointed as the head of the silk factory. From then on, Shen Aiqin gradually improved every aspect of work in the factory. In 1980, Hangzhou Jianqiao Silk Factory passed the national quality inspection and appraisal and obtained the license to sell its products in the department stores across the country. In 1981, Shen Aiqin recruited nearly 100 educated young people. In the next year, she sent a group of outstanding workers to study at Zhejiang Silk Institute of Technology (now Zhejiang University of Technology), who later became the backbone of Jianqiao Silk Factory. Shen Aiqin also began to ponder the entire silk production process. At that time, the key dyeing process was outsourced, which was not only costly but also delayed the production procedures. Therefore, she decided to launch the silk dyeing project. But the project would cost up to 5 million yuan, an astronomical figure at that time. Shen Aiqin wrote a letter of guarantee to the Jianqiao Township Government before she was given the green light to go on with the project. In 1984, a four-story silk-dyeing building was completed. In the first year, it secured a profit of 600,000 yuan.

Zhang Zuqin, the incumbent vice president of the Wensli Group, joined the Jianqiao Silk Factory in 1982. She started as a loom tender and was sent to the Shanghai Printing and Dyeing Technology Research Institute to study and plan a new factory. She recalled the situation at the time, "When I came back from study, we started to build the silk dyeing factory. In May 1985, *Hangzhou Daily* published a full-page report entitled 'Shenzhen Speed in Jianqiao', saying that the construction of the silk dyeing workshop of Hangzhou Jianqiao Silk Factory went so rapidly that the workers completed one story every seven days, with quality being ensured. This was never seen in Zhejiang before, and it could rival the 'Shenzhen speed', referring to the famous Special Economic Zone known for its rapid construction speed. In the same year, the dyeing factory started operation, and the company began to develop rapidly."

In the 1990s, Shen Aiqin began to consider technological upgrading. She visited the United States and Europe and discovered a huge gap between Chinese silk production and foreign technology. When she learned that a large state-owned Hangzhou factory had given up their attempt to introduce the Japanese Mitsubishi water jet looms because of lack of funds, she decided that she would become the first silk factory in China to introduce this technology. She applied to the Ministry of Agriculture and the Ministry of Textile Industry, and submitted reports to the township, district, and city governments, and finally secured approval of the project from the Zhejiang Provincial Planning Commission. After a huge effort, the project obtained the approval of the State Council, and 50 million yuan was invested. Later, Shen Aiqin invested another 200 million yuan introducing printing production equipment from Italy, Switzerland, and Japan, which boosted the annual output value by 7 times and increased profits by 4 times, and paid back all bank loans within three years.

During this period, Shen Aiqin wasted no time establishing and acquiring factories related to the silk industry chain, such as chemical fiber fabrics and garment production, brand processing, and import and export trade. She named her conglomerate Wensli and expanded to new areas such as real estate. In 2000, Shen Aiqin transformed her township enterprise into an equity company with a total of 28 shareholders. She became the controlling shareholder, holding 57.9% of the shares. The rest of the shareholders included her family members and the corporate executives. Shen Aiqin said, "Restructuring is an attempt to improve the mechanism. As a controlling shareholder, my greater role is to work as decision-maker. Our company belongs to the bigger community, so is our wealth. It is not so much that everyone works for me, but rather that I am responsible for society, working for everyone." After the restructuring, Shen Aiqin accelerated diversification and expanded to the biotechnology and pharmaceutical industries. In addition, Zhejiang Krent Paper Co., Ltd. was also established. In 2004, she obtained the qualifications for running hospitals and founded Hangzhou Wensli Hospital, and also invested in other hospitals.

Plan for Selecting Her Successor

Shen Aiqin has two daughters: Tu Hongxia and Tu Hongyan. Tu Hongxia is physically frail due to premature birth, and Shen Aiqin makes an effort to keep her away from difficult work. After graduating from high school, Tu Hongxia first joined the Jianqiao Rural Credit Union to work as an accountant and then as a credit manager at Hangzhou United Bank. In 2002, Hangzhou Cultural Mall, which consisted of wholesale and retail book selling, IT supplying, office buildings, and warehousing, opened for business. After several bungling general managers, Shen Aiqin appointed Tu Hongxia as the general manager of the Mall. Shen Aiqin said, "I have always doted on my eldest daughter. She is a smart and capable woman. She grows up in a comfortable environment and finds work in the bank to her taste. She gets along well with her colleagues in the bank and is very approachable and generous. I did not ask her to help me until the restructuring is completed. Everyone is satisfactory with her management (of the Mall). Conversely, when a professional manager reaches a certain level, his requirements will be higher, and he tends to change his mind; so, I have no worries when I know I trust the person in charge here."

Her younger daughter Tu Hongyan is stronger physically, and Shen Aiqin has always treated her as a boy. To Shen Aiqin, her younger daughter is shrewd, magnanimous, selfless, courageous, and dedicated to work. In 1992, Tu Hongyan graduated from the Department of Business Management of Shenzhen University. It was the time when Hangzhou and Fukui City of Japan were establishing sister city relationship and exchanging graduate students. Shen Aiqin encouraged her daughter to go abroad to gain experience. So, Hongyan went to Fukui, where she studied the art of clothing three days a week, and worked as an intern in a clothing company the other three days, starting as an assembly line worker. She said, "Although the Japanese company is not as big as our company, we need to learn from their management approaches."

One year later, Tu Hongyan returned to China, intending to open a small company with friends to earn enough money to support herself. However, Shen Aiqin suggested that she join the Jianqiao Silk Factory and start as a frontline worker. Tu Hongyan said, "After the restructuring of the company, mother is perhaps trying to train me. But I am not aware of that and don't want to take much responsibility. I know my mother works very hard." First, she worked on the assembly line and had a few senior workers to teach her. Then, she was transferred to the business department. Later, the Jianqiao Silk Factory obtained the right to import, and Tu Hongyan went to Hong Kong to be in charge of the establishment of a branch company to carry out import and export trade. In 1997, Tu Hongyan became the deputy general manager of Wensli Garment Co., Ltd. Two years later, she became the general manager of the garment factory with more than 300 employees. She became the executive chairwoman of the group's board of directors in 2004 and began to exercise the right to sign, officially taking over the business. Shen Aiqin said, "I make sure that my elder daughter agrees to my younger daughter taking over the business. They are blood-related sisters, and they get on well with each other. The younger one always asks her elder sister for advice with regards to major issues of business before she makes her decision. The elder sister would also support her younger sister at meetings to uphold her prestige. So, there are no factions in our factory, because there are no factions in our family."

By 2004, her two sons-in-law had also joined the group. Tu Hongxia's husband Wang Yunfei entered the Jianqiao Silk Factory after graduating from high school in 1981, as one of the first batch of rural educated youth who was hired by the Jianqiao Silk Factory. He first worked in the financial department and then was promoted to be the chairman of Hangzhou Wensli Biotechnology Co., Ltd. The younger sister's husband Li Jianhua graduated from Suzhou Silk Institute of Technology in 1984, and worked consecutively in Jiangsu Soho Group, Jiangsu Soho Garment Factory, and Shenzhen Southeast Silk Garment Co., Ltd. He met Tu Hongyan in 2001 when they were both members of a group surveying the silk industry in Europe. They got married in 2002 and Li joined the Wensli Import and Export Corporation as the general manager in 2003, and served as the group president in 2004, assisting Tu Hongyan to take over the business. Shen Aiqin said, "The two sons-in-law are even better than my two daughters. Li Jianhua is a generous, selfless, and hard-working man. He is the perfect match for my little daughter. When my girls tied the knot, they would assume the role of mother and daughter-in-law, and phase out of the businesses. The couple needs to manage such a big conglomerate, and mutual understanding is indispensable. In fact, Li Jianhua gives in to Tu Hongyan more often as she is known for her quick temper. The older son-in-law, Wang Yunfei, is selected and trained by me. He is down-to-earth and did a magnificent job managing the biotechnology sector."

Difficulties Surrounding the Business Succession by Daughter & Son-in-law

Relationship with Mother

In 2004, Tu Hongyan became the executive chairwoman of the group's board of directors, with the right to sign contracts. With the support of her husband Li Jianhua (the president of the group), she officially started to take over the business and was determined to develop the business vigorously. She also had to face generational conflicts with her mother Shen Aiqin, who was the chairwoman of the group's board of directors. Shen Aiqin believed that they should possess more factories and tangible assets to remain in the industry, so they should continue to expand and diversify. On the contrary, Tu Hongyan advocated focusing on the main business of silk, and Li Jianhua believed that share holding should be concentrated. They began to churn out a series of reforms, and disagreements and conflicts between the couple and Shen Aiqin were frequent for a few years.

Li Jianhua recalled, "Actually, the period from 2004 to 2008 was a very difficult time for Wensli, a time that laid a good foundation for its future development. However, that was not obvious to everyone. What is the most difficult part in the succession of the company? The first priority is for the three of us to reach consensus." First, in 2004, the No. 4 People's Hospital of Hangzhou was on sale, and a piece of land in Rizhao, Shandong Province had also been put up for public auction. Li Jianhua and Tu Hongyan believed that the financial situation at that time would only allow them to choose one of them, and the board of directors agreed with the couple. But Shen Aiqin believed that they should acquire both. Tu Hongyan and Li Jianhua finally accepted Shen's decision, and Wensli became the first private enterprise to acquire a state-owned hospital in China. Li Jianhua explained, "The old chairwoman insists on doing this. What could we do? We couldn't stop it. We could only back her up. We will then find a way to deal with financial and funding problems. We are not supposed to argue with her."

In 2005, Shen Aiqin formulated the strategic goal of "Three Threes". First, to establish three bases: Clothing base, printing and dyeing base, and biotechnology base. Second, to forge three markets: Clothing market, commercial and residential building materials market, and cultural mall market. Third, to build three brands: Wensli Silk Garment Brand, Wensli Biotech Brand, and Southern Home Commercial and Residential Building Materials Brand. In Shen Aiqin's view, enterprises should have fixed assets and size of the group was important.

At that time, the profit from silk, Wensli's main business, was low, and their business model relied heavily on foreign trade and OEM. Tu Hongyan, who had just taken over the business, advocated focusing on the main business of silk. She and Li Jianhua tried a series of reform measures, which met with strong opposition from Shen Aiqin. Tu Hongyan explained, "I have always had a dream — to make Wensli 'China's Hermes'. Around 2000, we were also engaged in other businesses such as real estate, and our main business was not clearly defined. We adjusted our strategy in 2005. We should have core capabilities, core products, and core industries. We started to sell out products that were not our core business. We also shut down businesses if the profits were not good, the industrial development was not clearly defined, and the prospects were poor. So that we can focus on silk, our main business. We plan to make our silk business strong in five or six years."

Zhang Zuqin recollected, "At the time, our manufacturing factory had been suffering losses for a few years, and the boss was not willing to shut it down. She had a special attachment to the factory, as it was from here that she first started up her business. Although it was losing money, she said she could compensate using the group's other profit making businesses. When the board met, their opinions were not uniform. Later on, following the instructions of Li Jianhua, many other industries unrelated to the main business of silk, such as real estate companies, were to be closed even if they were profitable. The decision was controversial. It definitely takes time, particularly when it is related to the transformation and upgrading of the enterprise."

Tu Hongyan believed that it was normal for a family to have disagreements between two generations, for they grew up in different environments and received different types of education. Their representation totally differed as a result of the market conditions. She said, "What worked well for my mother in the market at her time will most probably not work in today's market." Tu Hongyan felt that it was essential to understand the roots of the disagreements and find a solution. She said, "There were a lot of disputes in principle, but we have to go back to work the next day after the quarrels. When it came to major issues of principle, we would hold meetings of board of directors, or family meetings, and would also ask my mother and senior executives and friends that we trust to come to listen to our ideas and finally reach a consensus. Since my mother has a strong sense of self-esteem, you have to communicate with her calmly and patiently. She is not opinionated. The important thing is that we share the same goal — we seek the growth of the company, not personal interests. This is very important, and it is what I call the break-in period."

The silk factory under the charge of Tu Hongyan's third uncle Shen Baijun suffered serious losses and was finally shut down. Li Jianhua arranged for him to serve as the supervisor. Both Shen Aiqin and Shen Baijun were satisfied. Li Jianhua said, "The most important thing in the process of inheritance is how to deal with the internal relations." Tu Hongyan added, "Family ties never change; we will always stick together despite all the quarrels and disputes. But it would be different with professional managers."

The 28 shareholders were family members and senior employees of the group. Li Jianhua believed that it was necessary to concentrate the equity in order to smoothen the decision-making process for implementing the new strategy. So, while consolidating the main business, he persuaded the shareholders to sell their shares to Shen Aiqin. To facilitate this process, he bought from those who asked for a high price for their shares. He explained, "We offered this equity exchange. We asked them to give back the group shares in exchange for profitable companies, along with their equity, customers, suppliers, and brands, plus additional preferential policies."

Shen Aiqin agreed to the practice of equity exchange: "In the past few years, we had been concentrating on reorganizing the management team. For example, the older executives have been with me for 20 years, and now they are not accustomed to the leadership style of Tu Hongyan. I will satisfy their wish to be their own boss. I give them 65% of the shares, and the remaining 35% are enough for us. For us, the risk is not big, and they can do their best to be good bosses. But they must listen to the headquarters, which is integrated."

In the later period, there were only eight shareholders left: The shares of six family members accounted for about 90% of the total shares, and the remaining two were senior employees. Among the family members, Shen Aiqin had more shares than before. The remaining shareholders were Shen Baijun, the two sisters of the Tu family, and their husbands. Li Jianhua said, "I bought all my shares with my own money. I think my position in the company is very clear. I am a special high-level employee in this company."

Husband & Wife Work Together for Business Development

Tu Hongyan regarded herself as an entrepreneur and Li Jianhua a silk expert. She was very satisfied with their collaboration: "Silk has brought us together. We enjoy our time working together because we appreciate, tolerate, and understand each other. We have shared values and hobbies, and the same career goal. He said that he wants to do a good job in the inheritance of silk, to establish a flagship brand in the Chinese industry, and to delve deeper into, inherit and carry forward the 5,000-year-old silk culture in China. This is our shared mission as the second generation of silk businesspeople."

In 2011, Shen Aiqin officially handed over the group to her daughter and son-in-law, making Tu Hongyan the chairwoman of the board of directors of the group. The couple are now working together in perfect harmony; they are committed to upgrading the traditional silk industry to a new cultural industry, as well as promoting the internationalization of brand, management, and technology, and integration with the mobile Internet, in the hope of building "China's world-class silk luxury brand".

Industrial Upgrading

Developing Silk Gifts

Tu Hongyan realized that a business relying solely on exporting fabrics and earning the little profits from acting as an OEM company could not survive in this era and transformation was urgently needed. Li Jianhua believed that silk could be a high-end cultural gift. Therefore they set up Wensli Silk Gifts Co., Ltd. to serve enterprises, government agencies, large-scale events such as the 2008 Beijing Olympic Games, and meetings of heads of state. Tu Hongyan commented, "A piece of silk fabric that earns two yuan per meter can earn 20 yuan per meter when it is made as a gift. After it is made into a wall decoration, the profit per meter can reach 200 yuan. When silk is made into a work of art, the profit per meter may rise up to 2,000 yuan, or even 20,000 yuan." In 2009, silk culture gifts emerged as the best profit-making products in the group. Tu Hongyan added, "Now our domestic market is bigger than the export market. We want ordinary Chinese people to have a better understanding of silk and add to its value through cultural elements."

Delving into and Promoting Silk Culture

In 2010, Li Jianhua led a Wensli team on a journey along the Silk Road. When passing the Mogao Grottoes, he was informed that some ancient silk-embroidered paintings kept in the caves had been taken overseas. Later, Li Jianhua went to France three times and got the electronic photos of the 12 ancient silk paintings. He successfully copied and restored the Dunhuang silk paintings with high-tech patent technologies and presented them to the Dunhuang Museum for collection and research. In 2012, Wensli launched a new high-end art project by commissioning intangible cultural heritage trustees to produce silk works of art. In the same year at the International Silk Expo, Wensli displayed the eponymous silk embroidered artwork based on Luo Zhongli's famous painting "Father", handmade by the "disorderly embroidery" technique and priced at 680,000 yuan. After that, Li Jianhua took advantage of various forms of media to promote silk culture, such as producing a TV documentary "Silk World", publishing a series of books on silk culture like *What We Should Know about Silk* and *Everything about Silk*, holding seminars, delivering speeches, receiving interviews, and founding the first private silk culture museum in China — the Wensli Silk Culture Museum.

Establishing an International Design and Development Team

In order to build the brand of Wensli, Tu Hongyan first improved the team of designers by inviting designers from France and Hong Kong to join her team. Su Minyi, a famous modern watercolor painter from Hong Kong and the president of the Hong Kong Women Painters Association, joined Wensli in 2011 as the design director, combining the elements of water-color and silk. She would spend some time in Hangzhou every month to work with the design team. Han Binghua, who was selected as one of the world's top 100 graphic designers by Phaidon Press in New York, also joined Wensli as artistic director. He used to be the chairman of the Hong Kong Designers Association and the vice president of the International Graphic Design Association. He was also the designer of the regional flag and emblem of the Hong Kong Special Administrative Region.

Research into New Technologies and Materials

In addition to design, technology is also the foundation for silk companies to build brands. Tu Hongyan said, "If a brand does not have its own core technology, it will be useless to do any more marketing." In 2011, Wensli's Enterprise Technology Center became the country's only national center of the silk industry. It has four research institutes: New Materials Research Office, Ecological Dyeing and Finishing Technology Research Office, Modern High-tech Textile Digital Research Office, and Silk Culture Creative Design Office. Wensli invested heavily in the introduction of the world's top dyeing and finishing equipment and hired professors and even academicians — either members of the Chinese Academy of Sciences or members of the Chinese Academy of Engineering — as research and development personnel, and also cooperated with universities and research institutes to develop their products. But Tu Hongyan said frankly, "Despite our efforts, there is still a big technological gap between us and leading foreign brands."

Implementing Multi-brand Policy and Integrating with Mobile Internet

Tu Hongyan and Li Jianhua, in the exploration, gradually came to have a clear picture of the brand composition of Wensli. As a brand mainly tar-geting middle-level consumer groups, Wensli needed to forge brands for high-end consumers and consumers sensitive to the latest fashion as well. In 2011, the flagship store of Wensli officially entered the Internet-based

Taobao Mall. In 2012, Wensli established Hangzhou New Silk Road E-Commerce Co., Ltd. to integrate the operation of e-commerce platform. Through this platform, it launched the fashion consumption B2C brand "Shineline", targeting younger consumers born in the 1980s and 1990s. In 2013, Wensli launched the "Good Chinese Silk" B2C marketing platform featuring design silk scarf — the first of its kind in the industry — an attempt to actively secure a position in the mobile e-commerce field.

Chinese Brand, Made in France

Acquisition of French Silk Luxury Brand MARC ROZIER

As for products for high-end consumers, in 2013, after two years of negotiations, Wensli spent more than 5 million euros to officially acquire the French family silk company MARC ROZIER, holding 95% of its total shares. MARC ROZIER was founded in Lyon, France in 1885. It started to produce silk scarves 50-plus years earlier than Hermes. It is one of the two factories in Europe that has mastered the highly complex jacquard method. The manufacturing process from raw material procurement to design, jacquard weaving, printing, and dyeing is all done in France. It has many special counters around the world. It has designed and manufactured scarves for more than 40 international luxury brands, which has made it the second largest silk company in France.

Li Jianhua maintained that the future of silk lay in developing luxury goods. China had become the second largest consumer of luxury goods, but none of the world's 75 luxury brands were Chinese. Among them, half of the top 15 luxury brands were French brands, and the famous Hermes was made in France. Hence, Wensli would like to add "made in France" elements to its own brand. He said, "Now this company belongs to us and will contract manufacture for Wensli. In the future, this company will contract manufacture for some of the world's top brands, with the decision-making power in the hands of Wensli. In the past, Chinese companies felt proud to be OEM companies for international brands. Now we turn the table, letting foreign companies manufacture and process for us. This is a huge change." Wensli would also promote this luxury brand in China by organizing fashion shows and opening brand experience stores there.

Tu Hongyan added, "Their equipment is 30 years behind us, but the quality of the products is higher than ours. We have to learn from them."

In the same year, the central government proposed the national strategy of building the "Silk Road Economic Belt", which spurred on the silk industry and encouraged the internationalization of Wensli.

Appointment of a French CEO: "Modern Marco Polo"

In July 2014, Wensli officially hired the previous CEO of Hermes Silk Division, Patrick Bonnefond, as CEO of Wensli Silk Culture Co., Ltd. and MARC ROZIER, a subsidiary corporation under the Wensli Group. He was responsible for cultivating Wensli talents, introducing high-calibre European designers, and studying and implementing brand composition and international development strategies, and also in charge of MARC ROZIER's development in the Chinese and European market. He would spend most of his time in France and often fly to Hangzhou. The president of the Hangzhou Silk Industry Association commented that Bonnefond's appointment was an important milestone in the development of the silk industry in Hangzhou.[4]

Li Jianhua met with Mr. Bonnefond in Paris in March 2014. He recalled, "I imagined that a high-ranking executive of Hermès would be arrogant and self-satisfied, but when we sat down and exchanged the first few words, I could feel the rapport between us. We had many things in common when we talked about silk, culture, and the Silk Road." Li Jianhua pointed out that Wensli was a small company compared to Hermes. He felt that if he talked about how much they would pay Bonnefond every time they met, it would not be long before he found the seat opposite him empty. As long as Bonnefond could help Wensli achieve its goals, he should be able to get a higher pay than he did in Hermes. Bonnefond said, "When we met each other, our communication was not very smooth because of the language and cultural barriers, but our mutual love for silk united us and drove us to take on the important mission of inheriting and forwarding the tradition in modern silk."

---

[4]Yan, Yiqi. (2014). Wensli Has Designs on European Silk Market. *China Daily USA*, July 3, 16.

Having accepted the offer, Patrick Bonnefond came to Hangzhou to visit Wensli in May 2014, and exchanged views with the group's executives. The governor of Zhejiang Province and the mayor of Hangzhou met with him. In their meeting, the mayor made the following observation: "'Do your best to make it a good luxury brand, set up your own base of raw materials, combine the skills of France and China to expand to the global market." In Bonnefond's opinion, the purchasing power of luxury goods was shifting to Asia, and the Chinese market in particular was increasing rapidly. China's silk brands were at an important stage of development where ordinary brands were transiting to high-end brands and luxury brands. The reasons why he finally accepted the offer were: the cohesion of the Wensli management team, their dedication to silk culture, their understanding of and familiarity with the silk industry, the charisma of Tu Hongyan and Li Jianhua, and the couple's dream of creating a "Chinese luxury brand" that was totally consistent with Bonnefond's vision. The French CEO added, "I was born in Lyon, the capital of silk, so I have a personal love for silk. I believe a Chinese luxury brand will emerge on the Silk Road between Hangzhou and Lyon, and this brand will most probably be Wensli."

It would take some time for Patrick Bonnefond and Wensli to become attuned to each other's way of doing things. Take raw materials for example. When Bonnefond worked at Hermes, 80% of the raw silk came from Brazil, while 90% of the world's raw silk was made in China. He believed that the temperature in Brazil was relatively stable, and the Brazilian silk farmers worked on silk farms, which ensured stable output. They also had good production processes and techniques. However, silk production in China was family-based and output was therefore unstable. Li Jianhua thought differently: "In fact, there are many good sources of silk in China that Bonnefond are not aware of. I hope that after he joins Wensli, we can share such information with him so that he can spread this information in Europe. We are also pleased to promote the French silk culture here in China, so that the new Silk Road will be smoother, more exciting, and brilliant."

In addition, Patrick Bonnefond hoped that China would have a deeper understanding of the luxury industry. He said, "I don't want to call it Wensli Group, when it is better to call it a 'maison'. For example, we never say Louis Vuitton Group or Chanel Group, instead, we use the word 'maison ', whose Chinese translation is 'Shijia', meaning house or home, such as the Hermes Shijia. The French word 'maison' also has another connotation, that is, a family of craftsmen. In France, I would not say I visited this luxury goods company; I would say I visited this maison."

A few months later, Li Jianhua took great delight in what Patrick Bonnefond had achieved. He was totally surprised by what Bonnefond would be able to bring to Wensli. He said, "He made a three-year plan and then reported it to us for 12 hours. He told us about the sales task he would complete this year; how much comes from group purchasing and how much comes from retailing. He also told us which the group's purchasing companies are and why; for now he has these companies as his customers, what other companies he would expect to add to his customer list, why he would be able to develop these companies, and how he is going to make these companies his customers; what his strengths are, how confident he is of winning over this company as his customer; what products does he need to roll out to serve this customer and who will be responsible for this work; how do we recruit people, and how many people do I have to help complete these tasks, etc. He brings to Wensli the brand spirit and corporate management culture, as well as the meticulousness of doing things. Since we have such a reliable cooperation with him, I believe that both sides are very honest and very happy. One thing we didn't think of at the beginning was that he has access to huge human resources in Europe and wants us to join hands with some of the largest silk companies in Europe. He is an international talent who appreciates the diverse cultures of the world. He has been to China, Brazil, India and knows the cultural background and history of each country. In addition, we continue to communicate and exchange views with him. If you ask me the question whether we have any cultural differences? Definitely. In Europe, a company focuses on one product only. If you want to release four or five products, you must set up another company. You can't get things mixed. This is the part of their culture that we need to accept. I feel that the most important thing in our internationalization is to learn from them, not to impose our values on them, but it is very difficult because in Europe they do not recognize such Chinese business practices."

With the appointment of Bonnefond, Wensli accelerated the pace of brand building and international cooperation. For instance, in January 2015, Wensli released the "Phoenix's Nest" light luxury brand. The raw materials used were the highest grade of 5A or 6A natural mulberry silk. The design incorporated many Chinese elements, and the price was set at 1,500 to 3,000 yuan. The products unveiled included silk scarves and silk home textiles. The "Phoenix Nest" Living Concept Hall would be launched in the autumn and winter. They specifically adopted phoenix as the main symbol of the brand, similar to how Hermès used the horse.

By the end of 2014, Wensli's main business — silk was still the industrial leader in China. Its business earnings increased by 10% compared with 2013, and its profit increased by 7%. In 2015, Tu Hongyan pondered over the long-term development of Wensli. She came up with many plans: "We will go public in China. We are a leading company in the silk industry, and we must achieve the goal of sustainable development, including opening specialty stores both at home and abroad, and acquiring domestic and foreign excellent brand enterprises. I feel that we must focus more on quality rather than speed in the current enterprise development. In the process of pursuing wealth, we must have a healthier lifestyle and let our grassroots employees get more benefits from the development of the company. The dismissal rate of our company is very low. There are many couples, and both of them work in our company."

To implement these plans, talents were indispensable. Regarding professional managers and inheritance, Tu Hongyan's view was: "It is true that we are a family-owned group; but in the future, we will invite more professional managers to join us. The family business can be passed down, and the equity can be owned within the family. However, business management must be professionalized."

Family Relations: Mother, Daughters, & Sons-in-Law

The succession of many family businesses in China is based on the typical father-to-son model, but in the case of Wensli, the mother passes the baton to her daughter. In this particular process, the son-in-law also plays a particularly helpful and constructive role. The handover from Shen Aiqin to

Tu Hongyan is not smooth. Although communication between mother and daughter may be milder than that between father and son, the conflict between the first generation's strong personality and the second generation's new thinking is inevitable. The main reason for the conflict between Shen Aiqin and Tu Hongyan is the intergenerational difference between mother and daughter. Compared with Tu Hongyan, Shen Aiqin has relatively limited formal education, and Tu Hongyan has not only received a good education, but also studied and worked abroad. At the beginning of Shen Aiqin's career, she experienced the turmoil of the Cultural Revolution and the opening up and reform. For all the adversities, she had a strong belief to lead the company to move forward steadily and overcome difficulties. She was also alert enough to seize the opportunities brought about by the reform and opening up. Comparatively, Tu Hongyan was quick to take advantage of the time when China's economy was growing at an unprecedented pace to reap maximum benefits. The different growth experiences and background of the two generations caused them to have differing ideas on business management and operation. Shen Aiqin's management philosophy is the same as that of the majority of the first-generation uncultured entrepreneurs, lacking the sense of standard management. Tu Hongyan is different in that she puts more weight on business models, management concepts ,and practices, and hopes to run a business by a well-established commercial system like in the Western countries. To the older generation of entrepreneurs, the size of an enterprise is most important; they believe that when an enterprise is big enough, it will not easily be squeezed out of the market by its rivals. Therefore, in the process of promoting the development of Wensli, Shen Aiqin paid special attention to making it big, building up Wensli as a diversified corporate group. When Tu Hongyan took over the business, she believed that silk was the core of Wensli, and the development of this core business and related capabilities should give Wensli the edge to come out victorious in the competition.

Meanwhile, because of the different growing-up backgrounds and personal experiences, the generation of Shen Aiqin is more inclined to show the spirit of collectivism when dealing with the government, employees, and local communities, and put more emphasis on establishing good personal relationships. The second generation entrepreneurs represented by Tu Hongyan will consider more of rational factors and investment-return ratio of capital rather than personal relationships. The first generation of Chinese family-owned enterprises grew up in the bleak wilderness of the private economy. For entrepreneurs such as Shen Aiqin, their primary goal is to ensure the survival of enterprises, and secondly to maximize profits in order to contribute to the local and national economy. Therefore, the history of the first generation entrepreneurs getting prosperous is also the history of the growth of China's private economy. At the same time, while accumulating assets and wealth along with the expansion of their own family businesses, they also made an indelible contribution to the development of the Chinese economy and boosted local employment. Most of the second generation entrepreneurs like Tu Hongyan stand on the cornerstone of their parents' success. The pursuit of profit is not the primary driving force for their business development. They are willing to take over the business because they have dreams about the industry, such as establishing an international luxury brand of their own family. They tend to emphasize the establishment of a brand based on culture, and the promotion of a life philosophy.

If Shen Aiqin must rely on firm conviction to keep moving forward on the journey full of ups and downs, then Tu Hongyan, in the new economic situation, must learn to constantly follow the trend and adjust the strategy. Therefore, the mother and the daughter have been arguing over the bottom-line issues, but Tu Hongyan understands her mother and can accept her mother no matter what. In order to solve these problems, Tu Hongyan worked hard to find the root of the disagreements between them and used her leadership and communication skills to convince her mother. For example, she asked some trusted and experienced leaders and relatives to mediate their conflict. With the help of her husband, she figured out why her mother was unwilling to close down the last and worst-performing factory managed by her brother Shen Baijun. Subsequently, the couple persuaded Shen Baijun to shut down the factory and become the group's supervisor, eventually breaking the deadlock. This arrangement also made her mother feel satisfied.

Over the years, all members of the Tu family have been working together and living happily together. As a mother, Shen Aiqin is quite discreet in making her second daughter Tu Hongyan the successor, and has done all she can to make sure that her elder daughter has no misgivings about the arrangement. The two sisters are very close friends. Tu Hongyan respects her elder sister; and Tu Hongxia supports her younger sister by never interfering in her business decisions and giving her total independence to handle the company's affairs. For example, when Tu Hongyan and her husband went on a business trip, Tu Hongxia would offer to take care of their daughter. The two sons-in-law have always remained modest and have never irritated the mother and daughters of the Tu family. In addition, after handing over the company to the Tu Hongyan couple, Shen Aiqin put a lot of energy into painting and gives Tu Hongyan total freedom in managing the company.

In this process, we can see the compromises and concessions of the two generations. The smooth succession is due in large part to the fact that they essentially have more things in common rather than differences. First of all, the mother and the daughter have a highly consistent belief in the family, that is to maintain the unity and harmony of the family, and that any arguments on business management will not affect the relations of family members. Secondly, their love and passion for silk have prompted them to work hard to develop this business; although their methods may be different, they still stay true to their original goals. Thirdly, both the mother and the daughter maintain their entrepreneurial curiosity and an open mind to advanced concepts, methods, and techniques of their counterparts in developed countries. Moreover, the two generations have the courage to assume their responsibilities to the family and the company, which also contribute to keeping Wensli's leading position in the industry. Last but not least, it is also the most important point in the intergenerational inheritance of family business: The spread of entrepreneurship. Both the mother and the daughter are very hardworking, resilient, never afraid of any difficulties, daring to develop the enterprise and expand the industry, and able to rise up to challenges. They can also seize the opportunities. It is because of this sense of responsibility that they can positively and effectively promote the inheritance and transformation of Wensli.

Compared with the first generation of entrepreneurs, the second generation has a different background while they are growing up and receiving education. Thus, they have three advantages: One, they help family businesses move from personal relationship-based management to professional management; two, they help family businesses transform and upgrade and participate in international competition; three, they know how to take advantage of financial capital and the Internet to further their business. Since the takeover, Tu Hongyan has helped redefine the family brand, integrating the vision and dream of silk culture into the development of the company, and has made great achievements in the strategy of internationalization through adopting three major measures. In particular, appointing the Frenchman Patrick Bonnefond as the CEO in charge of Wensli's main business sector has demonstrated her great vision.

The significance of marriage in family businesses is far more than finding someone to be your life partner. Especially for the second generation of the family business, a good spouse often plays a vital role in the process of inheritance.[5] Some scholars have found that the value of the family business will be affected by the marriage of the family members who are controlling shareholders, because the marriage will form a lifelong relationship between the two connected families. Family networks created by marriage can facilitate the exchange of information and resources and boost business synergies between family businesses in the network. The benefit of doing so is that the larger the business, the more its business is highly dependent on proprietary information, political relationships, and exclusive resources. Marriage may also contribute to the close connection of families and the business alliances of the companies. As a result, this form of business alliance can eliminate competition between enterprises if it involves horizontal competitors or upstream and downstream suppliers and customers.

Apart from the two generations of female leaders, Tu Hongyan's husband, Li Jianhua, has played an important role in the inheritance and transformation of Wensli. The husband and wife are good partners in both life and business and are united with one mind. It should be said that the two systems of family and business have been perfectly integrated in them. As husband and wife, they must strike a good balance between their family roles and job roles. In the company, Tu Hongyan is the chairwoman and Party secretary, who is responsible for the general direction and strategic development of Wensli. Her identity is very clear, i.e., an

---

[5] Bunkanwanicha, P., Fan, J. P. H., & Wiwattanakantang, Y. (2013). The Value of Marriage to Family Firms. *Journal of Financial & Quantitative Analysis*, 48(48), 611–636.

entrepreneur whose priorities are to develop external connection such as establishing personal relations, resource networks, communicating with the media, etc. Tu Hongyan represents one of the best business cards of Wensli. Li Jianhua is the president of the group and a member of the board of directors. He is more like an expert and scholar, focusing on the research and promotion of silk culture. He spends most of his time handling the internal affairs of the enterprise, including formulating and implementing group strategy and taking charge of daily business operations. When Tu Hongyan is actively performing in the spotlight, Li Jianhua provides her with the strongest support from behind the scenes, as both a business partner and a husband. The couple are full of enthusiasm for the family business and spare no efforts to inherit and promote the silk culture. They hope that Wensli can become a model of the industry.

At home, Tu Hongyan is a daughter, sister, wife, and mother. Each identity has a special influence on the family and business. As a daughter, she is filial to her mother; as a successor, she is not afraid of proposing new concepts to persuade her mother to change her mind; as a sister, she is taken care of by her elder sister in life, while she takes more responsibility in the enterprise. The relationship between the sisters extends from the family to the company, as the elder sister is tasked with some of the group's business. These multiple roles require Tu Hongyan to distinguish the responsibilities of the family and the business. As a wife and mother, she needs to care for her husband and love her children in everyday life, but occasionally the group affairs will take up all her time. Although Tu Hongyan and Li Jianhua work together, they do not stay together for 24 hours daily because of the clear division of labor within the group. When both are free, they will have lunch together in the office, and discuss the company's business or talk about the latest in the family. Although Tu Hongyan is Li Jianhua's "boss" in the company, she is a loving wife at home. As long as she has time, she always packs up for him before he goes on a business trip.

As a son-in-law, Li Jianhua perfectly knows his role in the Tu family and Wensli Group. He is good at dealing with various relationships and has contributed to the family and the company, which is an indication of his unusual strengths. It is not easy to handle his relationship with Tu Hongyan well because, as a couple, they are supposed to support each other at home and be good business partners in the company. Li Jianhua and his wife make a point of engaging in positive communication and frank exchanges of opinions. They have even established some principles regarding the division of labor in the company and at home, the handling of a bad mood, and the resolution of disagreements and conflicts. Both of them know how to find a balance between one's ego (self-esteem) and compassion for the other (the needs of the other; being cared and respected).

Li Jianhua supports his wife's succession of Wensli from the very beginning. For example, he pursued an MBA degree, which enriched his management knowledge and expanded his network of contacts; he propelled the transformation of the company through equity concentration; he even offered to buy at a high price the stocks of other shareholders in order to speed up the progress of the main business. To prove that there is no nepotism within the company, he bought the company's shares with his own money. He knows very well that in the transitional period of the succession, the most important thing is to unify the thinking of himself, his wife, and his mother-in-law, and to handle properly their relations with the older generation. When a disagreement occurs between him and his mother-in-law or his wife, he knows when the appropriate time is to give in. He often mediates between his wife and his mother-in-law when they have a dispute. Over the years, he has proposed many new ideas to promote business transformation, such as the development of gift business, using the elements of culture to enhance the value of silk, the launch of mobile device-based sales platform, etc.

At home, Li Jianhua is a responsible father, husband, son, and son-in-law. He respects the members of the Tu family. At the Li household, he is a typical Chinese-style "head of the family" and can provide support for Tu Hongyan. The success of this couple can be attributed to their mutual understanding, tolerance, trust, and appreciation, and their dedication to the silk industry. Their goal is unified in both career and life. They know how to balance the positioning and functions of different roles, how to avoid any role confusion, therefore resulting in harmony at home and smooth management cooperation at work. The mutual support between husband and wife is advantageous to the development of the company.

Regardless if it is emotional, financial, or human capital support, their mutual assistance will have a long-lasting impact.

Husband and Wife as a Team

Husband-and-wife pairing has always been the most important partnership of Chinese family businesses. Two people with similar backgrounds and common hobbies will enjoy a high degree of unity for future planning as they live in the same environment or are put under the same pressure. Driven by the common goal, the entrepreneurial passion that arises from the foundation of the husband-and-wife partnership can better promote the development of the family business, and the experience that the two of them have built up alongside the development of their enterprise is also vital.[6]

In the process of enterprise development, partners often face a variety of management issues. When a partnership consists of people who are both career and life partners, personal feelings will be involved in business management. For husband-and-wife pairings, they need to pay attention to the following three aspects of management:

The first is conflict management. In business management the occurrence of conflicts is inevitable, thus conflict management is a vital part of the family business. If two generations or other blood relatives can emotionally neutralize conflicts by blood-is-thicker-than-water bonds, then for couples, how to resolve conflicts without adversely affecting their relationship is of great consequences. In the initial stage of the enterprise, making clearly-defined rules on decision-making can effectively avoid conflicts. The husband and wife should clarify their roles and division of labor in the enterprise, draw a clear line of their respective rights and responsibilities, and communicate thoroughly with each other to reach a consensus on their common responsibilities and goals when it comes to matters that require joint decision-making. Of course, with the development of the enterprise, the respective division of powers and

---

[6] Lee, Siew Kim Jean, Lu Yunting. (2014). Across the Gap between Husband and Wife. *Relay*, 9, 62.

responsibilities of the husband and wife can be continuously adjusted accordingly, but once consensus is reached, the decision making rules should be followed to avoid unnecessary conflicts.

What comes next is role management. The husband-and-wife pairing adds business partners to their roles in marriage, so the management of the shifting between the two roles is of vital significance. Both husband and wife must have a good understanding of the definition of their own roles and make a clear distinction. In the course of switching between corporate affairs and family affairs, it is necessary for them to clearly recognize that they should play different identity roles at different moments and in different situations. If the role of husband or wife is brought into the process of corporate affairs, the business development will be infused with too many emotional factors, which will affect the normal development of the company. If the role at work is brought into the family environment, it will affect the harmony of family relationships, which is not conducive to the couple's marital relations. This is why people often say that we should not bring work issues home with us.

Finally, mood management. The marital relationship is a very special relationship of interdependence, and there are both passion for love and family-like affection. However, when husband and wife become business partners, the duality of roles between them will inevitably affect their exchange of personal feelings. In the survey conducted by Professor Cappuyns[7], in contrast to their male counterparts, women in family businesses are more sensitive about and conscious of the pursuit of excellence, and emphasize work ethics and frugality. Therefore, the mood management of women in family businesses has become essential. Effective mood management can avoid conflicts between husband and wife, improve the efficiency of communication, and enhance the relationship and trust between each other. Spouse could help to relieve some work-related stress. However, when faced with a husband or wife playing dual roles, outlets of mood need to be transferred elsewhere. This requires the entrepreneurs of the husband and wife to have greater tolerance for each other and a certain amount of private space. Only when mood is well

---

[7]Cappuyns, K. (2007). Women behind the Scenes in Family Businesses. *Electronic Journal of Family Business Studies*, 1(1), 38–61.

regulated and managed can the relationship between family and business be well balanced.

With the development of Chinese family businesses and the arrival of the handover period, more and more husband-and-wife pairings are found in the second generation that is ready for the succession. For the second generation of couples standing on the shoulders of the first generation of entrepreneurs, growing together would pave the way to the dual benefits of career and marriage.

At the same time, one issue that calls for attention by husband-and-wife pairings is the management of the biological family of both parties. In addition, how to handle the relationship with the first generation is also an important factor affecting the harmonious development of both the family and the enterprise. Couples must reach a consensus and set a consistent goal in life so that they can face the dual challenges of life and career. At the same time, the distribution of gains is also a problem that needs to be dealt with cautiously. Especially for entrepreneurial couples, it is easier to overcome hardships than to live in comfort. Only when the profit distribution mechanism is reasonable and clear will it be beneficial to the long-term and stable development of the enterprise and will make sure that an individual's whim or personal interests will not hamper the sustainable development of business. Particularly in the case where complex relationships concerning many relatives on the two sides are involved, a clear interest distribution mechanism can effectively protect family wealth and corporate assets as there is a clear distinction between the two.

Therefore, for the husband-and-wife pairings, in the double-track development of family relations and corporate goals, working together to form a mutually agreeable tacit understanding requires both parties to work together under the premise of mutual respect. Husband and wife must have consistent values and life goals in order to balance the difference between business and individual needs. The way of communication and inclusiveness of the two people directly determine what kind of story the husband and wife can write in the business world. Couples who share many things in common while retaining their respective strengths, and who can cooperate with each other are destined to achieve a win-win situation for both career and family.

11

Daughter Succeeds Father as the Pioneer of Strategic Transformation

The founders of many family businesses have found it hard to decide on their successors, how to cultivate them and complete the transition, the delegation of power, and the distribution of wealth. Since everyone has only one life and business opportunities wait for no one, it takes great courage and wisdom to build an everlasting family business in such a rapidly changing time. The previous chapters have discussed the most popular "a son inheriting his father/mother" model in Chinese culture, the increasingly important model of professional manager inheritance, and the relatively rare "a daughter inheriting her mother" model. How does "a daughter inheriting her father" model look like?

A good example of "a daughter inheriting her father" is the Zhang family-owned Qingdao Red Collar Group, which completed its transformation and upgrading in the process of power transition. Zhang Daili had been working in the clothing industry for nearly two decades before he and his younger brother co-founded Qingdao Red Collar Clothing Co., Ltd., (Red Collar Clothing for short), in Jimo District of Qingdao, specializing in garments. He started doing business in the clothing industry soon after the implementation of reform and opening up policy in China.

In 1986, he founded Laixi Jiali Garment Factory, which produced jackets by replicating Hong Kong and Taiwan garment samples. In 1988, he established Qingdao Xisida Garment Co., Ltd., the first garment joint venture on the Chinese mainland in cooperation with a Taiwanese garment company.

The newly established Red Collar Clothing Company followed the old way of doing business: Mass production, OEM and shopping mall sales. The company became a group in October 1998 and then implemented a shareholding reform in June 2000, completing its transition to a modern enterprise system. At that time, the work of the two brothers was divided clearly. Zhang Daili was mainly in charge of the production, procurement, and customization of clothing while his younger brother was mainly responsible for sales. At the end of 2002, the younger brother switched to real estate business, and Zhang Daili took over the retail business of Red Collar Group.

As the largest exporter of clothing, China accounted for 1/6 of the international market share and was a huge potential market for clothing at that time. In 2002, the annual clothing consumption in China was about 240 billion yuan, 95% of which was from the domestic market. Traditional clothing companies could make money just by following the traditional model in such an era when market demand was much greater than supply.[1]

However, Zhang Daili saw a different future. As a manufacturing industry, the traditional clothing industry was losing its cost advantage, and was faced with the increasingly complicated inventory problems due to the prolonged production cycle of design, production, and consumption, as well as the problem of product homogeneity. Besides, it seemed to him that the business model of traditional clothing manufacturing was very unhealthy, in which manufacturers' products had to pass through agents or other intermediate traders to be sold to customers, and the prevalence of deduction, fraud, and deception in the process were posing serious problems to the entire business ecosystem. Zhang Daili realized that the "low cost + low price + channel" pyramid was not a solution for

---

[1] Jiang, Hengjie. The Influence of China's Entry to WTO on the Clothing Industry. *Textile Economy Weekly*, 2012(1),13.

manufacturing in the long run.² So, how could companies break through the traditional clothing industry model?

"Personalization"

Zhang Daili, who had worked in the clothing industry for years, was convinced that the clothes that fit one exactly are the best. He decided to build his clothing company into a business featuring "personalization". Generally speaking, clothing personalization consists of three types: the first is simple customization, i.e., the clothing is manufactured according to the standard pattern without making any change; the second is semi customization, which refers to pattern grading based on the standard pattern, changing the length of the specific parts; the third is full customization, i.e., to manufacture a single piece of clothes in a customized pattern by taking the customer's measurement, creating an exclusive pattern, applying the appropriate process — all in accordance with the customer's requirements.³

However, the traditional clothing customization industry had the disadvantages of strong dependence on experience, prolonged time of making, high cost, to name but a few. In order to solve these problems, Zhang Daili went to Germany, Japan, and other countries several times to visit custom clothing enterprises in the 1980s. Deeply impressed by the advanced technology and efficient productivity of a full-custom clothing company in Germany, Zhang Daili introduced their first custom-made production equipment from Germany. "I am very sensitive to these digital things and I like it very much," Zhang said. As early as 1986, he bought a computer and hired a computer teacher for his children. "I was trying to make good use of their business concept; I was perceptive enough to do that." Zhang had full confidence in himself, "I can do it well! Innovation is associated with huge risks and costs, but it can also create a bright future." In his view, the best future meant the highest efficiency, the lowest cost and the

---

²Red Collar Group: Achieve 150% Increase of Sales with Zero Inventory. http://info. texnet.com.cn/content/2015-03-28/510060.html, March 28, 2015.
³The Trend of Clothing Customization — The Full Customization. http://www.redcollar. com.cn/detailed.aspx?nid=122, October 26, 2015.

strongest profitability, and large-scale personalization was the only way to achieve it. He believed that it was the industrialized streamlined custom production model of "one pattern for one customer, one style for one garment, and one-piece flow" that Red Collar should develop.

It should be said that Zhang Daili first thought of how to make the company live longer and better before its inheritance. Where would the manufacturing industry go in the Internet era? Zhang Daili had a clear plan for the development and transition of the Red Collar Group, and it was with the entrepreneurial spirit of tenacity that he survived the initial difficulties.

The Subverter of the Traditional Clothing Industry

Many people consider personalization and mass production inherently contradictory. However, Zhang Daili saw it in a different way. He believed that the fundamental requirement for scale production was standardization, while personalization was the maximization of standardization; large-scale customization could be realized if each link of customization became standardized. To prove this, Zhang Daili devoted quite a few years to building a factory lab of more than 3,000 people and, based on big data technology and Internet thinking, creating the RCMTM (Red Collar Made to Measure, for custom suits) platform with independent intellectual property rights.

Big Data Technology Drives Mass Customization

The RCMTM platform was launched in April 2012. Consumers in every corner of the world can place an order for a customized suit through the RCMTM platform as long as they have access to the Internet. The entire production process consists of more than 30 sub-systems, all based on data.[4] The data system makes it possible for all the details of the garment to be customized and realizes mass industrial production on the assembly line. This system was developed after research into the personalized data

---

[4]Li Jinzhu from the Red Collar Group: Data Could Be Gold as well as Garbage. http://finance.sina.com.cn/leadership/msypl/20141016/140920557774.shtml, October 16, 2014.

of more than 2 million customers that were collected by the Red Collar over a decade. The change of any data would cause a simultaneous change of 9666 items of the data, as these data are closely connected to each other. It would thus ensure the fit of the clothes.[5]

The Original "Three Points and One Line" Body Measuring Method

Usually, the making of a customized suit includes such steps as body measurement, pattern making, cutting, sewing, fitting, and modification, all of which are basically done manually. The experience-based processes completed manually are where the high added value lies, because no one has exactly the same body measurement as another person. In order to find a way to measure quickly and accurately, Zhang Daili consulted many experienced body measurers and experts in the clothing industry. Yet, they all said that there was no short cut to learning how to measure. Thanks to his many years of experience working in the clothing industry, Zhang Daili eventually worked out a measuring method with independent intellectual property rights. Known as the "three points and one line", or the "infallible method", it requires only a ruler and a dedicated shoulder slope gauge. Using this method, the customer will get all the details of his body shape after obtaining the 24 figures from 19 body parts within 5 minutes. It only takes five days for the Red Collar Group to train a new hand to become a professional body measurer.[6]

Creating a 3D Intelligent Printing Factory

The key to the RCMTM platform is to replace the manual pattern making with 3D intelligent printing. As long as customers collect the data of their body through the "three points and one line" method and enter them into the RCMTM platform, the system will create a customer-specific pattern with 3D intelligent printing through digital modeling, which is based on the big data to ensure the accuracy of digital modeling. The Red Collar

---

[5] http://info.texnet.com.cn/content/2015-03-28/510060.html
[6] http://www.tedcollar.com.cn/detailed.aspx?nid=122

Group has a database of over a trillion patterns, which covers more than 99% body shapes across the world.

   After the formation of digital pattern, the system will split the garment data into specific processes (about 300), which will be processed by the computer identification terminal before being transferred to the stock preparation department, and then to the automatic cutting machine. All the cut pieces will be hung on a hanger (something like the train track), with an electronic tag with customer information attached to it in order to store each customer's specific needs. By scanning the electronic label of each piece of cloth with the computer, the workers on the assembly line can obtain the technical standards and operation requirements of the customer from the Internet cloud and sew the garment manually or with machine according to technical data such as lining, buttons, and cuffs.[7] The whole production workshop is very clean and tidy, the operation of the entire assembly line is extremely smooth, and there is no backlog of excess workload between the handover links. Employees of each department work in synchronization on Internet endpoints, obtain data from the network cloud, and interact with customers and users in real time despite the geographical distance, national borders, and language barriers.[8]

Subverting the Past, Fostering Strengths, and Avoiding Weaknesses

Based on 3D printing technology and the combination of informationization and industrialization, Red Collar Group has created a flexible factory, finally realizing the personal and flexible garment production in large scale, with high efficiency and low cost. The industrial customization model of the Red Collar Group has surpassed the original homogenized garment mass production mode in many ways: Sales have increased by 100% in the past three years, compared to the 10% increase under the

---

[7] Zhang, Xiaoying, Zhang Shuang, Liu Cheng. (2015). Red Collar Group: The Pioneer of Internet plus Clothing Customization. http://www.ce.cn/cysc/newmain/jdpd/fz/201507/07/t20150707_5857055.shtml, July 7.

[8] Chinese E-commerce Research Center. (2015). Red Collar Group: Internet plus the Intelligent Industrial Manufacture Model. www.efpp.com.cn.

original model; the profit garnered by the new model is 5–10 times more than that under the original model, with only a 10% increase in the production cost. The industrial customization model has a shorter production cycle, lower design cost than the old model, with the inventory dropping to zero; the per capita profit of this new model is six times as much as that of the original model; and so on. These data give the industrial customization model a much stronger competitiveness than the original model.

Apart from that, the new model has not only avoided the shortcomings of traditional suit tailoring, such as low production efficiency, long production cycle, and high labor cost, but also filled the gap in individual demands left out by industrialized assembly line production. In general, the production cycle of a high-end, custom, and hand-made suit is about 3–6 months, and the price of an ordinary piece, the channel price, is 2 times the mill price, which is often 5 times as much as the production cost. Using the new model, the Red Collar Group can finish and deliver a custom suit 7 days after the order is received, with a price about 2 times of the production cost. A custom suit can cost as low as 2,000 yuan, depending on the quality of the fabric.

Organizational Structure Reengineering Contributes to Business Model Transformation

The mass customization model has high requirements for the supply chain, R&D and design, production logistics, customer service, and other systems, and requires quick response from each system. Therefore, in order to cope with the disruptive changes in the business model, the Red Collar Group has continued to adjust and reform the management and organizational model to fully integrate internal and external resources. In 2013, the group formed an organizational structure led by a board of directors, with coordinated management of the process control center, investment and financing center, key account service center, and supply chain center.

Since the strategic transformation, the Red Collar Group has fully integrated the original 30-plus departments and eliminated redundant departments. "It has switched from hierarchical management to platform management, and it is node-to-node. The supply chain center, for instance, includes warehousing, supply, R&D, equipment, production, and other departments. The integration aims to coordinate the departments better and more efficiently meet customers' needs," said Li Dexing, director of the Red Collar Group supply chain center.[9]

This node-to-node, flat management with high efficiency is the node management model adopted by the Red Collar Group. For example, the customer service center gathers information about customers' demands and can send node-to-node orders to any position in any department of the group. That is to say, the customer's demands can be directly sent to the node staff rather than the department head, and the staff of the customer service center contact relevant departments according to customer's demands and consult with the supervisor if necessary. As soon as the task is finished, the performance of the head of the department that undertook the task will be evaluated by the department that assigned the task, and the department head will evaluate the performance of his subordinates, which is typical of the node-to-node mechanism under which the department heads assume full responsibility. With standardization, procedure-based management, and systemization as its core, the node management model solves the problems at each node that used to require extended experience and strong ability. Since the responsibility of each position is clearly-defined, the employees only need to execute the tasks, yet are obliged to provide feedback once a problem is discovered.

In addition, the Red Collar Group has also set up a traffic-light signaling mechanism to assess the integrity of employees. When the integrity of an employee or manager is compromised, a red light means that he/she needs to leave the company; a yellow light means the suspension of salary raise and promotion, but it can be compensated by doing charity activities; and a green light means that the employee or the manager has priority in salary adjustment and promotion. The traffic light mechanism is set in line with the organizational restructuring of the Red Collar Group to get rid of departments, the hierarchical levels, and unnecessary leadership. In addition, the Red Collar Group has also established a point mall to provide

---

[9] Pan, Dongyan. (2014). Red Collar Group: Subversive of the Manufacturing Industry? CEIBS Business Review, 8.

buffet-style benefits. Just like at a buffet table, employees can choose whatever they like in the mall with the points they have earned, such as a tour, a bike, or a dinner with the chairman.[10]

Through Wind and Rain, the Transformation Was Completed after Ten Years of Struggle

Behind the remarkable success of the RCMTM platform is the obsessive persistence of its founder, Zhang Daili, despite the opposition from all the employees. Pioneers of an industry are always alone from the very start and faced with lack of understanding and support. It is a worthy career, or more accurately a belief, that Zhang is holding on to. Ten years ago, with bright prospects in the clothing industry, no one understood why Zhang Daili would rather break new ground by investing in such a platform that did not seem to have a future. As a great deal of difficulties came up against him in the pursuit of transformation, Zhang cried and struggled, but he never thought of giving up.

Zhang found the most difficult part was to change the way people think. An employee who joined the Red Collar Group in 2009 said, "At that time, we all called him crazy behind his back. While accepting the tasks he had assigned us without saying anything, we would instead often delay or not do it at all." The objection of and resistance from the employees greatly embarrassed Zhang Daili, but he believed that the employees would cooperate willingly once they could see what the future holds for them. As a result, Zhang Daili convened one meeting after another to educate them and organize various training programs for them. For example, before the transformation, all the employees of the Red Collar factory came from the countryside and needed to be trained to learn such basic skills as turning on and off the computers. On one or two occasions, Zhang Daili had to take very tough steps. For instance, in order to facilitate the informatization construction and reduce the error rate at the same time, Zhang Daili required that the measurement department and other departments that they "must work with computers, or you will not be needed for the work!" Some employees who had not been able to change

---

[10] http://www.toutiao.com/i6209846269848027649/

the traditional working methods and thinking were dismissed; some other employees who could not put up with Zhang's reform chose to leave the Red Collar.

In addition, the R&D and innovation also encountered many bottle-necks. The underlying logic of RCMTM platform construction was designed by Zhang Daili, but the programming and construction of the system was very difficult. In 2003, as the domestic ERP system could not meet the requirements of mass customization, Zhang Daili decided to set up an information technology department consisting of more than a dozen people. When trying to build the system, the information technology department often worked late into the night, and from time to time had to start all over again due to lack of experience. Mi Qingyang, director of information technology of the Red Collar Group recalled, "The greatest challenges lay in the whole process from the research and development of information system to its online operation, as no software company had ever developed such a system. All we could do is talking to the employees slowly to get to know what their work involves, what are the processes and how efficient they are, so as to develop a system that can meet the needs of work and improve production efficiency." Li Jinzhu, vice president of the Red Collar Group who witnessed the whole process of enterprise transformation, observed, "Each step was a challenge then, as there was no experience to draw on, nor was there any precedent to refer to. When we made a step forward, something even harder loomed before we had time to savor the joyfulness."

In order to build this unprecedented system, Zhang Daili also pur-chased professional platform and equipment of assembly line customiza-tion system, and even introduced advanced hanging systems and logistics systems from abroad, but none of these readily met all of his production needs.[11] Therefore, Red Collar Group built a talent pool of more than 500 professional information technology engineers who were experts in big data, cloud computing, and other professional information systems by acquiring some professional IT companies or by working together with

---

[11] Liu, Meiqi, Zhang Yuting. (2015). Red Collar Suits: A Reform of Personalized Customization. www. CBRAND.com.cn.

some others. These engineers helped him build the exclusive platform system.

The ever-increasing investment in employee training, technical innovation, equipment purchases, factory construction, and so on had never shaken his confidence. "I was so determined to do this that I put more money into it progressively, investing as much as I can no matter how much it needed and putting it off when I was running short of money. These plans were not made overnight but were worked out as we moved one step at a time. In this way, from 2003 to the end of 2013, Red Collar Group had invested 260 million yuan in this production line."

Daughter Volunteers to Take over the Business and Works Alongside Father to Transform It

In the critical moment of enterprise transformation, who should decide the future development suddenly became a matter of great importance for Zhang Daili: "Who can adhere to the transformation concept as he did, and who can be devoted to the Red Collar without regret?" As he considered the transformation of the company to be a progressive process, he adopted a progressive approach in cultivating his successor. With the passage of time and after continuous attempts, Zhang Daili was convinced that he needed to alter his plan to hand over the company to excellent professional managers during the transformation of the enterprise.

Unlike many entrepreneurs, the selection of successors had been on Zhang Daili's mind since the beginning of the Red Collar Group. He has two children, a daughter and a son who is three years younger than his sister. Since he proclaimed that he would not hand over the company to his children, neither of them had ever worked in the Red Collar Group, even as an intern. While his daughter Zhang Yunlan was studying abroad, Zhang Daili was looking for a successor. He hired a succession of professional managers and endeavored to transform the enterprise into a limited company through the separation of ownership and control. However, none of the professional managers made a qualified successor for Zhang.

"Having achieved initial success, now I need to find someone to take it over and lead it to the future." Zhang Daili said, "I had been training professional managers, but I found a problem in the process: At that time, many professional managers in China were pursuing economic benefits only and would not change their ways no matter how hard I had tried to correct them."

In the view of Zhang Daili, the problem of these professional managers lied in their overall quality rather than their professional or management ability. "The fact that the cost of breaking the law is relatively low compared to the benefits behind it would make a manager tend to lose himself and step out of line." Zhang Daili commented on the professional managers whom he had hired before. He believed that this was induced by the social context at the time. Much improvement needed to be done to the professional manager system in China. When people's material needs had yet to be fully satisfied, they often gave in to the temptation of interests and violated the rules.

In his search for an excellent professional manager to be his successor, Zhang Daili came to realize that his two children were capable enough to do the business along with him. Since they were materially satisfied, well-educated, and raised properly, they were highly professional and ambitious. Having thought it through, Zhang Daili reached out to them.

Having started a business of his own, his son, Zhang Yan, did not accept Zhang Daili's offer to work in the Red Collar Group by his side. Zhang Daili then turned to his daughter, Zhang Yunlan, who studied at the University of Northern British Columbia in Canada after high school, and graduated with two degrees in marketing and international trade. After graduation, she returned to China and worked in a foreign company in Shanghai. However, the daughter was not ready to take over her father's business at first. She was expecting life to be calm as usual. "I did not really have a plan for my life, because I thought that life is about killing time and I really enjoyed doing that," Zhang Yunlan recalled.

One day in 2005, Zhang Daili went to Shanghai to tell his daughter about his plan for the company, including informatization construction and strategic transition. Zhang Yunlan, who knew nothing of the clothing industry, was touched by her father's description. "He painted such a beautiful picture that I was deeply touched." Zhang Yunlan said yes to her father. "I had a feeling at the time that my father needed me. Besides, I always believe that nothing is unachievable as long as I work diligently and learn as much as I can."

Naturally, Zhang Yunlan joined the Red Collar Group without hesitation. "Even when I was a little girl, my parents would tell me about the importance of 'harmony and unity' in a family, and I believe I should sacrifice my own interests for the wellbeing of the big family if necessary." Although supportive of her father, she did not know much about the strategic transition described by her father. She also knew absolutely nothing about the business, organizational structure, and culture of the entire enterprise.

Groomed as Father's Successor

Just like how he conducted the strategic transition, he did not give away his presidency to his daughter immediately. Instead, he let her start at the bottom to get experience in different positions, while he observed her work silently. During this period, the father and the daughter arrived at a certain degree of tacit understanding, although it was a painful break-in period.

Being new to the Red Collar Group, Zhang Yunlan was eager to know about everything at the frontline of the business, including business processes and professional knowledge. She was first assigned to the International Business Department as a customs broker, responsible for customs clearance, inspection applications, quality control, and international business negotiations. A year later, Zhang Daili sent her to take charge of the marketing center. After that, at her own request, she was sent to a production workshop.

This might seem to be carefully planned, but all of these were actually done without any planning. Zhang Yunlan recalled, "I was not even aware of how much I should learn in a position. I just went there to study and let him know when I had learned enough so that he would transfer me to another post."

In her first two years working in the Red Collar Group, Zhang Yunlan was known to her colleagues as a regular diligent coworker rather than daughter of the chairman. She used to come early in the morning and leave late in the evening; she was always polite to all her superiors as well as colleagues. Due to her effort, she won the recognition of her father and was popular with other workers.

However, she took some daring moves even when she was in a basic position. The first bold decision made by Zhang Yunlan was still fresh in her memory. Zhang Yunlan was pregnant that year when she was in charge of the marketing center, yet she was still immersed in her work. Many of the employees in the marketing center were friends and relatives of her fourth uncle, who started the business with her father, so they often enjoyed certain "privileges" in a sense. However, Zhang Yunlan did not allow "privilege" to proliferate in the enterprise, so she talked with employees every day, but it didn't seem to work. As a result, she decided to get the backbone of the entire marketing team replaced. When she reported the decision to her father, he did not show any signs of disapproval, but encouraged her to make the call by herself.

Later, Zhang Yunlan made some adjustments to the entire marketing team, dismissing those who did not agree with the enterprise strategy and related instructions (accounting for nearly half of the entire team), and recruited and built a new team consisting of "post-80s". Although the new team was much younger than the old one, her move sent shock waves through the business of the Red Collar Group. In that year, the annual sales of the Red Collar Group decreased by half, and it took the enterprise a year to recover from it. At the same time, Zhang Yunlan was criticized for being a "spendthrift" and people said that the Red Collar Group should not have removed these talented people without a second thought.

While Zhang Yunlan was somewhat upset by the outcome, her father, who heard all the negative comments about Yunlan, did not mention a word of it to her diligent daughter. Instead, he encouraged his daughter to win back the lost market share. "He would let me fix it myself, reflect on my own, review it myself, and make it up by myself, yet with everything under his control." Zhang Yunlan concluded, "I think my father did a particularly good job in this regard. I am especially grateful to him."

Despite her father's support, Zhang Yunlan also had a hard time reconciling her style with her father's. "He did not praise us. We would feel greatly relieved to not be criticized by him." As the employees saw it, the father and the daughter differed in management styles but shared the same business philosophy. They both placed strict demands on integrity and quality. Zhang Rubo, business manager of the Red-collar Group for the Americas, said, "There is a slight difference in their focus: The chairman's extremely high requirements for product quality and production details have made us feel that high-quality products are the lifeblood of the company, which we can't afford to compromise on. Having studied abroad, Ms. Zhang has caused us to think more about the market, focusing on the customers from the beginning to the end. With products on one side, and the customers on the other, the two have shaped a unity."

There were many disagreements and conflicts between the father and the daughter, but every time Zhang Yunlan would successfully reach an agreement with her father in a clever way. At the beginning, Zhang Yunlan, who had lived overseas, often expressed her opposition to her father's ideas directly, but she gradually realized that it not only could not help solve the problem, but would also hurt each other's feelings. Later, she would first accept her father's advice, then refine her idea based on deep thinking, and then express her ideas to her father via email in the fullness of time. She considered it to be an effective way of communication. For one thing, she could comb through her argument and express her ideas rather well. For another, her father would "listen" to her suggestions more objectively. Zhang Yunlan's approach represented a good reference for how to deal with intergenerational conflict under various circumstances.

A New Broom Sweeps Clean

Zhang Yunlan is anything but a typical Shandong woman. Behind her gentle look and soft voice is a tough style. In March 2009, Zhang Daili said to her daughter, "I think it's time for you to take this position. I am going to hold a ceremony and invite a few friends of mine. Get ready for a speech about the future planning of the company." In this way, Zhang Daili handed over the presidency of the company to Zhang Yunlan. In her speech, Zhang Yunlan mainly talked about the "customization" strategy of the Red Collar Group, and expressed gratitude to her father. She believed her father not only handed over the power of the company's presidency to her but also pointed out the right direction. She may go slowly in that direction but prospects are good. This direction is the strategic transition to mass customization.

As she just turned 30 when she became the president, Zhang Yunlan was under great pressure from the powerful senior managers and employees who were skeptical about the strategic positioning and institutional reform of the company. In order to assert her authority, she invested a lot of time and emotion to communicate with employees, only to find that there was still opposition to the strategy of the group despite how genuine she was. She then decided to run the company in accordance with the rules and regulations without too much emotion involved.

Based on this principle, Zhang Yunlan fired a very influential veteran, who had represented a big obstacle to her management and implementation of the company's strategy. "I talked to him. I said from the bottom of my heart that, as the chairperson, I hope that he can take the lead in giving me support from the perspective of work and in the capacity of my elder." Zhang Yunlan recalled, "He said he would be supportive, but failed to put it into practice." Once, the veteran manager failed to attend a company meeting and could not be reached. The next day, Zhang Yunlan told the human resources department that he was to be dismissed. After that, she euphemistically told her father that she might have made another mistake. Even so, Zhang Daili expressed his approval for her daughter's decision. This incident came as a shock to the other veterans of the Red Collar Group, causing them to follow the rules.

In addition, in order to establish a sounder system to protect the corporate culture from being eroded by "privilege" and "nepotism", Zhang Yunlan almost removed all her family members from the Red Collar Group, leaving no one from her family in the core management positions. Apart from the institutionalization of the organization, Zhang Yunlan also made full use of the construction of mass customization to recruit young talents in a drastic manner, forming a leadership mainly consisting of "post-80s", among which many managers were "post-85s".

The team was getting more international while getting younger. It was after Zhang Yunlan took office as president that the international business of the Red Collar Group began to take off.[12] Before the transformation,

---

[12] Around 2014, half of Red Collar Group's revenue came from the overseas market, of which 80% were from the US and New York was its best market in the US.

the foreign trade business of the Red Collar Group was mainly OEM processing with low profits, and any mistake in the process could result in a loss. Besides, the company never went abroad to attend exhibitions, and therefore had no say in the international market. Zhang Yunlan proposed to attend exhibitions in the US after taking office and recruited some college students fluent in English. The core competitiveness brought by the RCMTM platform enhanced the Red Collar Group's bargaining power in the international market and greatly increased their profit margin. Zhang Rubo, general manager of the American business, who was recruited and cultivated by Zhang Yunlan, talked about the changes in the international business before and after the transformation of the group: "Before the transformation, we were one of the OEMs of M&S in the UK. We faced many rivals, a price only enough to cover the cost, as well as the possible move of production to Southeast Asia. After the transformation, we began to cooperate with other brands in the UK in MTM business through RCMTM platform and seized the market share quickly. M&S came to us to renew our cooperation in MTM, with a price several times higher than before and mutual respect."

In addition, in order to coordinate with the mass customization model launched by Red Collar Group, Zhang Yunlan continued to break new ground in market expansion and established more diversified custom brands. For example, she launched the R•PRINCE specializing in wedding dress, the international custom brand CAMEO, the latest Cotte, as well as brands specializing in women's clothing and children's clothing.

Zhang Daili is very glad to see his daughter Zhang Yunlan sacrifice her own interests to fight alongside him for the future of the enterprise that he established. In his view, the strategic transition of the Red Collar Group is inseparable from the cultivation of its successor. Zhang Yunlan said, "I was not growing by the day but by the hour." Ten years ago, young and fearless, she joined the Red Collar Group at her father's invitation. Six years ago, she talked about the beauty of the era of "customization" at the succession ceremony with confidence. Today, she is still working diligently at the production line after the development of the Magic Manufactory APP and the building of the Kutesmart platform, embodying the spirit of the Red Collar Group. But all the things behind it, the conviction and hesitation, the happiness and pain, the hard work and gains, constitute a story that only she knows.

Differences and Generation Gap Between Father and Daughter

In the mixed process of inheritance and transformation, Zhang Daili and Zhang Yunlan did have many differences and conflicts in ideas and methods, but they would keep trying to explore the direction that was most suitable for the Red Collar Group. Their way of getting along can actually provide a reference for family businesses that are going or will go through succession.

First, they differ in the way of management. Zhang Daili is strict with his children and employees, setting high standards and requirements for them. For example, employees were required to take notes with a computer at meetings rather than paper and pen. He even made rules about Zhang Yunlan's dress and hairstyle. Different from her father, Zhang Yunlan has a gentle attitude and is very polite to other leaders and colleagues, which has won her the recognition of others.

Second, they differ in how they communicate. Both of them have dismissed employees who do not cooperate with the company's strategic transition but their way of communication is very different. Zhang Daili is rather tough with employees, and he used to educate them at meetings, while Zhang Yunlan prefers one-on-one conversations. Aware of her father's feelings, she always keeps her father informed of each move and the reason behind it.

Third, they focus on different things. Zhang Daili puts a high value on product quality and other details of the production, while Zhang Yunlan is more focused on the market and pays more attention to customers. Besides, Zhang Daili is good at seeing the overarching picture and focuses on strategic management, while Zhang Yunlan pays more attention to details.

Fourth, they differ in the extent of openness. Zhang Yunlan is more open-minded than her father about expanding international business by introducing young, international talents. She also attempts to attract customers in more fields by promoting brand development.

Fifth, they differ in pioneering spirit. Zhang Daili is more entrepreneurial, daring to innovate and take risks, good at discovering and exploiting opportunities, and more committed to his dream. As the successor to such a successful entrepreneur as her father, Zhang Yunlan tends to follow her father's path and expand business in specific areas.

The different approaches of Zhang Yunlan and Zhang Daili mean different things to different people.

Embracing the Internet

In 2013, Zhang Daili's hard work finally paid off — the company had been successfully transformed. Fighting alone from the start, then with his daughter, he won the support of all the employees at last, and the Red Collar Group was also ushered into a new era of "manufacturing customized products with industrial production efficiency". Today, the Red Collar factory can automatically make over 20 sets of completely different suit patterns per second. In 2014, it achieved 150% increase in sales with zero inventory and a turnover of 6 billion yuan. "This once small clothing company has now become a platform, an e-commerce platform in the Internet industry," Zhang Daili said in an interview. After the successful transformation, the "Red-Collar model" hit the headlines and was covered twice by CCTV News Broadcast, attracting many well-known entrepreneurs to visit the factory. Zhang Ruimin, chairman of the Board of Directors of Haier Group, commented after the visit, "Changing from mass production to mass customization is essential but also the most difficult thing for traditional enterprises in the Internet era, in order to give customers the best individualized experience. The Red Collar made it. It is the outcome of years of dedicated hard work."

New Strategic Positioning: Contributing a New Force to Internet Industrial Civilization for Mankind

In 2013, the Red Collar Group organized a discussion on the company's strategic positioning and finally proposed the positioning of "Internet plus Industry". Zhang Daili said that "Internet plus" is to integrate Internet thinking into the vein of the enterprise, rather than simply adding a bit of Internet elements. The Red Collar Group, with its origin in industry, has proposed a C2M (Customer to Manufactory) model based on Internet thinking, which is to build an Internet-based direct interaction platform between consumers and manufacturers. "The core value of the Red Collar model is its development of a new paradigm of deep integration between traditional manufacturing and information technology, which includes the Internet thinking of industrial production, the whole process of production driven by data, and the debureaucratization of the organization. The operation model of direct connection between customers and manufacturers makes it possible to meet the individualized demand with industrialized mass production," commented Huang Kainan, deputy dean of the Center for Economic Research of Shandong University.

Kutesmart: Building a C2M Business Ecosystem

After the completion of the transformation of the entire enterprise in 2013, the strategic positioning of the Group has changed from the "mass customization" proposed by Zhang Yunlan when she took office in 2009 to creating a personalized customization platform for consumers based on the "Internet plus Industry" concept, or C2M business ecosystem, allowing consumers to make direct contact with the manufacturer. At the same time, the Red Collar Group is determined to promote "transformation of traditional industries" across the country and provide "one-stop solution". This critical task is undertaken by Qingdao Kutesmart Co., Ltd. (or "Kutesmart" for short). At the end of August 2015, Kutesmart launched its core strategic product, the "Magic Manufactory", under which the production of factory is directly driven by consumers' needs.

The "Kutesmart[13] C2M Business Ecosystem" proposed by the Red Collar Group aims to integrate the Internet with industrialization and connect customers directly to manufacturers. For customers, their demands are directly sent to the manufacturer instantly through the Internet platform, rather than through layers of agents in the traditional manner, making consumption and production a community of shared future in the market ecosystem. For manufacturing plants, the use of Internet of Things, the Internet and other technologies have helped them to build a connection

---

[13] Kutesmart is Qingdao Kaimiao Garment Co., Ltd. that was registered in 2005. Before that, Zhang Daili intentionally introduced the enterprise's transformation scheme with core competitiveness to this company. In 2013, the company was renamed "Kutesmart".

between people and people, people and factories, factories and factories, and services and services, realizing the horizontal, vertical, and "end-to-end" integration. Zhang Daili believes that it will provide solutions for traditional industries to be upgraded to the Internet-based industry. To this end, the Red Collar Group is building the Kutesmart ecological platform and has developed a product with completely independent intellectual property rights and source code — the SDE (Source Data Engineering), whose core competence is to provide enterprises with "Internet plus Industry" solution.

The Magic Manufactory is a strategic product of Kutesmart, an e-commerce platform that represents the C2M model. The mobile App called "Magic Manufactory" was officially launched at the end of August 2015. Zhang Yunlan said that its magic lies in that "the factory can quickly respond to the individual needs of customers". The Magic Manufactory beats the platform launched by the Red Collar Group previously in many aspects. For measurement, customers can go to its off-line store, or make an appointment for home service. The upcoming technology-based method can accurately collect the customer's data within 5 seconds. With regards to logistics, the delivery will take only 5 working days at the end of 2015. Customers can either pick it up at the store or take delivery at the designated address. In addition, in order to promoting its online activities, the Magic Manufactory is opening brick and mortar experience stores[14] in 24 cities across the country, which also provide measurement services.

The Implementation of Strategy: Challenges and Reflections

In the past 20 years, Zhang Daili has paved the way for the development of the Red Collar Group and led the company in achieving great success. He knows that everything is still in the process, and many strategies have yet to be carried out. (See Figure 11.1). He has just turned sixty and plans

---

[14] By October 21, 2015, Magic Manufactory had totally 15 stores, two in Jinan, one in Tianjin, one in Beijing, one in Shenyang, one in Dalian, one in Chengdu, one in Xi'an, one in Qingdao, two in Shanghai, one in Suzhou, one in Hangzhou, one in Shenzhen, and one in Kunming.

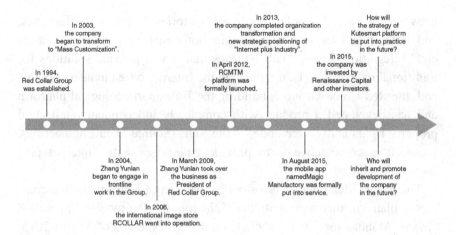

Figure 11.1   Timeline of Major Events in the Strategic Transition and Succession of Red Collar Group

to retire completely in three years. In order to make Red Collar a public company, he plans to complete the listing of the company within the next two years, and has so far completed two rounds of financing and introduced three investors including Renaissance Capital.[15] The shares holding by outside investors in the Red Collar Group will be less than 10% to ensure family holdings. According to Zhang Daili, the scale of the company will soon reach 10 billion yuan in the next two years, and the target is to reach 100 billion yuan when the enterprise is listed.

However, the strategic transformation of the company is ongoing, as the Kutesmart platform and Magic Manufactory launched by Red Collar Group have not truly impressed the consumers. The company's priority remains to be how to find the first consumers and satisfy them. If the company can succeed in attracting the first group of consumers, it will have its consumers multiplied more easily and faster, as Red Collar Group is full of confidence in the Red-Collar model and its products and services.

In the Internet era, companies tend to pursue faster growth, steady development, and longer lives, of which the latter two are the core

---

[15] Before introducing investors, Zhang Daili, daughter Zhang Yunlan and son Zhang Yan held shares of 51%, 25%, and 24% respectively.

elements of building evergreen foundation for a company, according to the Red Collar Group. So, the key for the Group to seizing the market opportunity is not fast growth, but stable development. Today, the smart factory has completed the transformation and upgrading, but lack of qualified personnel has delayed the implementation of strategy at the customer end. "High-salary fails to attract people who can implement the strategy. The higher the people are paid, the emptier their words are. They are just not able to do tangible work to put it through", Zhang Yunlan said.

"I am particularly grateful to my father. I think one thing he did the best about the inheritance is that he did not just pass a company to his children but provided a direction and relevant methods for them." Zhang Yunlan summed up the six years after she took over the company. "But everything is still under progress and we have yet to put our plan through. If the company is no longer developing, there will be no inheritance." Zhang Yunlan does not think that she has successfully taken over the company. "It is just the beginning, but how far I can go and how stable I am are dependent on my own performance and ability." This 30-plus-year-old woman of second generation entrepreneurs said softly, "I believe that my father and the entire group will remove me from my post without hesitation if I turn out to be not competent for the job one day."

Enterprise Heritage: The Succession Is Still on the Way

Although Zhang Daili has passed the presidency to his daughter, he still insists on building a public company. "The idea of building a public enterprise has not changed; I am still looking for a good professional manager who I know exists in the world; the only problem is that we need to find him/her." Zhang Daili said. Zhang Yunlan really understands her father's thought and said, "Of course, it's totally fine with me. I think it is right, and I totally agree with my father on that. He has such an ambitious vision that all the plans are based on that." Zhang Daili believes that the current Kutesmart platform created by the company can be spread and applied to all industries, enterprises, and organizations, contributing a new force of Internet industrial civilization to humanity.

Zhang Yunlan is convinced that her father's strategic plan is great and ambitious, but she also knows that the future will be full of challenges, and there is still a long way to go before the strategy is implemented successfully. "Actually, from the first day to the present, I have never been able to confirm whether I can lead this enterprise to the future, for the plan of C2M ongoing now is too large and the major problem lies in that there is no successful case for us to refer to." Zhang Yunlan finds that everything is no longer as simple as when she took over the presidency from a global perspective. "So, I'm not sure how long I can stay in this position and lead the company in its development, for a chairperson cannot play the role of CEO after all."

Zhang Yunlan is influenced by her father's tenacity, and his idea on reforming Red Collar to achieve industrialization has become a goal for the whole family. Zhang Yunlan has been carrying out reforms with no unnecessary worries because of her father's staunch support, during which trust and tacit understanding has grown between the first generation and the second generation. She clearly knows that the company must be transformed to reach the goal of C2M model set by her father. Zhang Daili would support all the moves of his daughter on the way to succession as long as she does not go against the common goal. This good intention also allows the second generation to have more confidence in creating a new world.

As the Red Collar's strategy of personalized customization became clearer and attracted more attention from the outside world, Zhang Daili and Zhang Yunlan were doing all they could to accelerate the implementation of the strategy at the customer end. In 2015, the Red Collar decided to create a new brand which requires planning for online products. Zhang Yunlan looked around only to find that no one was more suitable than her younger brother. Therefore, Zhang Yunlan asked her younger brother Zhang Yan, who engaged in investing at the time, to come back to the company, "I asked him to come back to help me as my father did a couple of years before. He dropped what he was doing immediately and returned with no hesitation."

Compared with the situation in her father's time, the C2M model has been accepted by more and more people due to greater penetration of the Internet. Thus, the promotion of the model is smoother than expected.

Zhang Yunlan and her younger brother have a clear division of work: Zhang Yunlan is responsible for popularizing the concept of Red Collar's C2M, and her younger brother Zhang Yan is in charge of the implementation of strategy and actual operations. Zhang Yan repeatedly stressed, "The current popular practice of the Internet is not suitable for the Red Collar. The Magic Manufactory will not splash money on web traffic. It must be financially viable, for profit represents the company's dignity. The apps of start-ups count on web traffic to raise money, but we are leading an industrial revolution." This also represents the views of Zhang Daili and Zhang Yunlan who repeated this view when presenting the Red Collar 4.0 industrial revolution in public.

The whole family is surprisingly consistent in pursuing this ultimate goal, which is attributable to the workings of genes, as said by Zhang Daili. For several years as he relinquished the thought of employing a professional manager in favor of selecting his daughter to take over the company, he has become more convinced about this: "The reason why my daughter can take over the company successfully lies not in the process, but in our consensus."

"Father has already led the Red Collar through the transformation of the supply chain despite great resistance. As the second generation, I must carry on father's values and spirit of the craftsman." Zhang Yunlan said frankly. Zhang Yan thinks that as successors they consider it a pressure as well as an impetus: "My father said to me that since everything is ready now, it's all on you now."

Now realizing that she has not given enough time to her children, Zhang Yunlan finally begins to work fewer hours. "I am trying to give priority to my family as much as work and spend more time with my family. This is a healthy balance." In addition, the return of her younger brother to the company has also taken much of the pressure off her, allowing her to spend more time with her children.

In order to ensure a smooth succession, Zhang Daili began the handover at the age of 55, but he is currently still not completely reassured: "I think I have to stay and assist them for a few more years, for the handover should be completed strategically rather than all at once." In fact, Zhang Daili has his own unfulfilled wishes. Having led the Red Collar in strategic transformation for more than ten years, he sees a huge market in the transformation of traditional enterprises. As thousands of small and medium-sized enterprises now face this challenge, the Red Collar can export this set of transformation plan to help more traditional enterprises with their transformation, which will spare them the intermediate links and bring higher profit.

Zhang Yunlan has not asked her father's plan regarding the successor in the future. She believes that her father would choose whoever is the most suitable and what she needs to do now is to do the work well step by step. Zhang Daili does not consider it to be a problem: "Even when my daughter takes over the company, my son will still be a shareholder. This enterprise belongs to both of them. I have no intention of working until I am advanced in age. The development of the company is their business after I fulfill my dream." Now it seems that they constitute a solid triangle: The elder sister takes over the business and controls the general direction of the Red Collar; the younger brother is in charge of operation, ensures that the plans are carried out and in the right direction; and their father manages the supply chain and provides his children the support they need.

On the shoulders of the giants, can Zhang Yunlan lead the Red Collar Group in implementing the strategy perfectly when her father completely withdraws from the Red Collar Group in three to five years? Now with the help of her younger brother, what is the future that lies ahead for the Red Collar Group? Whichever path should they take toward transformation in the future, they will need to understand and rely on each other, supporting each other strongly with no hesitation when necessary. All of these make the Red Collar a good example for the second-generation successors and the enterprises in transformation to learn from.

12

When Succession Meets Transformation

In the earlier chapters, we have studied several issues that Chinese family businesses are currently facing. From the perspective of corporate inheritance, should the first generation let the children or professional managers take over the business? From the perspective of wealth inheritance, should they reasonably divide the property among family members or concentrate it? Should they let corporations go public or maintain the absolute control and management by the family? From the perspective of enterprise transformation, should they choose business specialization or diversification, internationalization or localization, low-end or high-end, and online or offline? A series of survival and development issues are imminent. In light of the analysis of the cases, we will discuss these problems in this chapter by using four figures to summarize and describe the succession and transformation of family businesses: Figure 12.1 shows four models of family business succession; Figure 12.2 specifically depicts two ways of internal equity allocation in the family; Figure 12.3 shows the four sources of successors to family business management; Figure 12.4 shows several options for strategic transformation. The popular saying known as "crossing the river by feeling for the stones" describes gradually drawing your own blueprint by observing how others have done it.

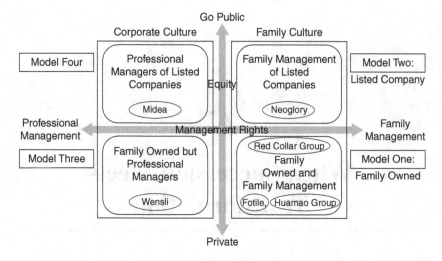

Figure 12.1   Four Succession Models of Family Business

Four Models of Family Business Succession

The succession of family businesses actually includes two dimensions: One is the shift of management rights, and the other is the transfer of ownership (namely equity). However, we often get them mixed up. Speaking of management rights, they can be retained by the family or transferred to professional managers; as for equity, it can be retained within the family, or (part of the) equity can be transferred to those outside the family such as employees and the public. Based on these two dimensions, we classify family businesses into four types (see Figure 12.1): First, the company is owned and managed by the family; second, the company goes public but is managed by the family; third, the company is owned by the family but managed by a professional manager, and fourth, the company goes public and is managed by a professional manager. We will explain them one by one in the following.

Model One: Centralization of Dual Rights — Owned and Managed by the Family

In the management and inheritance of family businesses, the core is to achieve the optimal allocation of management rights and equity. Among the existing models, the most common one is the centralization of two rights. Most family corporations develop themselves from scratch, thanks to the strong personal ability and judgment and decision-making of the entrepreneurial generation. At present, most family corporations in China are still in such a state: In most cases the equity and management rights are controlled by one family, in particular by one individual. The stability of control and management rights will guarantee the sustainable development of a firm, especially for family companies. When rights of ownership and management are centralized, however, the correlation between the future of the enterprise and the will of the family will become more closely connected.

In light of traditional Chinese thinking, the most conventional way of family business succession is the model of dual rights centralization, namely the equity and management rights are retained by the family. The inheritance of equity in family firms, in nature, is the distribution and inheritance of family wealth, while family business management rights are corporate rights of control over the actual operation of the enterprise, reflecting the management behavior of family members. There are usually two steps in the model of "father-son/daughter" succession. The sign of completing the first step is that the second generation becomes chairman (namely management rights are passed from the first generation to the next), and the sign of completing the second step is that the second generation gains the actual control of the corporation (that is, the equity is passed on from the first generation to the second). Obviously, under this model, the choice of successors is crucial. Many time-honored Chinese brands declined because of the incompetent successors, and some withdrew from the market due to the lack of successors.

In the cases discussed earlier, we discover that Fotile, Huamao, and Red Collar have the dual rights in the hands of the family. Likewise, the domestic business and the overall decision-making of Wensli are basically implemented based on dual rights. But adopting such a model does not mean that they exclude the involvement of professional managers. In fact, these firms inevitably need the support of professional teams in the course of growth, and they have also perfected the establishment of corporate specialization and standardized governance structure before the second generation takes over the business. When it comes to family business, they have chosen the path of "father-son/daughter" and equity privatization.

The Agency Theory holds that when ownership and management rights are unified in the family, the agency costs within the enterprise are minimized.[1] In addition, there is the concept of "differential mode of the association" in China that makes it difficult to establish a high level of trust between family and non-family members. The imperfection of the professional manager market also increases the cost and risk of introducing external managers. The existence of domestic family corporations is generally short, and most of them are still under the control of the first-generation leaders. The founding entrepreneur's courage, vision, social relationships, and his/her absolute authority in the family can effectively reduce the cost of family management, which allows people to fully utilize its strengths and makes it easier for family members to show trust and loyalty to one another.[2] This is an extremely favorable condition for the handover and development of the enterprise in the first peak of family business in China.

However, in the case of dual rights centralization in the family, the more family members participate in business operations, the more outstanding talents abound and the more family members the board of directors accumulate, the more difficult intergenerational will be. This point has been explained in detail in Zone 7 of the Three-circle Theory. Therefore, we notice that for Fotile or Huamao Group, the selection of successors is very clear. Although the two families have different methods in the inheritance of dual rights, both management right and equity are firmly under the control of the family. Both Mao Lixiang and Xu Wanmao handed over the management right of the enterprise in its totality to Mao Zhongqun and Xu Lixun through the mechanism prepared in advance, avoiding frictions arising from jostling for management right by other family members. The focus of management right transfer is not on wealth but on talent. Thus, only when the next generation possesses the ability to

---

[1] Jensen, M. C., & Meckling, W. H. (1976). Theory of the Firm: Managerial Behavior, Agency Costs and Capital Structure. *Journal of Financial Economics*, 3, 305–360.
[2] Pang, Zhu. (2012). Family's Control Power, Management Power and Corporate Performance — A Research Based on the Listed Companies of Chinese Families. *Tourism Overview*, 9.

manage family companies, then the interfamily succession of management right is beneficial to the long-term sustainable development of the company. This is also the main reason why family corporations need to adopt a modern corporate governance model and hire competent managers from outside the family to serve as executives if their family members are no longer qualified for business management once the company expands. Mao Zhongqun of Fotile showed a strong sense of innovation and management skills over the course of succession. He grew up with the company, and thus excelled in both professional skills and management philosophy, which is a key guarantee for Fotile's strategic focus and concentration.

The smooth of Red Collar should be attributed to Zhang Daili, a liberal-minded first generation entrepreneur. He begun to reflect on the direction of corporate governance and how to select successor fairly early when he made the decision to lead the enterprise in transforming into high-end customization service by taking advantage of the Internet. After employing several professional managers, Daili was convinced that he must rely on his own children. A decade after she took over the power from her father, Zhang Yunlan demonstrated that she was capable of running the family business independently. Meanwhile, the return of the son Zhang Yan made the company all the more powerful. However, given the industry features and future development needs of Red Collar, perhaps like Wensli, they will rely more on the expertise of professional managers and the financial support from the capital market in the future. We are eager to see what inheritance path it will take in the future.

In a word, currently most Chinese family firms belong to this model. If there is enough management talent in the family who are willing to assume the management responsibility of the businesses, then family management, which boasts unique strengths, is never a bad idea. In the event where more resources are needed, or competent successors are not found in the family over the course of corporate development, then family companies will have to take other succession models.

Model Two: Managed by Family and Going Public

When an enterprise is in a high-speed development and encounters a transformation bottleneck, the original capital accumulation method may not be able to meet the funding requirements for further expansion. Under such conditions, bringing in strategic investors or going public to quickly obtain the funds required for development have become the preferred choice for many family businesses. After more than a decade of growth, many family companies have started to turn to financial investment fields, especially after the second generation with a background of overseas education are involved. When the enterprise transformation covers multiple fields, the demand for the capital market becomes particularly obvious. Therefore, going public has remained a concern for almost every family business in the past five years. Once a firm is listed, its original management structure and development model will be impacted to a certain extent. For family corporations, the balanced allocation of equity and management rights will no longer be based on family control only but will be oriented to specialization and institutionalization.

Even after going public, many family corporations still retain the management right of the parent company. That is to say, the listed company is a subsidiary, but its equity and management rights are still in the hands of the family who holds controlling shares in the parent company. Due to the late start of Chinese family businesses, many of the first-generation entrepreneurs are in their mid-fifties and have not considered equity arrangement for the second generation. According to the 2015 survey[3] by Forbes (Chinese Edition), only 20% of family companies listed on the A-share market hold corporate equity, and nearly 50% of the second generation hold stock between 5% to 15%. In a small number of enterprises which have completed the handover, the second generation holds over 20% of the shares. On the issue of property rights, the control of family firms still remains in the hands of first generation. When the second generation joins the corporation, most of them start from lower positions and gradually take charge of the firm's management and not until then will the transfer of property rights begin.

As for A-share listed family businesses, most of the second generation hold the post of corporate directors, which accounts for 53% (including general managers and concurrent directors). Wang Sicong, son of Wang

---

[3] Mao, Jingjing. (2015). Game Between Inheritance and Tradition — A Survey Report on Family Businesses. *Forbes* (Chinese version), 9.

Jianlin from Wanda Group, and Xu Shitan, son of Xu Rongxiao from Shimao Group, for example, are both on the board of directors although they are not directly involved in the management of the company. Secondly, 27% of the second generation have been appointed as general manager. On the path of succession, some families choose to let the second generation start from the basic level or branch companies, so that they can be familiar with all aspects of management, such as Liang Zaizhong, successor of Sany Heavy Industry, who started as workshop supervisor, and Xiu Yuan, the heir of Xiuzheng Pharmaceutical Group who got down to business from the branch in Guangdong. Some families tend to let the second generation get direct contact with the operation of the company in management positions, grasping the overall corporate development as decision makers. Take Lu Weiding for example. He served as deputy general manager of Wanxiang Group at the age of 21.[4]

On April 27, 2016, Neoglory Prosperity Co., Ltd., a subsidiary of Neoglory Group, officially went public after restructuring and a name change, which is a milestone that Neoglory Group has achieved after multiple twists and turns. Since the completion of restructuring, Neoglory Holding Group Co., Ltd., with a shareholding ratio of 71.05%, has become the largest shareholder of Neoglory Prosperity. In addition, Yu Yunxin holds 96,943,581 shares of the company, accounting for 7.89% of the total shares after the issuance. For Neoglory Group the succession plan is well in place. Yu Jiangbo, Zhou Xiaoguang's eldest son has been implementing his plans in the family corporation's main business sectors. After a series of drastic reforms, Jiangbo has played a key role in improving the jewelry company's performance. At the same time, in light of his own interest, he has expanded into the new frontier of e-commerce, which has injected new vitality into the traditional enterprise. With the stable development of the core jewelry business after transformation, Yu Jiangbo is starting to get engaged in the family's investment business, and along with his parents, will take Neoglory to broader domains.

Neoglory's persistence in going public is because doing so can bring large amount of funds for its real estate business and investment sectors, which has always been the strategic vision of this company. Since Yu Jiangbo

---

[4] Ibid.

took over as general manager of Neoglory Jewelry, he has been assisting his parents to fulfill this wish. Zhou Xiaoguang spent ten years fostering three professional managers without success, and has finally turned Neoglory into a leading jewelry producer with the full support and dedication of her son. So, considering the current performance and the personal ability of Yu Jiangbo, Neoglory, as a family business, will undoubtedly keep management rights within the family. Going public will help Neoglory to access the capital market. In the future, Neoglory will still focus on industry and commerce, supplemented by investment and finance, with the intention of broadening its scope of business. For those family businesses troubled by the imperfection of professional manager system, this is a possible choice of path for them.

After a family business goes public, it has to publish its financial reports on a regular basis to improve the transparency of corporate information, which is beneficial for investors and banks to assess the development plans and operational risks and therefore reduces uncertainties of the corporation. Additionally, the shares of listed companies can be cashed at any time, lowering the credit risk of the company and making it easier to obtain loans from banks. Hence, family businesses are more likely to gain financial support, whether it is from the capital market or the banking system, and less likely to encounter capital chain rupture. Moreover, after going public, family companies will become better known to the public and customers in a wider area, which will no doubt help increase the reputation assets of the firm. After going public, it is easier for family companies to win the respect and trust of customers, and they are in a better position to take orders from VIP customers, and increase the possibility of long-term cooperation with them. For companies like Neoglory, family image and brand equity will reinforce each other.

Firms like Neoglory conditionally separate ownership from management right. Although there are non-family shareholders, family members still control the overall situation. To maintain family management right and list on the stock market, part of the family business can leverage funds from the capital market while maintaining the family's power in the business. This may prove to be a win-win path for young Chinese family businesses.

Model 3: Private Ownership by Families and Management by Professional Managers

For every family business, the first generation often wants their offspring to succeed in order to obtain the dual inheritance of ownership and management right. However, what are they supposed to do when their children are unwilling or unable to take over the business? Whether they are domestic, Western or other mature family corporations, their first choice is to separate equity rights from management rights and to introduce professional managers to run the business. In China, the entrepreneurial generation often has a very strong personality as they are the people who started the business. They like to get actively involved, regarding the company as their own home, and particularly trust the veterans who have worked hard with them all along. Contrastingly, they do not place complete trust in professional managers. When the second generation takes over the business, they must learn to delegate the management power to professionals so that they can maximize their management abilities within the framework of well-established rules. Meanwhile they can also establish their own management team and change the overarching philosophy and practice of the enterprise.

As a result, a feasible model is to employ professional managers to implement professionalized management while the family maintains their equity right. In recent years this management model has been accepted by more and more family firms. In the process of inheritance, family companies have gradually transformed the former family governance model into specialized management.

In fact, many Western family enterprises are not completely ruled by a certain family but rely on majority shareholders to control the company. In terms of equity right, these family firms have adopted two major methods. Most of the larger family businesses adopt decentralized equity right, while the smaller ones mostly have centralized equity right.[5] Decentralized equity right allows as many family members as possible to hold company shares. In this type of family firms, the family members mostly play the

---

[5]Liu, Qiongna. (2011). Secrets of Long Lasting Family Businesses. *Grand Garden of Science*, 12, 77.

role of policy makers, and daily operations are conducted by hired professionals. Centralized equity right means that stock rights are only distributed to family members who hold posts in the company. Therefore, when family corporations grow stronger regardless if they are diversifying, expanding into the international market, or entering a new technological field, they need the support of professional managers. For the succeeding generation, the retention of equity right within the family can ensure they have the final say in strategic decision-making and maintain the family wealth; nevertheless, the introduction of an excellent professional manager team will help them to take over the business, make transformation, and build their own team, and fundamentally break away from the influences and constraints of some outdated management methods of the first generation.

The first generation leaders in family businesses generally have an authoritarian management style. They will not tolerate dissenting views. Relatively speaking, high degree of centralization of power means a lack of institutionalization in management, which is one of the reasons why many of the second generation are reluctant to work in their own family businesses. Given such circumstances, if family control and management are separated, and the decisions are no longer made by one individual or one family, then a sounder decision-making mechanism can be put in place. Doing so will perhaps weaken some of the strengths such as early and efficient decision-making, but it can reduce the impact of personal prejudice on many family businesses and weaken family constraints and influences on corporate development.

Wensli is an exemplary case; it is currently a family controlled firm and its management right is split between professional managers and the family. By controlling equity right, the couple who started the business hold on to the power of making overall strategic plans for the group, but the specific management rights have been properly delegated. The reason why Wensli can follow this path is because it has brought in a mature and outstanding professional manager and adopted a proper incentive mechanism. In the future, Wensli will also aspire to go public. For Wensli which is expanding into the international market, going public can help it establish the brand image and make it more well-known. However, in this model, ownership and management rights are moderately separated, and ownership enjoys the privilege of "veto power" over management rights, which sometimes causes "boss to fire managers arbitrarily".

Model 4: Listed Companies that Are Managed by Professional Managers

In the US and Europe, joint stock limited companies have become one of the cornerstones of family business transformation. Theoretically, traditional family businesses generally emphasize unlimited liability, namely individuals or families have full liability for enterprises. However, modern firms often underline limited liability and isolate the company and shareholders in finance and liability through limited liability, which means a complete separation of management rights and ownership. For example, Walmart, the number one among family-owned businesses, and Ford, the second, are both publicly listed companies. Although the Walton and the Ford family hold 38% and 40% of the enterprises' shares, the two companies are managed by professionals.

In the long run, this model may be the only choice for many Chinese family companies. Even if family businesses like Huamao and Fotile insist on never going public, the equities are also clearly defined in the family through family agreements. Without a clear separation of equity right and management right, family wealth will mix up with corporate assets, which eventually leads to great trouble and consequences for many family businesses.

If anything goes wrong in the process whereby Chinese family businesses' first generation begins to transfer power to the second generation, it will be a devastating blow to the family businesses. If the second generation is unwilling or unable to inherit and manage family firms, then it might be a reasonable choice to break the bottleneck in family management resources by going public in an attempt to attract professional managers to participate in and maintain the sustainable development of enterprises. Along with listing, the shares originally concentrated in the hands of family members will be gradually diluted. Especially after going public, family businesses will turn into a public company, which is also the choice often made by a large number of family businesses after they have grown greatly in size. Additionally, with intergenerational replacement and the involvement of more family members, their connection with the family businesses becomes looser. Some family members may not want to retain their shares. After the company goes public, their shares can be circulated, which removes barriers to their withdrawl and is conducive to the concentration of equities and more effective management decisions for big shareholders.

Before going public, family firms are usually controlled by family members and adopt an authoritarian-style management by the entrepreneurial parents. The positions of CEO and chairman are assumed by the founding entrepreneurs or their relatives. Going public can reduce the influence of family stock-holding and bring in other institutions and participants, which will accelerate the establishment of a reasonable and rule-based decision-making mechanism. Moreover, enterprises will be subject to supervision from external shareholders and securities regulatory authorities, and professional auditing institutions will be commissioned to conduct the audit, thus enhancing the transparency of business operation and management and improving internal governance structure.

In fact, the fourth model we talk about are listed family businesses managed by professionals. Compared with private family businesses, shareholding structure in listed companies is more transparent and the decision-making is relatively open. Especially for family corporate groups with more than one listed company, it is especially vital to adopt a specialized management model. Midea Group was one of the first family-owned enterprises to implement "de-familization" management. As early as 1997, He Xiangjian introduced the professional manager system, and through the multidivisional restructuring and decentralized management, he persuaded more than 20 of the senior managers, including his wife, to step down. By doing so he had hoped to downplay the influence of his family on the firm. In 2009, He delegated his power further, resigning from the post of chairman of Midea Electric Appliances, and handing it over to the professional manager Fang Hongbo. In 2012, Midea Group released a notice, announcing that He Xiangjian would officially retire from the post of chairman of the group. Fang Hongbo officially succeeded him as chairman of the group and concurrently served as chairman and president of

Midea Electric Appliances. By then, He Xiangjian had completed the 15-year-long "de-familization" process, and simultaneously created a new situation in which professional managers took over the business.

Although management right has been transferred to professional managers, He Xiangjian maintains the ownership of Midea. According to the announcement of Midea Group, He would step down as chairman of Midea Group, but would remain as chairman of Midea Holdings. He Xiangjian and his daughter-in-law, as representatives of the He family, hold 68.7% of stocks in the Midea Group. As big shareholders, Li Jianwei and He Xiangjian's son He Jianfeng, also serve on the board of directors of the Midea Group. As founder and a big shareholder, He Xiangjian would continue to care about and support the corporation's development.

"Family members are shareholders, not business operators or entrepreneurs," said He Xiangjian. He took the path of capital holdings rather than inheritance by descendants, which not only made full use of the talent of professional managers, but also invigorated the corporate mechanism and ensured that the family could share the fruits of the development of Midea. It was truly an ingenious arrangement. However, we must also notice that the "de-familization" model of Midea came with special conditions. First, Midea was in a period of strategic transformation, therefore, "de-familization" was urgent. Secondly, he had weighed the pros and cons of the plan for many years and implemented it step by step so as to minimize opposition. Thirdly, Midea had a well-established management mechanism and talent cultivating mechanism and the final result came naturally and smoothly. Because both internal and external conditions were right, Midea embarked on a path of "de-familization". In the absence of necessary preparations, to rush things over in "de-familization" will do harm to enterprises and the holding families.[6]

Two Ways of Equity Distribution within the Family

Among Chinese family companies facing the issue of inheritance, whether they are private family firms such as Fotile and Huamao, or public

---

[6]Yang, Binqi. (2012). Inspiration of Midea: How Should a Family Business De-familialize? Ifeng.com, August 31.

enterprises such as Midea and Neoglory, the founder's family is in a controlling position. However, at the beginning of establishment, these enterprises all faced the problem of unclearly defined property rights. Most of these corporations that have survived and expanded have almost all undergone shareholding reform, MBO, or equity acquisitions, which clarified the property rights relationship of the company and ensured the founding family's control over the corporation.

Over the course of facilitating the concentration of equity in the founder's family, the most important is to handle properly the two types of property rights relationship. First, since many were township and village enterprises at the initial stage, such as Midea, Wensli, and Huamao, it was necessary to resolve the property rights relationship with the local government. Take Midea as an example. An industry insider in home appliance who had business dealings with Midea observed: "The MBO of Midea was crucial to its subsequent success. In 1997, Midea's annual sales were a little more than one billion yuan, ranking the tenth or so among home appliance makers in China. What's more, it ranked relatively low in terms of the size of assets. But in the following decade, a large number of leading Chinese household electrical appliance manufacturers encountered various problems (such as frequent change of leadership and management team, repeated transfer of holding rights, compulsory government acquisitions, etc.), leading to slower growth and poorer performance, which finally resulted in mergers and acquisitions by their counterparts. The most fundamental reason behind these problems was the fact that the management who held no stock rights and the local government who had holding rights fought over the right of control over these enterprises."[7]

Secondly, in some cases initially the founder did not start the business alone but with a group of people. As a result, these founding members also held shares. For the founder, the usual practice was to buy shares from them to increase his own stock rights in the company. In the case of Wensli, the original 28 shareholders were family members and senior employees. Li Jianhua, husband of the youngest daughter of Shen Aiqin

---

[7] Jensen, M. C., & Meckling, W. H. (1976). Theory of the Firm: Managerial Behavior, Agency Costs and Capital Structure. *Journal of Financial Economics*, 3, 305–360.

(founder of Wensli), believed that to implement the new strategy, it was necessary to concentrate equity in order to make decisions. He persuaded shareholders to trade their stocks to Shen Aiqin. In return, they were granted profitable companies, along with their equity, customers, suppliers, and brands, plus additional preferential policies. In order to facilitate this process, Li Jianhua bought the over-priced shares with his own money. In the later period, there were only eight shareholders left in Wensli, including six family members and two veteran employees, with the family members holding 90% of the shares. Among family members, Shen Aiqin held more shares than before, and the remaining shareholders were Shen Baijun (the younger brother of Shen Aiqin), the two sisters of the Tu family and their husbands. Through asset replacement and share acquisition, Wensli realized the concentration of equity in the Shen family.

Then, after the equity is concentrated in the founder's family, can they solve the problem of property rights in the family business? In some aspects, this does resolve some issues. Owing to "differential mode of the association" in Chinese culture, people tend to trust those who have blood ties or marital bonds with them. Indeed, the strong mechanism of trust established by blood and marriage can guarantee the convergence of family interests to some extent. For instance, in Red Collar, when the founder Zhang Daili asked his daughter Zhang Yunlan to come back to help the family business, she joined the company without the slightest hesitation. Similarly, when Zhang Yunlan persuaded his younger brother Zhang Yan to come back to help, he promptly put aside his own career and returned. This kind of dedication to family businesses can hardly be expected from non-family members.

In an office building at Neoglory's headquarters, 30-odd members of the Yu and Zhou family lived together. Such emotional connections exist more or less in every family business. It is the emotional connections between family members that make family firms impose "emotional constraints" on family members, stimulating family members to struggle for the interest, honor, and future of the entire family.

Nonetheless, "emotional constraints" based on family relationships are never enough. Even within a family, different members have different interests and pursuits, so conflicts of interest and principal-agent

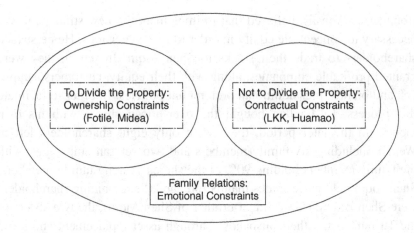

Figure 12.2   Equity Distribution and Constraints Within the Family

problems of property rights exist. Based on the previous cases, we find two ways of equity distribution in the intergenerational inheritance (see Figure 12.2).

The first model is to divide the family equity distinctly among family members, resulting in "ownership constraints": This is your property, meaning your own action will be the determining factor in increasing or decreasing this property. In his "pocket theory", Mao Lixiang, founder of Fotile, made a clear explanation of this model. To him, equity must be clearly defined and split evenly within the family. If siblings are of a strong character, they can hold shares in each other's company but they should not mix it up in operation. Otherwise, it may turn out to be a "time bomb" and eventually lead to the disintegration of the family and firm. Mao Lixiang prepared a "pocket" for his son and another "pocket" for his daughter. He also prepared a "pocket" for the senior employees who had been working with him from the very start of the business. Similarly, the He family of Midea adopted this model as well. On behalf of the big shareholders, He Xiangjian's son serves on the board of directors of Midea Group; He Xiangjian and his daughter-in-law are individual share-holders of Midea Holdings, the parent company of Midea Group; his two daughters have no shares in Midea but they have set up their own business outside Midea.

Comparatively speaking, this type of equity distribution is consistent with the principles of modern enterprise system, namely clear property rights. Through clearly-defined property rights, wealth and responsibility are passed down to the second generation. Mao Lixiang maintains that the successor must be a controlling shareholder, so that he will have the motivation to work harder and win people's trust. His "pocket theory" not only guarantees the wealth of his daughter, but also ensures that his son is properly motivated.

The second model is to not divide the property in a big family, but to define the rights, responsibilities, and distribution of interests among family members through a family agreement. Compared to the first model, this one, of which Huamao and LKK are good examples, replaces "ownership constraints" with "contractual constraints". Through the family agreement, Xu Wanmao not only established for Huamao the principle of "not going public" and "not splitting family property", but also appointed Xu Lixun as the sole successor to the family business. The advantage of this model is that family wealth does not dissipate owing to intergenerational inheritance. Moreover, this inheritance mechanism can maximize the convergence of family interests, realize benefit sharing within the family, improve the loyalty of the next generation and the mutually beneficial relationship between generations, and help to maintain corporate values from the family perspective. However, considering "contract incompleteness", it is difficult to clearly explain what may happen in the future and its countermeasures. In the case of Huamao, an obvious question emerges: After Xu Lixun, who will be the head of Huamao? What if Xu Lixun's son is reluctant or unable to take over the business? In addition, even if all adult family members sign the family agreement, its implementation and execution is not cost-free or risk-free.

The Zhou and Yu family of Neoglory appeared to be moving toward this model. Yu Jiangbo began to promote the establishment of a family committee in 2010. He talked about his concern for problems left unsolved from the first generation to the second generation. The family committee was initially composed of seven family members. Each family of Zhou Xiaoguang's seven siblings appointed one representative to discuss internal issues and development strategies. Furthermore, in 2013, Zhou began to formulate a family "charter", through which she hoped to clarify the interfamily rules of procedure.

According to the 2015 report of Forbes (Chinese version)[8], in the past six years, their survey of family corporations revealed that the main kinship in Chinese family businesses is evolving. Currently, couple, brothers, father/mother-child relationship, and marital bonds of the first generation still occupy the dominant position, but as entrepreneurs of the first generation are getting advanced in age, the second generation gradually comes on to the stage. Couple and father/mother-child relationship gradually surpasses the relationship of brothers and marital bonds built in the entrepreneurial period of the first generation. We have noticed that over the course of the expansion of family firms, the families keep exploring for ways to balance family involvement and modern enterprise system. Under the premise of guaranteeing family holdings, family companies are further presenting the trend in evolution from large families to small families. In other words, the first model based on "ownership constraints" with clearly-defined property rights seems to be more popular with Chinese family businesses than the second model based on "contractual constraints".

Four Ways of Selecting Successors in Family Business Management

In the earlier sections we discussed in detail equity distribution in families. Now we focus on the intergenerational inheritance of management right in family firms. In terms of the relationship between successors and family/corporations, we divide them into four categories (see Figure 12.3): (1) family members who have long served the family business (especially children of the founder(s)); (2) family members who hitherto have remained outside the family firm; (3) professional managers who have long worked in the family firm; (4) professional managers who have not served the family firm before. In terms of the enterprises' capacity

---

[8] Mao, Jingjing. (2015). Game Between Inheritance and Tradition — A Survey Report on Family Business. *Forbes*, 9.

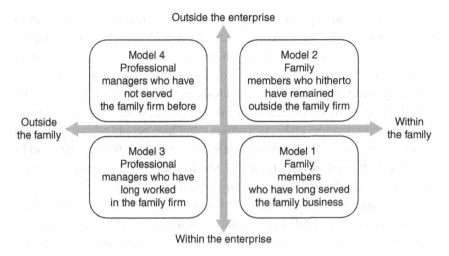

Figure 12.3   Four Ways of Selecting Successors in Family Business Management

requirement for strategic transformation, these four options possess both merits and demerits.

The first way is to choose a family member who has worked for a long time in the family firm. The prospective successor either joins the enterprise very early by starting work at the lowest level or directly joins the executive for the firm's management. Obviously, such a candidate is very familiar with the company, has a high degree of cultural convergence with the firm, and is apt to gain support from the family and other employees. Especially when he/she is the child (particularly a son) of the founding entrepreneur(s), he/she is more in line with the emotional needs of the "entrepreneurial generation" for family inheritance (not just the family business inheritance). Tu Hongyan of Wensli took over the family business from her mother, which is a case in point. Perhaps, because of the influence of traditional Chinese culture, the son-in-law is not taken for granted as a natural successor to family businesses. In Wensli, though Li Jianhua, husband of Tu Hongyan, played a major role in the firm's strategic transformation and business expansion, he did not regard himself as a "family member". He remarked, "I bought all my stock rights with my own money. I'm fully aware of my position in the firm. I am a special high-level employee in the company."

It is worth noticing that the limitation of this model is that companies do not look for the best inheritor out of consideration for the needs for strategic transformation but focus on one or even the sole candidate at an inopportune time. Hence, if the candidate proves to be competent, the company will thrive; and if the candidate is not competent, the company will decline. In this model, family business successors must have a good idea of their strengths and shortcomings and hire people whose skills and experience are complementary to theirs. For instance, Tu Hongyan and Li Jianhua employed an experienced French professional manager Patrick Bonnefond to help with the company's business in Europe.

The second model resembles the first one in that the successor is also a member (usually a child) in the founder's family, which satisfies many of the founders' emotional needs for "father-son inheritance". But in this model, the children do not grow up in the family firm, but work diligently in other people's company, or have started up their own business. Yet, should the family call for them, they will come back. The advantage of this model is the experience working in other people's companies and exposure to markets, technologies, and management methods that are different from those in their own family company, therefore broadening their horizons. Once they return to their family business, they are able to facilitate the development of family firms. Mao Zhongqun of Fotile and Xu Lixun of Huamao are examples of this type.

The shortcoming lies in the fact that at the initial stage of succession, employees may not trust and support the inheritor completely as he assumed the leader's post just because he has blood or marital relationship with the founder. He/she may also live in the shadow of the founder for a relatively long period. To solve such a problem, the most effective way is to prove himself/herself with excellent performance. A family business successor I interviewed once complained, "I studied in the UK, and lived there after graduation. Later my father asked me to return to China to inherit the family business. After the succession he frequently carped about me in the company; moreover, the seniors would also find fault with me." Another heir encountered the same problem. Her brother started up the business, and later he wanted his sister to join and lead the company. "The veterans who started the business with my brother did not trust me. On returning to the firm, I first took charge in the creation of a new business.

After winning their trust, I gradually re-focused on the main business." Xu Lixun of Huamao had similar experience, and only by displaying excellent performance did he gain a firm foothold in the company. Fortunately, although these family business successors met with difficulties in the early period, their family never wavered in providing them support, so they were given an extended period of "honeymoon" that allowed them to try, fail, and try again. They did not have to worry about being replaced by someone else once they failed.

The third model is to select a professional manager who has worked for a long time in the family business. Midea Group is undoubtedly the most successful example. Fang Hongbo, a non-family successor, joined Midea in 1992. By the time he took over the business as chairman of Midea Group in 2012, he had been working in Midea for two decades and thus knew the corporation very well and identified himself with it. He Xiangjian explained why he picked Fang Hongbo: "First, Fang has been in the company for twenty years since 1992. Certainly, it isn't a short period of time. Second, Fang is promoted step by step from an ordinary employee and he is cultivated by the company. Third, he has received good education. Moreover, he all along identifies with our corporate culture and philosophy. Fourth, he is now in his forties, in the prime of life. Fifth, since he joined the management team a decade ago, he has demonstrated his abilities through outstanding performance and picking him accords with the wishes of everyone. Last but not the least, he is a man of integrity and possesses professional ethics. What's more, he is always eager to learn and is enthusiastic about work. I'd say that he is the most ideal and most popular candidate in the whole team." [9]

Compared with the first method, this model has a lot more successors to choose from. Apart from Fang Hongbo, there are thousands of professional managers out there. The "first generation entrepreneurs" can compare multiple candidates and select the one they are most satisfied with. However, this kind of approach requires the "first generation entrepreneurs" to make preparations well in advance, by reserving and cultivating talents for their enterprises. As He Xiangjian said, "Succession is never

---

[9]Zhang, Yan. (2012). Midea Group Changed Its Leader. A Case from China Europe International Business School.

decided on a whim, nor is it a sudden arrangement. In fact, it took me twenty years or so to contemplate this: When conditions are right, I will step down, and we will no longer engage in family governance, but will hire professionals to manage the company. Especially in the past seven or eight years, I have made plans carefully to revise and improve the company's mechanism to support the succession."

The fourth way is to appoint a professional manager who has no previous relations with the company and the founder's family. Although this approach allows the company to choose the leader needed for strategic transformation in the biggest possible talent pool, in reality, it is usually the least satisfactory approach to be adopted only when the other three methods do not work. Of all the family businesses we interviewed, this method has the highest rate of failure. It is very hard to find a good candidate because professionals from outside the firm would have a hard time identifying with the family firm and the business philosophy of the family. Moreover, as professional managers from outside lack connections and strong supporters in the firm, they are a convenient scapegoat when problems arise.

Furthermore, .there is a two-way information asymmetry between the professional manager and the family business, which may lead to inheritance failure. The first kind of information asymmetry attracts much attention, i.e., the family firm does not know very well the actual abilities of the professional manager, and its judgment is only based on his/her résumé and the recommendation of the headhunting company. However, only after the professional manager assumes his post will the family find that he is not competent enough to run the business or that he is not the person the company needs. The second kind of information asymmetry, although not much attention has been paid to it, may exist. It is that the firm may not be as good as it has been described. According to a professional manager I know, he applied for the post in a family business and was ready to go all out to make the company thrive. After he took up his post as CEO, he soon found out that the boss personally kept the company's official seal, which meant that the boss could use corporate funds without telling him about it. Further, the boss had outstanding debts. The manager was not sure how deep the black hole was, so he left shortly after taking office.

Among the four models, the first and the third are intra-family inheritance, which are easily accepted in Chinese family businesses. From a positive point of view, in the foreseeable future, the main force of family business successors will be the second generation. The "silver spoon generation" with wealthy family backgrounds and good education will bring with them creative ideas to advance Chinese family firms to a new level. And with relatively less in-family competition, family infighting will also be reduced, thereby increasing the probability of smooth handover, which is conducive to the effective management after the transfer of management right. More and more families will replicate the good examples of intra-family inheritance. For talented heirs who are willing to pursue their own interests like He Jianfeng, they all hope that their fathers will be able to cultivate professional managers like Fang Hongbo to take over the business. After all, descendants of family businesses may not necessarily take over the management power from their parents, but they must learn how to become shareholders. Family businesses, whether they are privately owned or go public, must have a strict mechanism that clearly defines rights, responsibilities, and the distribution of profits.

Succession and Transformation Side by Side

The family businesses we interviewed all carried out strategic transformation of various degrees at the moment when intergenerational inheritance of management right took place. The garment business of Red Collar was transformed from offline to online. The kitchenware business of Fotile was upgraded to the high-end. Wensli and Midea actively tapped overseas markets in two different industries. Huamao and Neoglory both expanded their original main business to become more diversified. Over the course of these strategic transformations, the second generation played an important and positive role. Compared with the first generation, their biggest strengths are that they have received better education, possess more business resources, have a broader vision, and are open to unconventional ideas. Because of these, the strategic transformations of many family businesses not only result from the choice of the companies at the critical stage of development, but also from the

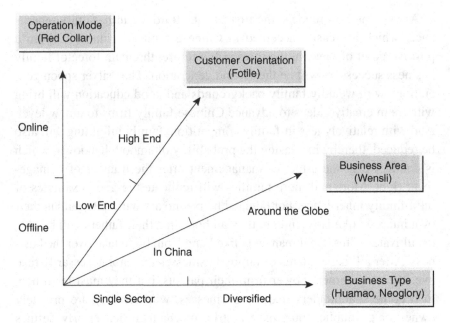

Figure 12.4   Four Strategic Choices for Family Business Transformation

initiation from the second generation. Figure 12.4 summarizes the choices of some family businesses on four strategic ideas, which we can use for reference.

Wensli: Brand Internationalization

When Shen Aiqin was in charge, she formulated the strategic goal of "Three Threes", to build three bases, open up three markets, and forge three well-known brands. In the early years, Chinese entrepreneurs paid particular attention to a firm's fixed assets and size. As supply fell short of demand at that time, they tended to embrace opportunism and policy orientation. Once an opportunity appeared in the market or where there was government support, they would get involved, which led to the decentralization and diversification of businesses.

Tu Hongyan, successor of Wensli, had differing ideas. She had her own dreams and pursuits, wanting to focus on silk and turn Wensli into "China's Hermès". After Tu became executive chairperson of the group in

2004, she began to reassess the group's business with the support of her husband, Li Jianhua (president of the group). Previously, as the corporation also engaged in other industries such as real estate, its main business was not clear enough. After 2005, she began to adjust the strategy to focus on the core capability, products, and industries of the firm. Under the new strategy, she started to sell off companies with non-core businesses, close those that were unprofitable, had no clear industrial logic or had bad development prospects, and switch to other products. Making such a decision put Tu Hongyan in a position that was in direct conflict with her mother Shen Aiqin, who was then chairperson of the group. Shen believed that to do business, one should possess as many factories and tangible assets as possible and continue to expand and diversify. Yet, Tu insisted on focusing on the silk industry and preferred the concentration of equity.

Tu Hongyan and her husband started to carry out reforms, which met with strong opposition from Shen Aiqin. Disagreements and conflicts occurred frequently over several years. Sometimes when she was unable to convince her mother, they had to make concessions. For example, though the manufacturing plant suffered losses for years, Shen Aiqin was not going to shut it down. It was because the plant was established when she first started the business, and even after it was running at a loss, she would still sustain it with the profits from other sectors. There were conflicting views during board of directors' meetings. In particular, when it came to the closure of many uncorrelated industries, it was easy to reach consensus about closing down those that were not making profits, but there were still disagreements about closing down the profitable ones. This process of restructuring lasted a few years, laying a solid foundation for the transformation and upgrading of Wensli.

Establishing a Chinese Brand and Positioning the Products

Tu Hongyan also realized that Wensli could not survive in this era if they relied only on exporting raw fabrics and earn low OEM fees. She firmly believed that Wensli must transform itself. Tu Hongyan and Li Jianhua have dedicated themselves to promoting silk culture, developing silk gifts, establishing an international design and development team, conducting research into new technologies and materials, and spending huge amount of money to obtain the latest technologies to set up the foundation of an international brand. Li Jianhua is also engaged in the frontier study of silk culture and promoting the integration of silk culture and the industry. They have a good understanding of the silk industry, and they know how to make the best use of high-quality silk raw materials, such as adding Chinese elements to better meet the needs of consumers. Meanwhile the couple also set up an excellent retail network to spread the industry and culture, connect with the mobile Internet, strive to establish the brand reputation and image, and cultivate brand loyalty.

The luxury goods industry is cyclical and faces many challenges such as picky customers and counterfeit products, so it is never easy working in this industry. In the meantime, overseas consumers have a poor impression on the quality and image of Chinese household goods. As Chinese luxury brands are still in their infancy, it makes things even more difficult. Hermès boasts a history of nearly 200 years, and the amount of investment in brand building is enormous. With only 40 years of history, Wensli still has a long way to go if it aspires to be in the same league with Hermès. In view of this, Wensli decided not to vie with Hermès, but to concentrate all its energy on establishing its own brand reputation.

Li Jianhua is leading the Wensli team to re-take the "Silk Road". They went to France three times, popularized silk culture by media coverage, founded the first private silk culture museum in China, i.e., Wensli Silk Culture Museum, and so on and so forth.

Chinese Brand with French Techniques

China is the second largest consumer of luxury goods, but none of the world's 75 luxury brands are made in China. Since Hermès products are made in France, Wensli proposes the concept of "Chinese Brand with French Techniques". In 2003, Wensli officially acquired the French family business company of silk scarf MARC ROZIER, which is one of the two factories in Europe that could weave intricate jacquard. The manufacturing process from raw material procurement to design, jacquard weaving, printing, and dyeing is all completed in France. Nowadays, the French company is part of Wensli Group and manufactures for Wensli. In the future, this enterprise will continue to offer "OEM Services" to the leading global brands, but the decision is in the hands of Wensli. In the past, traditional Chinese firms were proud of being OEMs of foreign brands. Now Wensli has made a great change. Tu Hongyan once said that as MARC ROZIER has a long history, the quality of its products is better than Wensli's although the French company's equipment is behind Wensli's by 30 years. She said that this is where Wensli could learn and improve.

Boldly Hiring International Talent

Over the course of building an international luxury brand, the couple always hoped to attract and cultivate more international talent, but there was no suitable candidate within the company who was able to internationalize the business. Fate of luck acquainted Li Jianhua with Bonnefond, CEO of Hermès, and they hit it off. Soon, Bonnefond is appointed as CEO of Wensli Silk Culture Co., Ltd. and CEO of MARC ROZIER, and he is responsible for cultivating talent, introducing top European designers, and researching and implementing brand architecture and international development strategies. He is also in charge of business development of MARC ROZIER in the Chinese and the European markets. The employment of a Frenchman as CEO of the group's subsidiaries reflects the determination and courage of Wensli to go global.

Bonnefond has brought new perspectives and launched unconventional activities that facilitated the removal of outdated ideas and practices in Wensli. As a senior professional manager in the luxury goods industry, he owns a strong network of resources in Europe and has a comprehensive understanding of the useful resources and information in the industry. He has the strengths of all external professional managers, i.e., excellent educational background, matching expertise and abilities, distinctive international vision, and cultural sensitivity. In addition, as former CEO of Hermès, he has experience in managing top international luxury brands, as well as a profound understanding of textile technologies and French production techniques. In terms of channels, he has established a fairly good global network of suppliers, distributors, and customers. All this is considered valuable experience for the internationalization of Wensli. Meanwhile, he has brought with him a team of executives and designers who would work alongside him in the new post. More importantly, he has brought with him new design ideas and new management modes, as well as ideas about the adjustment of the brand operation.

The participation of external professionals will also test the company's own system, and Wensli has made the necessary adjustment accordingly. A new brand, a new executive, and new ideas must be gradually integrated with the enterprise, which requires the overall cooperation and adjustment of the firm. In this process, how much authorization and resource support the family would like to give to the professional manager is of great significance. Family businesses must be mentally prepared for the upcoming self-reform in order to help the hired CEO to take root and integrate with the company and implement the strategy of internationalization through to the end.

Cultivating Globalized Chinese Talent

Key factors in the creation of an international luxury silk brand include high-quality silk, consummate craftsmanship, production processes and techniques, design, distribution, and outstanding brand DNA. Funding is not a problem at Wensli, instead, talent is. For this reason, how to attract and cultivate international talent is pivotal to the success of Wensli and Bonnefond.

In China, the talent pool in the luxury goods industry is very limited. There is a severe shortage of internationalized talent who is creative, proficient in English, and capable of supervising overseas business. Those who have a good command of French and other European languages are even rarer. By introducing talent from overseas counterparts, employing talent with relevant work experience in the fashion industry, and investing more to cultivate Chinese talent for globalization, Wensli is working hard to build a global corporate culture and human resources system that match its visions, traditions, and local employee preferences. What's more, it is cooperating with educational institutions to bridge the gap between China and overseas markets. In 2014, Wensli Group and MARC ROZIER brought in total revenues of 9.8 billion yuan and 28 million yuan respectively. Tu Hongyan and Li Jianhua are on their way to transform Wensli into "China's Hermès" step by step.

Red Collar Turns to Online Service

The story of Red Collar Group in Qingdao also encompasses the two key points of business succession and strategic transformation. Zhang Daili and his daughter Zhang Yunlan explored the inheritance and development of family businesses under the parallel management by father and daughter. Zhang Daili, who was once a carpenter and earned his first pot of gold through this skill, ventured into the business world in 1976. After more than a decade of hard work, he founded Red Collar in 1995. Adhering to the philosophy of "ethics comes before business", Zhang Daili regarded integrity as the essential trait of a man as well as a business. He was often quoted as saying, "A carpenter who doesn't know how to use a computer is not a good tailor." On hearing this for the first time, many might feel confused. However, switching to the clothing industry, he sharply noticed the niche market brought by the Internet. In some sense, information technology facilitated his personal transition.

To transform Red Collar Group was one of Zhang's dreams. He realized very early that providing "OEM services" or low-end manufacturing was not the path to success, so he had all along advocated altering the business mode.

He maintained that customization (the mode with customized production as the core) was the future development direction of traditional mass production. Hence, he devoted himself wholeheartedly to promoting his company's strategic transformation. The reform Zhang hoped to implement covered two aspects: One was to make RCMTM the creator, designer, and promoter of the C2M mode; the other was to take advantage of information technology to advance new-type industrialization. Starting from 2003, taking advantage of IT-based thinking and using Red Collar's 3,000- employee-plant as a laboratory, he spent 11 years and hundreds of millions of yuan to carry out an arduous experimentation on upgrading traditional Chinese industries. Finally he formed a completely personalized, large-scale, and industrialized Red Collar mode, achieved the deep integration of informatization and industrialization under the Internet thinking of big data, and came up with the values and methodology of the Internet-based industry. Red Collar Group successfully launched the global custom suits platform — RCMTM. Around 2013, it upgraded its strategy and built a solid support platform to provide a complete solution for the apparel industry and make unremitting efforts to realize prosperity of the industry.

Before and After the Transformation

Undoubtedly, Zhang Daili, through his conviction, perseverance, and hard work, contributed to the successful transformation of Red Collar Group. Over the course of achieving personal ideals, he possessed a firm business belief and learned from foreign advanced technologies to continuously carry out innovative practices. He also invented an efficient method for size measurement, insisted on employee training, and adjusted organizational structure to center on customer needs. Moreover, he fostered a people-oriented corporate culture, continued to invest in the group, and cultivated successors step by step, in order to bring about the transformation of Red Collar Group. Nonetheless, it was not simply a transition from OEM to high-end customization. Red Collar Group underwent great changes before and after the transition, mainly in relation to production

Table 12.1 Changes Before and After the Transformation in Red Collar Group

	Before the Transformation	After the Transformation
• Production Mode	• Similar to Other Traditional Manufacturers • No Core Competitiveness	• Flexible Production, through 3D Smart Printing • Big Data-driven Technology • High Efficiency and Low Cost
• Technologies	• All Traditional Technologies Applied to Clothing Manufacture	• Independent R&D Department • An Efficient Method for Size Measurement
• Employees	• Ordinary Workers with Little Knowledge of Computer and English • Friends, Relatives and Privilege	• Internationalized Talent and Educated People Proficient in English • 500 Information Technology Engineers • Young and Capable Manager Team Born in the 1980s

Table 12.1   *(Continued)*

	Before the Transformation	After the Transformation
• Core Business	• Ready-made Garments • OEM • Sales Stores	• Customization • E-commerce Platform • Provide Solutions for Other Traditional Manufacturers and Upgrade Their Production Modes
• Organizational Structure	• Multi-level Management • Over 30 Redundant Departments	• Flat Organization • Management Based on Platform and Node • Standard and Powerful Institutional System
• Corporate Culture	• No Common Goal for Employees • Lack of Organizational Identity	• Comprehensive Support for Customization • Common Mission: Use the Internet to Open up to a New Industrial Era

mode, technologies, employees, core business, organizational structure, corporate culture, etc. (see Table 12.1).

Overcoming Technical Problems and Transforming from Mass Production to Customization

In 2003, the domestic ERP system could not meet the requirements of customization. On the other hand, the imported equipment could not work in Red Collar Group. To resolve these problems, Zhang Daili purchased the professional platform and equipment of the streamlined customized system, and introduced advanced foreign hanger and logistics systems. Meanwhile he formed an information technology department composed of more than a dozen people working overtime to develop their own system. Additionally, he also acquired some professional information companies, and absorbed 500-odd information engineers who were proficient in various professional technologies such as big data and cloud computing. Based on these, the team built the unique platform named RCMTM and developed SDE products with independent intellectual property rights protection.

Changing Perceptions of Employees and Leading Organizational Change & Strategic Transformation

In the process of advancing transformation, Zhang Daili's biggest challenge was to change the perceptions of employees, as many of them had little idea about the strategic transformation. As an entrepreneur, Zhang had a forward-looking sense, but not all employees who were accustomed to basic manufacturing process were aware of the necessity of transition. To seek unity of thinking and pursue the common goal, Zhang did not take advantage of his authority to force his ideas on the staff. On the contrary, he understood the employees who had followed him all the way and did not blame them for the negative reception towards his reform. He held meetings to explain the strategic transformation to the employees to enhance their confidence. He also organized training programs for them to learn how to use the advanced equipment and technologies. Of course, some measures were still required to upgrade technologies. He imposed certain regulations, such as requiring the staff of the measurement department to work digitally. After all the efforts, he dismissed the employees who still refused to accept the new method of work after receiving training. To the progress of Red Collar, flexible personnel are indispensable.

It is commonplace for most employees to be not prepared for organizational change. Once the transition takes place, we can classify them into four categories in terms of their attitudes and psychological readiness: supporters, assistants, criticizers, and obstructors. Therefore, it is crucial to identify early backers who are open-minded and willing to accept the proposed changes. To win the trust of the majority, the key is to strive for a staged victory. In other words, the achievement of transition at an early stage helps the innovator win more support. Only when the transformation is supported by the majority can the reformer accumulate enough impetus and implement the initiatives smoothly. The reward and punishment system are conducive to sending the right signal and motivates the expected behaviors that support change, which is quite significant.

Cultivating an Outstanding Innovator to Inherit the Company in the Process of Transformation

Powerful and influential as Red Collar may be, eventually it will face the issue of succession. If the corporation is not successfully continued, its prosperity is just short-lived. Hence the third challenge for Zhang Daili is to find a competent successor. Since no professional manager candidates could meet his requirements, Zhang Daili finally appointed his daughter Zhang Yunlan to take over the business as president of Red Collar Group and to proceed with his unfinished mission. But Zhang Daili did not rush things, instead, he took a progressive and methodical approach. First, he communicated thoroughly with her daughter to help her form the same business values. Next, he had her start from the main business at the front line and rotate between different departments to acquire a comprehensive knowledge of the corporation. After she joined the company, he quietly observed her from behind and never took the initiative to influence her decisions. Most importantly, he encouraged her to make decisions on her own, and chose to unconditionally pay for any consequences of her daughter's decisions. Zhang Daili knew that some setbacks on the way to succession were inevitable, and his successor should not be afraid of demonstrating her courage and sense of responsibility because of the setbacks.

Over the course of the transformation, the father and the daughter played major roles in different fields. It is fair to say that today's achievement of Red Collar could not have been made without the hard work of the two generations, which involves compromises, mutual support, and more importantly, consistency in their ideas and effective communication. Both of them are exemplary in taking on the responsibilities. Zhang Yunlan has spent nearly a decade tempering herself since she joined the firm. As her father gradually delegates more power to her, she will assume more responsibilities for decision-making on the development of Red Collar. In the next two years, she will make sure the measures for the firm's strategic transformation will be fully implemented. When promoting the C2M mode, she has to attract more customers. Though it is the mission of Zhang Daili and Red Collar to aid other enterprises to implement the revolution of industrialization, the survival and growth of the firm itself is also crucial. As Red Collar constantly expands, she will also need to strike a balance between the employment of professional managers and her hands-on approach.

The return of her younger brother Zhang Yan has somewhat eased her burden. After she helped her father complete the industrialized transformation, the construction of the platform greatly facilitated the firm's growth, and the need for talent became more urgent. Like her father, Zhang Yunlan turned to a family member at the crucial moment. Accepting his sister's request without a flicker of hesitation, Zhang Yan resolutely joined Red Collar to assist his sister and father with the expansion. In an interview, Zhang Yunlan commented that women are under heavy pressure as they have so many roles to play. She deems it preferable to hand over the family business to a male heir. Although Zhang Yan currently serves as COO of Red Collar Group and takes charge of the specific operations, Zhang Yunlan remains the final decision-maker in the group. However, for the siblings, they never take it to heart. They know what they do is for the benefit of the family; they are working hard to realize their father's dream and toward a common goal. This is why the sister and the brother are courageous enough to forge ahead despite the challenges at this crucial time of succession and transformation.

In one or two years, on the platform of Red Collar there will be a great space for them to maximize their abilities and strengths. For example, the siblings can go on to establish the brand image of Magic Manufactory. Red Collar Group can organize various events and competitions in domestic colleges or universities, encourage the students to work out their own marketing strategies, and implement them in the Magic Manufactory. The reward for this competition can be a job offer in Red Collar Group or a company product, or both. This kind of event produces two effects. First, more people will get to know about Magic Manufactory and Red Collar Group, which increases brand awareness. Secondly, Red Collar Group is likely to reap good marketing tactics.

In addition, Zhang Yunlan is set about making Magic Manufactory a platform for college students or designers and fabric suppliers eager to start up a business. For consumers, they can have direct contact with these designers and suppliers on the platform. In fact, it has always been the common mission and dream of the three to popularize Red Collar Group's C2M mode and help other companies realize their strategic transformation. In this regard, Kutesmart has already carried out cooperation with the Alliance of Industrial Internet of China. Li Jinzhu, vice president of Red Collar Group and secretary general of the alliance, is also the main promoter of the initiative.

For Red Collar, or any family business, after a certain extent of development, especially after succession is completed, it will encounter the problem of talent selection. It is particularly important for firms like Red Collar that are carrying out transformation and upgrading using Internet technology to find a way of how to build a good team of professionals. Nevertheless, we must note that in the current social environment, the introduction of external talent has both merits and demerits. Zhang Yunlan is a key figure in proposing Magic Manufactory and formulating its business mode. Perhaps she knows better than any other person about how to develop Magic Manufactory. Furthermore, to independently put her own ideas into practice is also a golden opportunity for learning, which will facilitate her growing into an excellent CEO of Red Collar. However, if she does not employ other talent, she may not be able to jump outside the box and innovate, which potentially limits the growth of Magic Manufactory. Moreover, professional marketers may have a better understanding of the Chinese market and customers, which is conducive to securing more market shares more rapidly. We suggest Zhang Yunlan continue to cooperate with other senior executives of the group (e.g., Li Jinzhu), because this will not only help stabilize the firm, but will also harness their respective strengths.

To quote from Zhang Daili, Red Collar Group is no longer a clothing manufacturer but has grown into an Internet industry platform, which means that Zhang Yunlan assumes another responsibility — to promote the transformation of Red Collar Group from a non-platform-based firm to a platform-based firm. This transition is a fundamental change for the company, requiring the staff to change their values, adhere to a clear vision, adjust the interests of stakeholders, and then forge ahead. In other words, in the process of platform transformation, enterprises need to make adjustments to all VSOP (i.e., value, strategy, organization, and personnel) factors. At the value level, the firm needs to formulate a vision on the basis of a win-win philosophy, that is to say, it firmly believes that the core business first creates value for the society and then for the enterprise. It must be alert enough to identify the pain points of the industry, determine the company strategy based on the value chain analysis, and create a brand new ecosystem. It adjusts organizational structure to foster a new platform while it helps employees to achieve self-improvement, ensuring that talent and platform transformation synchronize.

Fotile Moves Towards High-end Products

China is a manufacturing power. As the cost of labor rises, the environmental carrying capacity approaches a critical point, i.e., the low-cost production mode at the cost of cheap labor and environmental pollution is no longer a feasible choice. The economic downturn makes industrial growth extremely difficult for the worse. As a result, the transformation and upgrading of the traditional manufacturing sector is imperative. For Fotile, the agreement reached by Mao Zhongqun and his father Mao Lixiang at the beginning of the business meant they chose to make a radical change in the products. When a company experiences a period of rapid expansion and has secured considerable market share, the initial business thinking and mode may obstruct its further development. Just like every declining industry which had its heyday, Mao Lixiang had to close down the production line of his once proud electronic gas igniters due to the ruthless price competition.

Obsolete enterprises result from outdated thinking. The Chinese manufacturing sector is gradually shaking off the label of the "world's factory", and the transition from "Made in China" to "Intelligent Manufacturing in China" is a period full of challenges. According to Mao Lixiang's own experience, the transition from igniters to range hoods was a significant move in terms of the width of the cross-sector change and the market risks associated with it. At that time, there were over 250 range hood manufacturers nationwide, and the market was basically dominated by Sacon, Yuli, and Robam. However, after three months of market research, analysis, and verification, Mao Zhongqun persuaded his father to launch a new product, which was the first step of Fotile's transformation. In this process, father and son took the overall interests of the family into account. In view of the common interests, the family members were ready to share the information about the market changes they had captured. Meanwhile, the authoritative leadership made it easier for members to reach consensus, make quick and flexible responses to market changes, and improve decision-making efficiency. Due to the smooth internal communication, the implementation of the decisions was effective.[10]

Fotile, entering the kitchen electrical appliance industry in 1996, embarked on the path of diversification like its counterparts. After obtaining the "first pot of gold", it turned to other fields such as household appliances, and for this reason, Fotile's core business was not prominent. In 2006, Fotile defined itself as an "expert in built-in kitchen electrical appliance" and adjusted the product structure based on this definition. For instance, it closed down the product lines and business segments that were not in line with this definition, giving up the projects of water dispensers, induction cookers, and later even the mid-range products of kitchen appliances. At the initial stage, disagreements and conflicts occurred between Mao Zhongqun and his father, but the son's perseverance drove the transition of the family business from low-end to high-end. Mao Zhongqun put forward the strategy of "specialization, high-end, high-quality" and stuck to it. Even in the period when Chinese traditional kitchen appliances brands confronted major challenges and turning points, Fotile did not alter its intention. It pursued long-term development, chose a single development mode of specialization, and focused on the high-end market. He maintained that Fotile, defining itself as a high-end kitchen appliance expert and leader, represented a high-end quality of life, and aimed to establish differentiated awareness in the eyes of consumers. Later, it turned out that after abandoning the mid-end market, its overall sales performance continued to grow at a high speed. It established its status in the industry as "China's high-end kitchen electrical appliance expert and leader" and successfully opened up new commercial space for the related industry in the high-end market. Over the years, Fotile has ranked first place in brand surveys carried out by third-party agencies, which proves that its brand status is recognized by hundreds of thousands of buyers.

---

[10] Mao, Lixiang. (2008). Evergreen Family Business. Zhejiang People's Publishing House.

The value of Fotile's success rests with its focus. The corporation has devoted all the core resources to the key areas of brand establishment and abandoned other auxiliary strategies so as to focus on building a sustainable competitive edge. For such an enterprise, customer experience and service come first. It was precisely for this reason that Mao Zhongqun was determined to transit Fotile to high-end. As the Chinese economy progressively matures, the advantage resulting from a cheap labor force no longer exists. Most Chinese family businesses have a humble beginning and are concentrated in the low-end market, which puts many private entrepreneurs in a dilemma when it comes to business succession. The fundamental solution lies in promoting the transformation and upgrading of sectors and enterprises, enabling firms to move from the original extensive, low-end, low value-added, manufacturing, and processing-oriented to high-end to achieve the brand upgrading. Fotile is undoubtedly an exemplary for this case.[11]

From Low Cost to Moderate Cost

In the past three decades, low cost was the competitive edge pursued by most companies, which was also the reason why Mao Lixiang's igniters were embroiled in a price war. To upgrade products, one must abandon the low-cost mentality. Many corporations produce whatever is profitable and some of them prioritize profit before everything else. They keep jumping from one industry to another or seek diversification blindly. As a result, enterprises do not have a solid basis but have to duplicate foreign products at a much lower price and engage in disorderly competition. Homogeneous and substandard products abound. Whoever offers the lowest price of the industry wins the "competition". This has brought the enterprises themselves and the industry as a whole to the brink of collapse, getting stuck in the mire of a vicious circle. "Made in China" products are labeled as "low-end", "cheap", and "fake". Since low-end products have to meet customers' requirements for low price and fairly good quality, keeping cost as low as possible is the top priority for enterprises, and all the factors

---

[11] Tao, Yunbiao. (2013). A Successful Transformation — Six Principles for Transformation from Low End to High End. *China Brand and Anti-counterfeiting*, 6, 24–27.

leading to cost increase have to be eliminated. Due to various constraints, a large number of family businesses go to great lengths to keep costs low in order to survive. Once Fotile decided to go after high-end consumers, it faced a market of upgraded consumption. Buyers value the degree of satisfaction derived from the products, which will inevitably cause increases in cost. This financial input can enhance the intrinsic value of the brand and thus gain the recognition of the high-end market. Carrying out transformation from low-end to high-end, a company must not begrudge the moderate increase in investment in its attempt to forge a high-end brand. Mao Zhongqun never hesitates in spending quite a lot of money on the research and development of products. Normally he spends 5% of sales revenue supporting product and technology innovation annually — a proportion far exceeding the industry's average — and it can go beyond 5% without an upper limit if they deem it necessary. Currently Fotile has three pillars supporting technological innovation, i.e., a state-accredited enterprise technology center, a national-level laboratory, and a national-level research institute. This includes over 200 R&D personnel, including Chinese and foreign experts in aircraft fans, submarine noises, aviation reliability, and industrial design who have over 70 invention patents and 500-odd other patents under their belt, making Fotile the undoubted leader in the technological innovation and transition of kitchen appliances. Fotile's effort has promoted the continuous upgrading of the national standard for range hoods. The increased cost that creates the added value is worthwhile as high-end customers are glad to pay for the difference. The increased revenue far surpasses the increased cost. Fotile thus explains its persistence in the high-end products: They do not think that they are luxuries enjoyed only by a very small number of people. Rather, they are products of better quality, higher performance, and with more comfortable usage experience, which consumers are willing to spend more money on.

From Homogeneous to Differentiated Products

When the manufacturing sector stays in the low-end stage, it focuses on low price as an attraction to consumers on the market. Products are made by mass production and characterized by homogeneity. Therefore, in the low-end market, products and brands are more or less the same. But for high-end customers, differentiation, not price, is what they are concerned about. A brand that differentiates itself from other brands through its own uniqueness will have a competitive edge and therefore a larger share of the market. The reason why people are willing to pay more for premium brands is because they are not completely substitutable. For high-end consumers, these features can satisfy their sense of identity amongst the elite and the need for personalization. Fotile has clearly and precisely segmented the market. In the early years, it aimed to defeat foreign brands by specializing in range hoods that are more in line with Chinese people's habits. Then Fotile established a unique premium brand image by tailoring its products to the targeted consumers. Gradually it created an image of quality products and good service that catered to Chinese cooking habits, establishing a competitive edge through its unique characteristics different from its competitors such as Robam and Bosch.

Fotile has built up a complete industrial system oriented to high-end consumers and covering all the links from product development, brand promotion, marketing to after-sales service that cannot be replicated by other enterprises in a short time. Mao Zhongqun believes that in the Chinese home appliance market, kitchen appliances are the only area in which domestic companies have the final say in the high-end market. But creating a brand for the high-end market is different from one for middle- and low-end market. You do not naturally have access to the high-end market after you have done well in the middle- and low-end markets. What Fotile needs to do is to keep developing better products to gain a firm foothold in the high-end market. In 2014, Mao Zhongqun once again emphasized the principle of "three nots, four adherences". "Three nots": Not go public, not engage in price wars, and not practice deception. "Four adherences": Adhere to high-end positioning and continue to lead and promote the transformation and upgrading of the entire kitchen appliance industry; adhere to original design and continue to lead the trend of built-in and complete sets of kitchen appliances; adhere to continuous innovation and create environmentally-friendly and healthful lifestyle of good taste for users; adhere to social responsibility and contribute to the progress of industry, society, and humanity. These will ensure that Fotile always provides consumers with a better product experience and commits to its core strategy.

From Product Branding to Corporate Branding

In the low-end market, buyers recognize products instead of companies, and at best they only pay attention to product brands. In the high-end market, consumers focus not only on the products themselves, but also on the enterprises producing the brands. Therefore, corporate branding has become the key force to support product branding. In the past decade Mao Zhongqun has been focusing on the establishment of Fotile's corporate culture. Consumption of premium brands is not only the consumption of products, the recognition of corporate culture is of more significance. Over the course of upgrading, Fotile abandoned the low-end market once and for all and built the high-end brand, by which it gained an advantage in the entire market. The combination of "quality product, corporate culture, and producer integrity" is the essence of Fotile's brand culture.

Since its founding in 1996, Fotile has stuck to the positioning of being a "professional, high-end, and responsible" enterprise and never stops innovating. Its line of products includes European style range hoods, side suction range hoods, powerful yet quiet ventilation range hoods, to name but a few. Apart from these, it has also developed other products like gas stoves, disinfection cabinets, built-in steamers, ovens, and microwave ovens. Mao Zhongqun said that Fotile will adhere to the high-end positioning and go on to lead and promote the transformation and upgrading of the entire kitchen appliance industry. It will also uphold the original design and carry on leading the development trend of complete built-in sets of kitchen appliances. Always aiming to outdo its own performance, Fotile will reform the Chinese kitchen and help Chinese people realize the dream of a quality kitchen. Fotile's every breakthrough that established its leading position in the industry always centers on one point, i.e., keep bringing pleasant surprises to users.

To a family firm like Fotile which had been very successful in the low-end market, entering the high-end market meant a thorough reformation. As the second generation heir of the family, Mao Zhongqun played a pivotal role in the process. But the reform he implemented in the business after his succession would not have been a success without his father's support and vision. Senior Mao showed the courage and ingenuity of an entrepreneur. He discarded the old practices that helped him succeed in the market, optimized his accumulated experience and resources, and braved himself for the challenge of the new high-end market and helped his son mature, all of which contributed to the transformation and upgrading of Fotile. The precise and accurate positioning of the company made it easier for consumers to remember. Meanwhile, the succession of the Mao family business was also clearly defined. At the beginning of his second venture along with his son, Senior Mao made a specific plan for the division of the family assets, which paved the way for Fotile's subsequent development and management. Through the "pocket theory" he not only guaranteed the respective rights and industries of family members, but also clarified the dominance of the family heir, which allowed Mao Zhongqun to successfully implement his strategies and put his ideas into practice and would not lead to family conflicts because of disagreements in corporate management. In Mao Lixiang's view, the successor should progressively assume the role of leader and organizer of management reform and promote the transformation and upgrading and management reform of the enterprise in the process of succession. Over the course, the successor would grow into the new leader of the enterprise. As Fotile was the product of his second business venture with his son, they learned a lot from the lessons of the father's first business venture. They conducted a series of explorations and attempts on setting up a modern management system with Fotile characteristics. They roughly focused on three aspects: First, introduce talent; second, weaken the influence of family; third, introduce rules and regulations.[12] After the son took over the business, Senior Mao proceeded with the research and education of family business succession. Now, when speaking of Fotile and the Maos, people usually come up with keywords such as startup business, traditional Chinese culture, and representative of family businesses, precisely because of the efforts they have made in the process of firm inheritance and transformation, persistence and promotion of traditional culture, the innovation and

---

[12] Mao. Lixiang. *Inheritance for 100 Years*. Zhejiang People's Publishing House.

application of the modern management system, and the insistence on the family business heritage. I look forward to the prosperity of this traditional family that will survive the third generation and beyond.

Neoglory and Huamao: Towards Industrial Diversification

Most Chinese family corporations start with single products, a simple business mode, and chaotic management structure. With the growth of business and the overall economic transformation and upgrading, they will encounter the problem of choosing between two paths: Diversification or professionalization. In the meantime, they will also face the handover issue. Therefore, a family firm needs to answer the question of leader selection and succession while making its choice from the two development paths. While Fotile took the road of professionalization, Huamao and Neoglory, also based in Zhejiang Province, embarked on the path of diversification in parallel with their process of succession.

In reality, the choice of diversification or specialization relies on the size of the company itself and its original business. Also, it depends on the interests and abilities of the succeeding generation. According to a study by Zhang Jianjun and Li Hongwei[13], the background of private entrepreneurs affects not only the diversification of a firm but also its corporate performance after the diversification process is completed. It is found that younger entrepreneurs who are highly educated and who have served as heads of business are more likely to choose diversification than the older entrepreneurs with lower academic degrees and no previous leadership experience. In addition, their choice of diversification will generate greater asset size and higher asset growth rate. Interestingly, people who have received higher or lower education perform much better than those with an average level of education after diversification. As a major decision of a corporation, the diversification strategy will inevitably be influenced by its family characteristics. Although both Huamao and Neoglory opted for diversification, their courses and reasons varied from each other.

---

[13] Zhang, Jianjun and Li Hongwei. (2007). Enterpreneur's Background from a Family Business, Diversified Strantegy and Performance. *Nankai Business Review*, 10.

Xu Lixun, the only son of Xu Wanmao, followed the arrangements of his father in his growth. The son once remarked, "I had no option and never thought about what personal interests meant." Although he knew he wanted a life of his own, he had to succeed to the family business in the face of a corporate crisis and took on the responsibilities of Huamao. Generally, many problems are covered up when a company is running smoothly, but they do get exposed in times of crisis. In 2001, the Ministry of Education unexpectedly launched a new policy aimed at reducing the burden on students, i.e., removing teaching aids from the procurement catalog of the education system in China, which had a huge impact on the main business of Huamao. The figure showed that from 2000 to 2005 the profits of Huamao fell sharply year by year from 200 million yuan when Xu Lixun took over from his father to its first loss in 2005, which was a time of great suffering for a new business leader like Xu Lixun.

Yet the market was constantly changing, hence the policy adjustment didn't fully account for Huamao's continued decline over six years. In the eyes of Xu Lixun, the fundamental reason for the loss of profit was the transformation Huamao was undergoing. Any corporation with a history of nearly three decades in a single industry was in need of a transformation sooner or later. For Huamao, the early succession of Xu Lixun brought the time forward.

The first day he assumed office as president, Xu Lixun made up his mind to prove himself by good performance. If he wanted to win everyone's trust in the company, he should make substantial achievements rather than embroil in the internal fight for power. For this purpose, Xu Lixun needed to push the transformation of Huamao. Back then he knew very well the predicament: How to break the restrictions caused by the old human resources structure? Obviously, he should focus on new growth points, good products, and profitable markets in order to bring huge benefits to Huamao, and in the process prove his worth.

From 2000 to 2002, it took Xu Lixun almost three years to transit Huamao Group from an industrial corporation to an investment one. The headquarters was transformed into an investment holding company responsible for investment only. Moreover, each business segment was separated into subsidiaries and branches with independent operations and sole responsibilities for their own losses or profits. The completion of the institutional and organizational changes did relieve the concerns of the young man as it meant that the declining performance of Huamao became controllable. This means that once the decline hits the bottom line, he would close off the subsidiary with heavy losses to ensure the health of the entire group.

What Xu Lixun took the most pride in happened at the end of 2005. At that time, he sensed that the Chinese stock market would recover and firmly believed his judgment. Not taking too much into consideration, he boldly invested a huge amount of capital into the stock market without informing the board of directors. In 2006, the bull market came as expected. Xu Lixun earned more than 100 million yuan from his investment for Huamao, taking up 80% of the group's total profit that year. As a result, the investment business of Huamao Group became an important source of income. Speaking of transformation through capital operation, the second generation with financial background can naturally play a key role. They are much better qualified than the first generation in terms of their market knowledge and interests.

At the end of 2007, Xu Lixun detected the imminent global financial crisis and proposed to make some preparations, namely shrinking the investment and maintaining a steady cash flow. After 2007, the sales revenues and profit of Huamao kept growing at a rate of 20%. The backbone team directly under his leadership matured day by day and was able to implement his ideas and strategies in an accurate and effective way. And all the staff placed great trust in him.

Currently, he centers the main business on three sectors, i.e., education, culture, and medical care. In 2015 the sales volume of the group exceeded 5 billion yuan, and Xu Lixun stabilized the growth rate of revenues and profits at around 10%. He believed this rate of increase, while satisfactory and beneficial, could guarantee the healthy function of the entire system. For this purpose, he formulated most of the policies based on sustainable development. In Huamao, employees may be punished for the over fulfillment of tasks. "What we need is quality development instead of great-leap-forwards," the young man commented.

The succession of Yu Jiangbo in Neoglory was much smoother than that of Xu Lixun. At the end of 2008, after finishing his overseas study, Yu Jiangbo returned to China to join the family group. In June 2009, he was responsible for Neoglory's participation in the Chinese Private Enterprise at Expo 2010 in Shanghai. In March 2010, he initiated the first e-commerce association in Yiwu and served as chairman. In the same year, two major events organized by him — the Launch of Popular Jewelry Trends and Neoglory Day at the Expo's United Pavilion of Chinese Private Enterprise — were a great success. At the beginning of 2011, he assumed the post of general manager of Neoglory Jewelry. Later that year, he founded Zhejiang Warehouse Technology Co., Ltd. In 2012, the self-owned brand "SU live" specializing in sterling silver jewelries was unveiled at London Fashion Week and earned much praise. Neoglory set up 100 direct-sale domestic stores and 35 "e-commerce warehouses". In 2016, it built 100 more at home and abroad, including some in Spain and the United States. Obviously, "Online + Physical Stores" is a new pattern of Neoglory.

Compared with the corporate accomplishments in the past two decades, Zhou Xiaoguang, founder of Neoglory, took more pride in her big family. The maturity and succession of her son Yu Jiangbo would not have been possible without the imperceptible influence and education of the family. Upon his return to the family business in his thirties, Yu successively established a few new-type enterprises such as Chuangdao Investment Management Co., Ltd., Zhejiang Warehouse Technology Co., Ltd. and Zhejiang Taoqu Network Technology Co., Ltd. On October 25, 2015, the day before Neoglory's 20th anniversary celebration, Yu Jiangbo had a dialogue with Jack Ma as a "maker" at the World Zhejiang Entrepreneurs Convention, and remarked, "Jack has always been my idol, but in terms of smart warehousing, I am proud to be ahead of my idol." He established the Warehouse in 2011, two years earlier than Cainiao Network Technology Co., Ltd under Jack Ma. In the field of automated intelligent warehousing system, Yu's company took a tough road with the system and hardware all independently developed by itself. After four years of efforts, the E-Commerce Warehouse created a unique open system and overall solution worldwide and became an organization which assisted the government in formulating standards for the e-commerce warehousing industry.

In 2015, Yu Jiangbo officially took over the business as president of Neoglory Group, a product of his parents' years of hard work. Before the financial turmoil in 2007, Zhou Xiaoguang perceived the future risks of the industry through inspection tours to overseas markets. As a traditional manufacturing industry dependent on manual labor, the jewelry sector inevitably experienced the throes, decline, adjustment, and transformation as well as the surge in labor costs in the ten years of professional management when Zhou Xiaoguang was in power and after the reform of her son upon succession. Therefore, Neoglory forged a diversified development structure quite early, integrating industries, real estate, investment, commerce, and trade. The significance of the diversification of Neoglory lay in the fact that profits from real estate, investment, commerce, and trade were used to support the group's development because the profits from jewelry were no longer a major source of income for the group. However, Zhou Xiaoguang and Yu Yunxin started up their business in the jewelry sector. Making jewelry meant a lot to the couple and their son Jiangbo, who grew up in the jewelry factory. It was their core business over a long period of time. Yu Jiangbo's enthusiasm for e-commerce added something new to Neoglory's diversification strategy.

One Decides to Go Public, While Another Never

When Yu Jiangbo succeeded as general manager of Neoglory Jewelry, his parents were making plans to go public in an attempt to open up broader prospects for the group through the operation of the capital market. It had proved to be an arduous path. Earlier, Neoglory showed the intention of going public after it had been growing in size but met with failure twice. First, as the major shareholder of the Zhongbai Holdings Group Co., Ltd., it was unable to sit on the board of directors. Subsequently, they were hoping to get listed via the shell of Jinlu Group and failed again due to non-market factors. On April 26, 2016, the moment Zhou Xiaoguang struck the bell in the Shenzhen Stock Exchange, Neoglory Prosperity was officially listed after official reorganization and a name change. It is a listed company with dual main businesses specializing in real estate development and commercial operation, supplemented by slewing bearing production and operation. It strives to build a diversified development pattern of the traditional machinery industry, the real estate industry, and the commercial operation industry. In Zhou Xiaoguang's view, though

Neoglory has assets of 40 billion yuan, resource integration is often constrained due to the lack of a capital operation platform. She deems that the listing will facilitate the expansion of Neoglory. After getting access to the capital market, the group will take the industry as the mainstay supplemented by the two pillars of investment and finance to pursue business development in larger and wider areas.

Now, let's take a look at the diversification plan of Huamao and Neoglory. Although they play different roles, the second generation has injected new industrial factors into their family firms. Xu Lixun's financial investment and Yu Jiangbo's e-commerce are both an important part of their group's diversified industrial setup. Nonetheless, behind the diversification, they also have different demands and choices for capital. A great number of Chinese family firms are unlisted holding companies with independent subsidiaries which may be listed and some of these listed companies are under the control of family holding companies. This is an option for many domestic family businesses in the face of transformation and industrial expansion.

As a family business, Huamao boasts two pillars: One is the consensus reached in the Xu Wanmao era, such as how Huamao will never go public; the other is the "Common Agreement of the Xu Family" signed by family members during the said era.

The consensus of never going public seems to be incompatible with the diversification that embraces the capital market, but all in all, it is determined by Huamao's goal of "sustainable operation". This is also the reason why Xu Lixun is still fully committed to Huamao's education sector which is the group's earliest important business even if the investment industry is more profitable. Speaking of the adherence to the main business, Yu Jiangbo and Xu Lixun happen to hold the same view. Nevertheless, the Xu family is more inclined to believe that outstanding companies do not necessarily go public, and such companies can still win the respect of society.

Why did Xu Lixun urge his father to draft the "Common Agreement of the Xu Family"? The answer is quite simple. He has three elder sisters; they do not want to see the scenario that family members become antagonistic towards each other owing to the division of family assets. They do not expect Huamao to fail within three generations due to the division of equity in the hands of later generations.

In 2008, the Xu family members signed the "Common Agreement of the Xu Family". According to the agreement, a trust fund is to be established to manage family members' equity in Huamao. The agreement has formulated the principle of "separating the family without dividing the property", meaning all family members have the right to distribute dividends, and each family will receive dividends every year. On one hand, this mechanism guarantees that several generations of family members have no worries about food and clothing. On the other hand, it fundamentally resolves the disputes over the inheritance of family property, and prevents the loss of the power of control due to excessive dispersion of shares after several generations of succession. In addition, the agreement also establishes the inheritance system under which the business will pass on to the eldest son and eldest grandson, and has provisions on the distribution of the remainder of property when the company is in risk or files for bankruptcy.

For Neoglory, going public means to seek more free financial capital, and to improve the professionalized governance of the company. When dividing the different industrial sectors of the group, it takes into account the high demand for funds in the real estate sector, whose profits can be separated from those of the group. Moreover, with the power of capital, Neoglory will cooperate with KW, the world's largest real estate franchise, to integrate high-quality properties with great value worldwide, and focus on developing new real estate products and businesses such as cultural, tourism, elderly care real estate, new commercial properties, and commercial real estate management. It will continue to expand and innovate in the fields of energy, mining, clean technology, etc. Furthermore, Neoglory will make full use of multiple investment platforms, effectively integrate international and domestic resources, and carry out investment & financing and mergers & acquisitions business more professionally, striving to build more than two listed companies in the next few years.

The 30 members of the Yu and Zhou family live together in a happy and harmonious state, which is the envy of many family firms. Yu Jiangbo and people of the older generation in his family have pondered the issue of inheritance and development. He invited Professor Joseph P.H. Fan from the Chinese University of Hong Kong to help draft the Neoglory Family "charter". For instance, a family council is established, and family members over 18 years of age are eligible to join and express their opinions. Major corporate matters must be discussed and voted through the family committee. The relevant rules for implementation are still being improved. The idea of going public has also taken the development of the enterprise into consideration, i.e., a more effective and reasonable operation or exit mechanism. Of course, the strength of the capital market can help Neoglory reach new heights in the next two decades.

13

Still on the Way

Family businesses in China are now pondering these questions: What course will their next generation follow and how are they going to take over the business? How much room do professional managers have to play their roles? In addition, how should family wealth be passed on? Does business transformation and upgrading mean diversification? Can the Internet and international markets help family businesses continue to open up new territories? Under such a background, how can Chinese family businesses carry out a smooth intergenerational succession? This will be an important topic of this era.

Reviewing the development of Chinese family businesses over the past 30 years, we can see that there are no more than three key points in every family business: Hand the business over or not? Split the family wealth or not? Transform the business or not? The first one is about the succession of family businesses, the second one concerns the distribution and accumulation of wealth, and the last one centers around the development of the business. In recent years, China has seen family businesses enter the peak of succession. A sizable number of excellent heirs of the second generation are taking over the business from their parents, while a fairly large number of them are unwilling to do so, which is related to the historical accumulation of Chinese family businesses. Under such circumstances, the cultivation of professional managers seems particularly important, but the credit system and incentive system of Chinese professional managers are far from satisfactory, which pose serious challenges to the succession of family businesses.

Family wealth is the top priority in family business succession. As the saying goes, "Inequality rather than scarcity is the cause of trouble." This suggests that the wealth distribution of family businesses is actually a very sensitive topic. Every entrepreneur needs to study this issue very carefully: How to be fair without decentralizing the family's control and avoid the excessive spreading out of wealth or the dispersion of equity because of the family's large fortune. At present, China's wealth management industry is booming, but many laws and regulations need to be improved. However, we should understand that the sole value of family wealth is not just money itself, but more of the responsibility that comes with it. The emerging family wealth trust can effectively help family businesses avoid the risks associated with wealth inheritance and make better use of wealth to make it play a greater role in society.

The last problem of transforming the business is significantly special in China because the transformation and succession of the company are parallel dual tracks, and the trains of the family business must run properly on the two tracks, otherwise any carelessness will cause them to overturn. If an enterprise fails to make a timely or correct transformation in the face of the changing times, it is very likely that it will be eliminated. Factors such as technology, market, and talent are changing rapidly in the age of the Internet. Business transformation is an optimization that adapts to the times, and it is also the only way towards sustainable development. A research report released by the well-known consulting firm McKinsey in 2013 showed that the average life span of global family businesses is only 24 years, of which only about 30% of family businesses can be passed to the second generation. The number of family businesses that can continue to the third generation is less than 13%, and only 5% of family businesses can still create value for shareholders beyond the third generation. Obviously, many family businesses which fail to be passed down are eliminated during the transformation process and the remaining 30% or so are better at seizing the opportunities of new markets, just like how the proverb goes, "A boat sailing against the current must strive ahead or it will be driven back."

No matter when inheritance meets transformation or vice versa, it will be a hard time for family businesses, not to mention that some enterprises encounter the two challenges at the same time. In China, family businesses are plagued by the solidified internal competition in the industry, the near saturation of overall industrial scale, and the gradually outdated marketing mode. Worse still, quite a few traditional manufacturing businesses are facing the survival dilemma and are in urgent need of finding new market opportunities to realize the business transformation and upgrading. At the crossroads of transformational change, enterprises need knowledge and talents that are different from those of the past, and intergenerational succession provides a good opportunity to solve the problem of updating enterprise leaders' knowledge. In addition, today's young people, especially the second generation of the family businesses, have grown up in completely different environments from those of the older generation. They are better educated and have more and better choices for career and life. Thus, if the enterprise they are supposed to inherit refuses to transform and change but still engages in the original low-end industry and adopts the original business model, and if they have to work together with the same people of the older generation — the same senior managers and under the same management methods — this will very likely turn them off. However, the needs of family business for transformation and upgrading may give them more space and motivation to use their imagination and maximize their abilities. Of course, the process is always tortuous as almost all the handover processes are associated with challenges. However, eventual progress will be achieved by addressing those problems. Time always stands on the side of young people. They have a stronger learning ability and a better understanding of the market trends as well as the technological innovation needs of the times. They are also braver to challenge the existing and established industry models and build a path of innovation completely different from that of their parents.

The succession of the second generation is essentially a process of starting a business venture a second time. The best way for succession is not to hand over the power from the first generation to the second, but to complete the transformation and upgrading of the enterprise through internal or external entrepreneurship or to make the second generation mature and experienced enough by doing pioneering work so as to best leverage the individual's strengths and optimize the business. In this process, the key to the succession and transformation of family business lies in the continuation of the spirit and culture of family business. All of this requires a long-term plan alongside preparing, cultivating, and reserving talents with a comprehensive and reasonable management structure featured by check and balance. When transformation meets inheritance, it is a vital challenge for many family businesses. However, whenever there is a crisis, there is also an opportunity for a favorable change. We hope this book will provide some experience and food for thought for businesses still on the way to success.

Acknowledgements

I published my first book on family business in Chinese in 2007 and its English version *Chinese Family Business — Wealth Goes Beyond Three Generations* the next year. At that time, I had just arrived in China.

Ten years passed by in a flash. When writing *Crossroads of Family Business in China: Succession and Transformation* this time, I focused on the development of Chinese family businesses, including many Chinese cases. This decade had not been smooth sailing. In fact, my research on this topic stagnated for nearly five years because it was particularly difficult to conduct interviews and study cases of family businesses at that time, and much more so to obtain the relevant reliable data. Family businesses were generally very low-key and unwilling to acknowledge or claim their family business identities. Yet, this trend changed significantly in the next five years. One reason for that was an increasing number of family companies doing very well, and the other was that many private enterprises must face the issue of business inheritance after more than 30 years of development. Therefore, the dilemma of whether the second generation should take over the business was placed on the agenda. Fortunately, the leaders of CEIBS, especially President Pedro Nueno, supported the idea that CEIBS should set up a research center on this subject to guide family business inheritance in China. Thus, in 2013, the CEIBS Center for Family Heritage was established with the strong support of all parties.

In the past few years, not only had we held seminars and forums and published white papers and cases every year, but we also conducted researches, visits, and field trips and organized a learning alliance to allow the second-generation members to visit and inspect different companies every two months. With several years of observation, reflection, and research, I thought it was time to publish a second book.

Writing a book is like going through a ten-month pregnancy, with both joys and worries. During the interview and writing process, I received help and support from many people. First of all, I would like to thank the entrepreneurs in the book for their help in my interviews and research, which was out of their love and support for education and sense of responsibilities to society. I am also grateful to the CEIBS Case Center for their generosity to allow me to use these cases in this book. Last but not least, my thanks would also extend to my collaborator, Professor Anthea Zhang, for her research and contribution to the topic of inheritance, which was exemplary in the academia. It was truly a wonderful experience working with her.

I always felt a sense of guilt to the research assistants who worked behind the scenes. As a boss, I could be devoted to work without rest all day long. Thus, if they had not worked hard, they would have failed to keep up with me and it would be extremely tiring to catch up with my pace. Therefore, I am particularly grateful to Lu Yunting for her work in the CEIBS Center for Family Heritage over the past three years. She had dedicated herself to the work with great perseverance and unmatched diligence. My thanks also go to Rebecca Chung, An Jing, Zhao Liman, and Zhao Ziqian who had been working with me to write the cases. I want to thank them for traveling long distances with me to do the interviewing and providing the much needed help. Additionally, I would also like to thank Zhao Hua for helping me proofread the manuscript in the final stage.

Finally, I would like to express my thanks to my late father. His life experiences had enlightened me to think about and explore on this topic and I have gained wonder and growth along the way.

Jean Lee
January 2017

Index

Printed in the United States
by Baker & Taylor Publisher Services